SEVEN ARCHBISHOPS

Seven Archbishops

by

SIDNEY DARK

*(Author of "Five Deans," "The Church,
Impotent or Triumphant?" "If Christ came
to London," "The People's Archbishop")*

1944

EYRE & SPOTTISWOODE

LONDON

First Published . . . *1944*

PRINTED IN GREAT BRITAIN FOR
EYRE AND SPOTTISWOODE (PUBLISHERS) LIMITED,
15, BEDFORD STREET, STRAND, LONDON, W.C.2

CONTENTS

INTRODUCTION

IN this year of grace, the Primate of All England, is for the first time for many generations, a great national figure, the spokesman of the nation's conscience, destined perhaps to have a more powerful influence in the shaping of the England of to-morrow than any other living man.

Even by the religious minded (by no means a mighty multitude) religion has come to be regarded as the ornament rather than the explanation of life. There are to-day far more First Day Relaxionists than Seventh Day Adventists. Consequently the churchman is expected to stay in church and to mind his own business, and Dr. Temple's suggestion that the banker may not be an instrument for the glory of God or the good of man has been resented as an impertinent irrelevance. With a modesty that has, in effect, been an abdication, the religious leader had for generations accepted the contention that his business is exclusively with men's souls, that nowadays God rests on six days out of seven, and, as most men are rarely interested in the welfare of their souls, the religious leaders in this country have had an ever decreasing influence on the development of secular affairs.

In my youth, Manning and Booth, and perhaps Spurgeon were the only divines whose names were known to the majority, who never went to Church or chapel. Booth was known, because with vulgar, histrionic exuberance, he preached to the outcasts and the miserable. Manning is still gratefully remembered because the Catholic faith made him the champion of the oppressed and the underpaid. Were he alive, the great cardinal would assuredly subscribe to the Malvern Findings and would be as emphatic as the Archbishops of Canterbury and York and the late Cardinal Hinsley have been in support of the recommendations of the Beveridge Report.

Latterly Dick Sheppard and Studdert Kennedy had " news value " in the popular press, because of their abounding humanity. But until, in a series of speeches that have been heard by many thousands and have been widely reported, Dr. Temple began to preach the social gospel with

all the authority of his high office, it is safe to say that only
the men and women, often in the pews, had any knowledge
of the contemporary ministers of the altar and the pulpit.
Even now I doubt whether the name of any diocesan bishop
is known to more than twenty-five per cent. of the people
in his diocese. This is regarded as natural and proper by the
people who contend that religion and politics should be kept
rigorously apart, although as a matter of fact a vivid religion
must affect every activity of individual and social life.

In the middle ages there was no sharp division between
the spiritual and secular. No such division occurred at the
Reformation. Calvin was a politician as well as a theologian.
The Puritans derived both their political and their social
philosophy from their faith. At the beginning of this
century, the English Nonconformists, under the leadership
of John Clifford, were the most powerful of the supporters
of Radicalism. The people, too, who are now bidding
Dr. Temple to confine himself to exclusively ecclesiastical
affairs, were quite content while the Church of England
was from the death of Queen Anne to the end of the Victorian
era the ally of the Tories.

In writing the following sketches of seven Archbishops of
Canterbury, living in different centuries and in vastly
different surroundings, I have been concerned with their
influence on the Church and consequently on the nation, in
the days when the Church's contact with the nation was
close and apparent and in the days when it became divorced
from the common life and was the obedient appanage of the
dominant party in the state.

From my own convictions, I have been naturally and inevitably concerned to point out that, so long as the Church has
been vividly conscious that the Provinces of Canterbury and
York remain the Church Catholic in this realm, so long has
it been able to fulfil its mission and to leaven the nation
with the faith once delivered to the saints and to fight the
battle of the poor and that when, poisoned by deference
to the power of money, it has humbly accepted the position
of one of the innumerable Protestant sects, it has ceased to
count for good or evil.

There have been saints and scholars and statesmen among the predecessors of Dr. Temple. There have been many more mediocrities and it is interesting that the men, who owed their preferment to the favour of kings, were of better stuff than the men who, from the days of Walpole, have owed their preferment to the favour of politicians, which has meant the favour of the rich.

There were great men at Canterbury in the days before the Reformation—Lanfranc, St. Anselm and Theobold, St. Thomas, Stephen Langton and St. Edmund, Chicheley, Morton and Warham. There were great men in the centuries of transition—Pole and Parker, Laud and Juxon and Sancroft. Then, with the establishment of the supremacy of money in the national life, for two hundred years the Primate was little more than an ornamental court official. The mission of the Wesleys, the Evangelical revival, the great Tractarian movement had neither sympathy, guidance nor understanding from Canterbury.

It is possible (even though it is absurd) to regard St. Thomas as the mere arrogant champion of clerical privilege. It is possible (though equally absurd) to think of Laud as nothing but the defender of royal tyranny. But at least they were men who died for what they believed.

The mitred Erastians of the Eighteenth and Nineteenth Centuries did not believe in anything very much ; they neither ruled nor controlled ; they were " blind mouths." In the first of these centuries, the English people were more degraded than ever in their history ; in the second, the smug Victorian era, pious wealth was the real ruler of the nation, whether the Government was Liberal or Tory, and the bishops sided with the rich Nonconformists in resisting the Factory Acts and every other attempt to hinder money from battening on the souls and bodies of the people. Ecclesiastical authority was indifferent to the existence of social conditions that stunted and frustrated the lives of the majority. It was uninterested in the ethical significance of the Manchester ideal of buying in the cheapest market and selling in the dearest. It was content, as Froude has said " to leave the present world to the men of business and the devil."

The Church was not unworldly. It accepted Locke's assertion that " the great and chief end of men uniting into commonwealths and putting themselves under government is the preservation of property." It was, indeed, very jealous for its own property and as for the ninety per cent. who had no property worth considering, the Church agreed that they must go on submissively adding by their labour to the property of the few. The Church was other-worldly in the sense that it promised Lazarus, if he were sufficiently humble, a place in Abraham's bosom in the world to come. When the Church abandoned its concern for the well being, in this world, of the majority, it ceased to have any spiritual influence.

It is impossible not to note that the complete abdication of that ghostly authority in mundane affairs, generally acknowledged though often resented before the Reformation, which Laud died to preserve and which was demanded by the Puritans, was accompanied in the Church of England by the repudiation by the hierarchy of the Laudian tradition. The comfortable practice of humble penitence, quiet and sincere confession and priestly absolution was forbidden. The significance of the Holy Eucharist was lost. It was no longer the supreme act of worship. It was certainly not recognised as, to quote a recent pamphlet, " the feast of fellowship witnessing to the unity of the Church and so to the potential unity in Christ of the whole of man's earthly life."

Religion was robbed of its beauty, its dignity and its mystery, and, in consequence, of its saving grace. Church services became deadly dull, as, alas they have remained in many parishes, and men were far more attracted by the excitement of the hell fire orations of fervent revivalists and the tambourine banging of red jerseyed Salvationists as they are now more attracted by Holywood films.

In the Eighteenth Century the farmers resented the open-air preaching of the Wesleys, because the excitement of " conversion " interfered with the drudgery of field work. Excitement is bad for the working man. That was why the American Methodists contrived, in alliance with " big business " to saddle the United States with prohibition and the real reason why well-to-do English Puritans have tried to prevent Sunday games in the parks and are constantly plotting to shut up Sunday cinemas.

The Catholic faith is tremendously exciting and it is one of the achievements of the Church of England, shared with the sedater Protestant sects, that it has made the Christian religion dull.

Thanks to the Oxford Movement, of which I shall have much to say, dullness has been largely dissipated. Thanks to the Christian social movement that has been closely associated with the Catholic revival, the Church has begun to recognise its real mission and to understand that half a gospel is no better than no gospel.

This new attitude has been summarised by the Bishop of Bradford who asks : " May the reason why we have so bitterly failed to christianize the world be that we have tried to be more spiritually minded than our Lord ? "

I am, of course, aware that my contention of the continuity of the English Church, and that Dr. Temple is the legitimate spiritual heir of St. Augustine, is open to not unreasonable challenge. That challenge has been often and adequately met. In the study of Laud, I have referred to the matter at some length. Here I am only concerned to repeat that my viewpoint in the following essays is that, equally with the Roman Church and the Orthodox Churches of the East, the Church of England is part of the One, Holy Catholic and Apostolic Church divinely founded on the first Whitsunday. I go further than this. With all its shortcomings—its failure through many generations to realise its birthright and the consequent responsibilities—the Church of England has preserved the essentials of the primitive faith without the superstitious excrescences of modern Roman doctrine and the arbitary claims of the Roman see, whilst its separation from Rome, deplorable as has been many of its results, has saved the English Church from any responsibility for the political alignments of the Vatican.

The long contest between the Pope and the English Kings from the Conqueror to Henry VIII was fundamentally political, the resolution to prevent the interference in English domestic affairs not of the supreme Christian pontiff but of a foreign sovereign, whose policy was swayed sometimes, as with Hildebrand by long-sighted consideration for the good of Christendom, but more often by the desire for the secular advantage of a secular ruler. This resolution was fully approved by the English people. Moreover, it is not to be denied that the scandalous immorality of the Renaissance Popes, which caused the righteous anger of Savonarola, was one of the causes of the Reformation and the break up of Christendom, and its bitterest critics would never suggest that, whatever their shortcomings, the Primates of England have, at any time, approached the iniquities of Alexander VI.

The mediæval Church denounced the sin of usury. Modern finance is usury under a polite name. Finance, with its complex ramifications and realities, is responsible for the wars, the want and the waste that are at long last bringing an historic era to an end in blood and tears. Usury, condemned in the middle ages, was condoned, if not defended by many though not all the Puritan leaders, and it has therefore been asserted that, when half Europe repudiated Catholic theology and Papal authority it, at the same time, surrendered to the power of money. But that assertion has to be modified by recalling the fact that Rome, before the Reformation, did not always practise what it preached, and that it sometimes encouraged what it denounced.

Professor Tawney has summarised the mediæval doctrine as " Labour—the common lot of mankind—is necessary and honourable ; trade is necessary . . . . finance, if not immoral, is at best sordid and at worst dishonourable." This was the basis of the theory of the Just Price which was primarily ethical, the implicit assertion that economics must be subject to morality. It has been stated as follows : " The Just Price implied that a man's work should normally be recompensed by an income which gives him a reasonable livelihood. Every member of society has a right to live, and to live a decent human life : to pay a price for his labour (or for the commodity produced by it) which will not allow of this, is unjust, and therefore sinful. Further, the doctrine that there is a Just Price of each commodity which buyer and seller alike must seek, implies that there is an economic reality, a complex of objective fact, and that action in this economic field must be just, i.e., in accordance with these real relationships of things and persons as they ought to be."

There is an evident intimate connection between the ecclesiastical demand for the Just Price and the Socialist ideal " from every man according to his ability and to every man according to his need." The Church, realising that business with every other human activity was part of its business, derived from the Gospels a definite social philosophy and it recognised, from contemporary experience, that " he that maketh haste to be rich shall not be innocent." So long as it was emphatic that it is the divine intention that all men shall live a good life on this earth, it was the effective champion of the weak and the source of sweetness and light. When it compromised with Mammon it was false to God. As Prebendary Kirk has said in accepting the gold standard, it abandoned the soul standard. That, I contend, is manifestly clear in the following short studies of leading figures in the English Church in different centuries. One hundred and ten years ago, the Tractarian fathers pleaded for the recovery of the theological teaching of the primitive church. To-day, the English Archbishops are pleading for the recovery of the economic and social doctrines of the primitive church. The future of religion and consequently the future of the world, largely depend on how far the Church understands the appeals and how far it responds to them.

CHAPTER ONE

THE PHILOSOPHER

THE eleventh century was one of the great creative periods in European history, an era comparable to the sixteenth century, when many old things passed away and most things became new. In the sixteenth century drama, there was an unparalleled number of outstanding figures, some good and some very evil. In the earlier age, William the Norman and Hildebrand were the chief makers of history, with, so far as England was concerned, the two Archbishops of Canterbury, the Italian Lanfranc and St. Anselm, of little less importance. These men stood for law and order. It was due to them that their age saw the recovery of law established by the Romans and more or less disregarded in the centuries that followed the fall of the Imperial city.

The Dark Ages were not entirely stagnant either religiously or culturally. There were saints in England in those days, a few scholars, of whom the Venerable Bede is best remembered, and an occasional enlightened statesman like King Alfred and St. Dunstan. There were some patches of light in the darkness, but they were always brief and when the tenth century passed into the eleventh, lawlessness prevailed in both the Church and in the secular states.

The primary objective of the great eleventh century Popes, Hildebrand, who reigned as Gregory VII, and his predecessor, Alexander II, was to compel obedience to the canon law both from the clergy and the laity. They realised that the Church must be internally cleansed and reformed that its authority might be generally respected. Its claim to jurisdiction over all temporal princes must be established, if law and order, justice and decency, were to be assured. That was the Hildebrandian contention. Similarly, William of Normandy realised the necessity for strong central secular power, able to command general obedience and he further realised that, to secure this obedience, authority must not be swayed by caprice but must be based on accepted and recognised law.

It is one of the strangest of historical puzzles that the Normans, barbarians outside the Roman tradition, who landed on the coast of France on piratical expeditions, intent on nothing but ravaging and destruction, should in a generation have become assimilated into the cultural life of the land that they had conquered and should have recovered for both France and England the priceless heritage of Rome. The puzzle becomes the more curious when it is remembered that it was only in north-west Europe that the Normans were the great civilisers.

The Normans who conquered Sicily and southern Italy were on the whole true to their piratical origin. They were certainly not the builders of a civilisation. It was clearly the genius of William, who was not only the greatest of the Normans but unique among the Normans, that made him the founder of the mediæval order in England.

The first sign of grace in the Norman lords in France was the building of churches and monasteries to take the places of those which they had destroyed. One of them, it is recorded, " built six churches in the name of the Lord out of his own means." But it was easier to build churches and religious houses than to find the priests to minister in them. The clergy were ignorant and self-indulgent. The bishops were either married or openly living with mistresses and most of them were as ignorant as the clergy. The monastery was the mainspring of religion, not only the retreat from a troubled world for men, eager for study and prayer, but the school, the seminary and often the hospital. And it was inevitable that the religious revival should have begun in the religious houses.

Reform was initiated at Cluny and in 1034 the famous monastery at Bec was founded by Herlwin, a Norman knight, who, before being ordained, had gained considerable reputation as a soldier. Herlwin was a man of ideas. He had a clear notion of what he wanted Bec to become, but he lacked the capacity to put his ideas into practice. This was effected by Lanfranc, an Italian from Lombardy, who came to the monastery by chance and remained to be its Prior for twenty years and to establish its continent-wide reputation for piety and learning.

Lanfranc brought with him from Italy considerable secular learning and experience as a teacher. As a novice at Bec, he acquired religious enthusiasm, and with his strong character, his sound judgment, and his ever-growing reputation as a teacher, he made Bec the model monastery of the times. Young men came from Italy, Germany and France, eager to be numbered with Lanfranc's students, and among them were the future Pope Alexander II and St. Anselm of Aosta, a future Archbishop. The monastery's income was constantly increased by gifts from the faithful. The Duke William visited the monastery and was impressed by the learned Prior, who was employed by him in various confidential missions. And four years after William became William the Conqueror, Lanfranc became the English Primate. From the beginning of their connection he was the Conqueror's confidant, indeed, his only confidant.

Lanfranc established the strict Benedictine order at Bec, with a common sense modification in some respects and in certain circumstances of the traditional discipline. The days were devoted to worship, improvement and work. There were ample opportunities for pleasant social life. Every monk had his definite duties. Monks and students had to take their share of the manual work of the community. Faults were fairly judged and sternly punished. It was a disciplined but friendly rule that Lanfranc instituted.

St. Anselm, his most considerable pupil, was born at Aosta in 1033. He felt the call of the religious life when he was fifteen, and a few years later, with the genius for wandering characteristic of the Lombards in the Middle Ages, he made his way across the Alps and through France to Bec. It is probable that he had heard at home of the distinction given to Bec by his fellow countryman, Lanfranc. The journey took him three years. St. Anselm went to Bec, Dean Church says, " as men later on went to universities to find the best knowledge and the best teaching of the day." A strong friendship sprung up between St. Anselm and Lanfranc, the Prior a man of great practical ability, the student to prove himself " an original thinker of great originality and subtlety."

It was some time before St. Anselm decided to become a

monk. He was well off. A comfortable life awaited him if he returned home. It seems probable that his decision was dictated by the desire to secure peace and quiet for his studies, and his writing, as well as by the call to the dedicated life. He became a professed monk in 1060. He succeeded Lanfranc as Prior of the monastery in 1063. He became Abbot in 1078 and he remained at Bec until, in 1093, he was compelled, much against his will, to become Archbishop of Canterbury.

It was in these years at Bec that St. Anselm wrote the books that have caused him to be recognised as among the great European thinkers. He was uninterested in the empty subtleties of finicky theological speculations. He was concerned with the eternal problems of human life. He was a rationalist, deriving as a thinker from Plato through St. Augustine, and anticipating Descartes, Leibnitz and Hegel. He insisted that faith is necessary for understanding but he also insisted that faith must be justified by reason. Eadmer, his biographer, says : " He bent his purpose most earnestly to this, that according to his faith it might be vouchsaved to him to perceive by his mind and reason the things that were veiled in them." By reasoning he was convinced men can realise the certainty of the existence of God.

St. Anselm spent the last troubled years of his life defending the rights of the Church and there is an element of irony in the fact that the Church has repudiated the philosophy that he spent the preceding thirty-three years in elaborating. Mgr. Knox says of St. Anselm : " He was a philosopher and a theologian, yet to-day his theological views are generally quoted to be refuted, and his most famous exploit in philosophy, the ontological proof of the existence of God, is not only discredited, but has, according to some, the dubious credit of being the parent of modern idealism." Be that as it may, the boldness and originality of this thinker of the early Middle Ages cannot be exaggerated.

The conquest of England by William of Normandy was made possible by the character of Edward the Confessor, the last of the Saxon kings and by the events of his reign. Before Edward's accession in 1042, England had been ruled for twenty-five years by Danish kings—Canute, a religious-minded statesman, who, following the earlier achievement of St. Dunstan, strove to make the conquered Saxons and the invading Danes into one people, and his two riotous barbaric sons, St. Edward was the son of a Saxon father and a Norman mother. As a boy of ten, he was taken for safety to Normandy and he grew up in an atmosphere of ordered piety. He was a man without any personal ambition. He was made king against his will, refusing to return to England until he was assured that the throne could be recovered without bloodshed. He was a gentle albino, and he had no idea how to govern a people whose language he could hardly understand and whose qualities he could never appreciate, and after struggling ineffectually with the help of Norman advisers, he not unwillingly surrendered the government to the Saxon, Earl Godwin, devoting himself to the building of the Abbey Church of St. Peter at Westminster in the pious hope that it might be the source of sweetness and light in a rude land. Ten years after St. Edward's coronation Godwin drove the Norman nobles and bishops out of the kingdom. Robert of Jumiéges, whom Edward had made Archbishop of Canterbury, was outlawed and the Primacy was bestowed by Godwin, in defiance of all canon law, on Stigand, the Saxon Bishop of Winchester. Godwin and his son Harold were to St. Edward and his mentor, William of Normandy, the champions of the ecclesiastical lawlessness which they both loathed.

The history of the English church before the Norman conquest consists of a series of periods of romantic progress followed by periods of stagnation and reaction. The legend of the journey of St. Joseph of Arimathea from Jerusalem to plant the Holy Thorn at Glastonbury is, I suppose, no more than a lovely legend, but it is certain that by the beginning of the third century Christianity had been introduced into the island by Roman settlers, though it probably made few if any converts from the Celtic inhabitants. The English Church had its proto-martyr, St. Alban, in this century. There were bishops of London, York and Lincoln in the fourth century, and they were present at the Council of Arles. At the beginning of the fifth century, St. Ninian, a Briton trained in Rome, became a missionary in North Britain, outside the Roman sphere of influence, and in this century Christianity was established in parts of the country by the Celtic missionaries, who, when the Roman Empire was destroyed and the continent of Europe overrun by barbarians, preserved the Catholic faith and Christian learning in Ireland. In England the Church was practically destroyed by the Anglo-Saxon invaders, though it lingered on in Wales, Cornwall and Scotland with scattered congregations at Glastonbury and some other places and a bishop in London.

In 597 St. Augustine landed in Kent, and in November of that year he was consecrated Archbishop of the English by the Metropolitan of Arles. It is important to remember that St. Augustine found a non-Roman Catholic Church in the land over which the Pope had given him jurisdiction, the church that counted among its saints St. Ninian, St. Columba and St. David. St. Augustine met the Welsh bishops and monks, who regarded him much as the nineteenth century Tractarians regarded the hierarchy set up in England by Cardinal Wiseman. St. Augustine had the typically Roman love of order and uniformity. The Celts obstinately adhered to their own tradition and practices and nothing came of the conference.

St. Augustine died in 604 and fifty years later, thanks to the zeal of missionaries, some Italian, some Burgundian, and some Celtic, of whom St. Aidan, who had many of the qualities of St. Francis, was the most famous, the larger part of England was Christian, in Kent and Wessex definitely Roman, in the rest of the country still definitely Celtic. It was clear that if the National Church were to continue as part of the Catholic world, there must be unity of doctrine, uniformity of practice and a common allegiance, and this vital end was attained by Theodore, a native of Cilicia in Asia Minor, who became Archbishop of Canterbury in 668. However English the English church may be it owes a heavy debt to foreign zeal and piety. Backed by the tireless activity of the Saxon Wilfrid, Theodore succeeded in two years in securing the recognition of his primatial authority from all the English bishops with the acknowledgement that they owed their orders to the Pope. The first provincial council of the English Church was held in Hertford in 673.

In view of the subsequent events with which I am largely concerned in these essays, the next event in Theodore's episcopate has a particular interest. The Archbishop properly felt the necessity of creating new bishoprics and he proposed to cut into four the huge diocese of Northumbria which extended from the Humber to the Forth, with its see city at York. Wilfrid was Bishop of Northumbria and bitterly resented the division, and when, with the consent of the King, Theodore ignored his protest, Wilfrid appealed to Rome. The Pope decided in his favour—and the decision was disregarded. This was the action of a Saxon king and a foreign-born English primate !

The episcopate of Theodore was a time of unqualified progress. Many new religious houses were established. In all the dioceses there were schools mainly for the education of the clergy. The parochial system was founded. The early Celtic monasteries in England had been the homes of hermit-like piety. St. Hilda's famous double foundation for men and women at Whitby was founded before Theodore came to Canterbury. But Theodore's Benedictine houses at Ripon and Jarrow were the first considerable English homes of learning.

In the early years of the next century, the English Church began its missionary work. St. Willibrand went from the monastery at Ripon to preach the Gospel in the valley of the Meuse and he was followed by St. Boniface, who was martyred in Frisia in 755.

Perhaps the loveliest figure of the English Church in this period was the Venerable Bede, the gentle modest scholar who, in the monastery at Jarrow, made the first English translation of the New Testament and from whose writing comes our knowledge of the Celtic and Saxon saints.

Theodore died in 690. Bede died in 735. And in the years that followed before the defeat of the Danes by Alfred the Great in 878, the church suffered greviously from the ravages of invaders, and the general political instability. Very few of the Saxon monasteries were governed by established rules, such as those of St. Benedict and St.

Basil. Most of them had their own local rules, which were never closely obeyed. In 747, an order was issued by a Church Council forbidding the religious houses to harbour " play actors, musicians and buffoons." There was, too, a decay in learning and it was said in 871 that there was not a priest, south of the Thames, who could translate the Liturgy into English. Indeed, when Alfred, who has been not inaptly called the St. Louis of England, began his work of religious and cultural regeneration, he was obliged to send to France, to Germany and to Wales for ecclesiastics of learning and character. Alfred, however, found in Plegemund, a hermit of Chester, a worthy and capable Archbishop who occupied the primatial see for over thirty years. Much was done for the revival of learning and for the reform of the monasteries, and the authority of Canterbury, which had been disregarded in both the north and the west was largely re-established. But it was left to St. Dunstan in the second half of the tenth century to establish the church as a powerful national institution. St. Dunstan was an artist, a musician, a man of deep personal piety, and the first of the English ecclesiastic statesmen. He introduced the Benedictine rule into the Glastonbury monastery, of which he was Abbot, and the example of Glastonbury was followed in other houses. In 955 he used the power of the church to dethrone Eadwig, who had made an incestuous marriage, and this is the first example in English history of the Church's intervention in politics. In 959, St. Dunstan became Archbishop of Canterbury and the most powerful man in the island. Politically he was responsible for the consolidation of the country into a single kingdom and for the beginning of the commercial importance of London. As an ecclesiastic, the reform of the monasteries was his most important achievement. Clerical marriages had become the accepted custom, but St. Dunstan forbade marriages after ordination and encouraged celibacy.

Unhappily much that St. Dunstan had accomplished was destroyed in the second Danish invasion in 988, during which Aethelgar, Archbishop of Canterbury, was martyred at Greenwich. Anarchy continued for nearly thirty years until the recovery of a measure of law and order by Canute, and after another twenty-five years the accession of St. Edward the Confessor. The glory of the early English church, that had produced its saints, its scholars, and its other administrators, had never been entirely recovered. The repeated attempts to regularise the monastic life had only been very partially and very temporarily successful. The episcopate was inefficient and its authority continually flouted. The schools were decadent. The secular clergy were generally ignorant and inefficient. The Norman conquest created the English nation and saved the English church. The Conqueror laid the foundations for the greatness of the nation. The two great Archbishops, Lanfranc and St. Anselm, whom he brought from Normandy, were the regenerators of the Church.

While William and Lanfranc were establishing law and order in England, the great struggle was proceeding between the Pope and the German Emperor.

In 1065, Henry IV of Germany attained his majority, and, in 1073, Hildebrand became Pope Gregory VII, not by formal election but by popular acclamation subsequently ratified by the cardinals and bishops. He was described as " a man of profound theological knowledge, a man of prudence, a lover of equity and justice, firm in adversity, temperate in prosperity ; according to the Apostolic words, of good conversation ; blameless, sober, modest, chaste, hospitable—one that ruleth his own house ; a man well brought up in the bosom of his mother, the Church."

With his tremendous vigour, Gregory at once set himself to the tasks of strengthening the temporal sovereignty and rooting out the abuses that continued within the Church. In a letter, written immediately after his consecration, he said :

" The rulers and princes of this world oppress the Church as if she were a vile slave. They do not blush to cover her with confusion, if only they can satisfy their cupidity. The priests and those charged with the guidance of the Church, completely neglect the law of God, are neglectful of their obligations towards Him, and towards their flocks. In aiming at ecclesiastical dignities they seek only worldly glory, and they waste, in their own presumptuous pomp and foolish expenses, that which should serve to save and aid many. The people, like sheep without a shepherd, are unguided and fall into error and sin and Christianity is a mere name to them."

In a letter to Lanfranc, Archbishop of Canterbury, Gregory urged him to whole heartedness in church reform and particularly exhorted him to be concerned with the Scottish clergy—Malcolm, King of Scotland, had done homage as his vassal to William two years before—who not only married but often abandoned their wives and even put them up for sale. But while the Pope was friendly to Norman William, the Normans in Italy had now become to Gregory "those vile little Normans" who must be brought to heel. They even regarded his excommunication with complete indifference.

In 1075, Henry IV had made himself the acknowledged master of the German states and he demanded the Imperial crown from the Pope. Gregory temporised. He refused to confirm the Emperor's nominations to bishoprics, he chided his arrogance and he reminded him that Saul " in the flush of triumph refused to listen to the words of the prophet and was punished by God."

Henry replied with equal vehemence. He declared that Gregory had not been legally elected, that he was "no longer Pope but a false monk," and, acting on his right as a Roman patrician, the Emperor declared the Pope deposed, being supported by the German and some of the Italian bishops. Gregory's principle was that it was his right as the successor of St. Peter to depose kings, while Henry withstood such an assumption, as an unheard-of novelty in Christendom. He claimed that, in temporal matters, he was independent of the Pope and subject to God alone.

In February, 1076, Gregory excommunicated the Emperor and suspended the bishops who had sided with him, and fearful that Henry might march on Rome he tried to arrange a military alliance with the Italian Normans, whom he thoroughly and reasonably suspected.

The excommunication released the German princes from their allegiance to the Emperor and his position became precarious, the bishops, who had sided with him, hastening to make their subjection to the Pope. Gregory journeyed from Rome to Canossa, a town on the borders of Lombardy, the province that has been foremost in resistance to the Papal authority, and there the German nobles and bishops came as bare-footed penitents to beg for his absolution. They were followed by the Emperor, who crossed the Alps in bitter winter weather. " In the penitent's garb and bare-foot, the King appeared before the walls of the fortress. He had laid aside every mark of royalty, and fasting, he awaited the pleasure of the Pope for three days." The humiliation was as complete as that of the English Henry II after the murder of St. Thomas. On certain stringent conditions the absolution was granted, the excommunication was withdrawn and the Emperor received Holy Communion.

The Imperial journey to Canossa has become proverbial. It has been described as " the triumph of sacerdotal Christianity in the humiliation of the temporal power " and another writer has said that " an Imperial penitent, standing barefoot and woollen-frocked in the snow, till the priest who sat within should absolve him was enough to mark a decisive change and inflict an irretrievable disgrace on the crown so abused." As a matter of fact, Henry was actuated by realistic political motives. He lost very little at Canossa and the Pope gained nothing.

Despite the reconciliation, the German princes chose a rival king and for years there was civil war in Germany, with the usual result of bitter suffering for the people. Gregory claimed the right to decide between the rivals, but his arbitration was refused and Henry continued to select and invest German bishops, and again the Pope pronounced against him a decree of excommunication and deposition. His rival was at the same time recognised as the German king and a vassal of the Holy See. But nobody was any the worse or any the better. The rival king was killed in battle. Henry remained comparatively secure, and, in 1081, Hildebrand was repudiated by a synod attended by thirty German and Italian prelates, the Pope being accused of " simony, bribery, licentiousness, heresy and necromancy," and a new Pope, who took the title of Clement III, was elected, the Emperor paying homage to him as the Supreme Head of the Church.

Gregory was now compelled to seek a real alliance with the Normans, for which he had to pay dearly. In the agreement signed in June, 1080, the Pope wrote : "As to the estates which you unjustly retain, I patiently suffer you to do your will at the present time, trusting in God and in your goodness, and in order that for the future you may conduct yourself in such a way as will tend to the glory of God and of Blessed Peter, as is incumbent both for you and myself."

This is a sufficient proof of the flimsiness of the subjection of secular to spiritual authority claimed to have been established at Canossa. The Pope indeed knew that he was beaten, he fulminated and excommunicated, but after two or three abortive attempts, Henry entered Rome in 1084 and Clement III put the Imperial crown on his head on Easter Day.

Then the Normans moved. They marched against Rome, the Emperor fled, the Normans occupied the city and after releasing Gregory, who had shut himself up in the Castle of St. Angelo, their soldiers and their Saracen allies had an orgy of plunder and destruction. " It is probable," says Milman, " that neither Goth nor Vandal, neither Greek nor German brought such desolation on the city as this capture by the Normans," and it could not be forgotten that the Normans were the Pope's allies.

Gregory died at Salerno in 1085. His last words were : " I have loved justice and hated iniquity, therefore I die in exile."

Gregory was a learned theologian, a master rhetorician, a man of austere piety, abounding with courage. But he was certainly not a subtle statesman. He was a bad judge of men. He was incapable of conciliation. His spirit, it has been said, was that of Elijah anathematising the prophets of Baal. He was the first of the Popes to claim, in virtue of his office, the right to appoint and to dispose kings and princes. Service to the Church was to be rewarded by the granting of secular sovereignty ; hostility to the Church was to be punished by the forcible withdrawal of that sovereignty. This claim was specifically stated by Gregory at a council in 1080. The authority to loose and to bind, divinely bestowed on the successors of St. Peter, applied to this world as well as to the world to come. The Pope was the supreme authority on earth in both spiritual and temporal affairs. It was this claim, maintained with more or less emphasis by Rome, that the German Emperors and the English sovereigns from the Conqueror to Henry VIII persistently repudiated and opposed.

After Gregory's death, Clement III disappeared and Victor II reigned for a year in Rome. He was succeeded by Urban II, a Frenchman who had been a monk at Cluny, another prelate of outstanding piety, who professed to be a follower of Gregory but who, with firmness and energy, had considerable caution and prudence. He was Pope when St. Anselm was consecrated Archbishop of Canterbury.

Through all these troubled years, St. Anselm pursued his quite protected life in his Norman monastery. He may have known very little of what was happening in Germany and Italy, but he must have had full knowledge of events in England. With other Norman religious houses, Bec was given English estates after the Conquest and, as both Prior and Abbot, St. Anselm frequently crossed the Channel on monastery business. The conquest was completed in 1071; Lanfranc was appointed Archbishop of Canterbury in 1070 and was afterwards the one man in England whom the Conqueror fully trusted. Dean Church quotes a contemporary estimate of William's rule in England, a tribute alike to his masterliness and his devotion to law :

" The King William that we speak of was a very wise man, and very great ; and more worshipful and stronger than any of his foregangers. He was mild to the good men who loved God, and beyond all measure stern to whose who gainsaid his will. On that selfsame place where God granted him that he might win England, he raised up a great minster, and set monks therein, and enriched it well. . . .

" Bishops he set off their bishoprics, and abbots off their abbacies and thanes in prison ; and at last he spared not his own brother, called Odo ; he was a very great bishop in Normandy ; at Bayeux was his see ; and he was the chief of men next to the king. And he had an earldom in England, and when the king was in Normandy, he was mightiest in this land. And him did he set in prison. Among other things it is not to be forgotten the good peace that he made in this land ; so that any one man, that himself were aught, might fare over this realm with his bosom full of gold, unhurt ; and no man durst slay another man, had this one done ever so much evil to the other ; and if any man harmed a woman, he was punished accordingly. He ruled over England ; and with his craftiness so looked it through, that there was not one hide within England, that he learned not who had it, or what it was worth ; and then he set it in his written book."

The king was above the law but he saw to it that all lesser men should obey the laws that he made. In the feudal social system that he established, he retained certain Saxon institutions, and, while there is no question of the ultimate benefits that Norman rule brought to England, it is also probable that the bulk of the Saxon population, the villeins and the serfs, the small-holders and the artisans, were no worse off under William than they had been under Edward. The Saxon thanes were dispossessed but those, who had little to lose, do not seem to have lost it. That is suggested by Domesday Book.

William as Conqueror showed a moderation that was unique in his age. When the Normans entered Rome, at the invitation of Pope Gregory, they pillaged and raped and burned. But when William compelled Exeter to surrender, the leading citizens were " favourably received and assured of their lives and goods," and the king " secured the gates with a strong guard of men, whom he could trust, in order to preserve the goods of the citizens from any breaches of discipline."

William claimed and maintained the overlordship of ecclesiastics as well as of the secular nobles. His claim was identical with that of the Emperor Henry IV and it was never seriously challenged. Five hundred years before Elizabeth he was, at least administratively the head of the Church in his realms. He regarded the responsibility very seriously. He was, says Dean Church, " a jealous and intelligent guardian, watching over all that went on in churches and monasteries, claiming great powers of interference, but interfering with an object and on a system." He appointed bishops and abbots and invested them with the insignia of office. Another contemporary chronicler records :

" He would, then, suffer no one in all his dominions to receive the Bishop of the city of Rome for the Apostle's Vicar, unless by his command, or in any wise to receive his letters, unless they had first been shown to himself. Further, he would not suffer the Primate of his kingdom, the Archbishop of Canterbury, if he were presiding over a general council of the bishops, to establish or forbid anything, unless what was agreeable to his will, and had first been ordained by him. To none of his bishops, nevertheless, did he permit that it should be allowed to implead publicly or excommunicate any of his barons or servants charged with incest or adultery, or any great crime, except by his precept, or to compel them by any penalty of ecclesiastical severity."

He deposed Archbishop Malger of Rouen, whose life was scandalous, and appointed in his place a saintly prelate of foreign birth. He called councils, at which he was present, to discuss theological doctrine and clerical discipline. He refused point blank to pay fealty to Pope Gregory. In a letter to Rome, written certainly with the knowledge of Lanfranc, he said :

"Hubert your legate coming to me on your behalf, admonished me, religious Father, that I should do fealty to you and your successors ; and that, touching the money which my predecessors were accustomed to send to the Roman Church, I should take better order. The one claim I have admitted, and the other I have not admitted. Fealty I neither have been willing to do, nor will I do it now, for I never promised it ; and I find not that my predecessors did it to yours. The money, for three years while I have been in Gaul, has been carelessly collected ; now, however, that by the Divine mercy I am returned to my realm, what has gathered is forwarded by the aforesaid legate, and the remainder, as soon as there is an opportunity, shall be sent by the envoys of Lanfranc, our faithful Archbishop. Pray for us and for the state of our realm ; because we have loved your predecessors, and you above all we desire to love sincerely, and listen to obediently."

He never recognised the excommunication of the Emperor and, in the struggle between Pope and Pope, he resolutely refused to take sides, but he never admitted the Hildebrandian claims.

William died at Rouen on September 9th, 1087. No sooner was the breath out of his body and the iron hand no longer to be feared than barons and bishops hurried away to guard their own interests. The master was gone ; it was now every man for himself. Orderic, the English-born son of a French father, to whom our knowledge of the times is mainly due, records :

"Behold ! I have with care inquired and with truth related what, in the Duke's fall, was pointed out beforehand by God's ordering hand. It is no fancy tragedy that I am palming off ; I am not courting the laughter of idlers by the quaint speeches of a comedy ; but to thoughtful readers I present the reality of change and chance. In the midst of prosperity, disasters appeared, that the hearts of men on earth might fear. A king once mighty and warlike, the terror of many people in many countries, lay naked on the ground, deserted by those whom he had nourished up. He needed borrowed money for his funeral ; he needed the help of a common soldier to provide a bier and bearers for it, he who had, up to that moment, such a superfluity of riches. Past a town in flames, he was carried by frightened men to his minster ; and he who had ruled over so many cities, and towns and villages, wanted a free spot on earth, that was his own, for his burial. . . . Rich and poor are alike in their lot : both are a prey to death and the worm. Put not, then, your trust in princes, which are nought, O ye sons of men ; but in God, the Living and the True, who is the Maker of all. Consider the course of things in the Old and the New Testament and there take for yourselves examples without number of what to avoid and what to desire. Trust not in wrong and robbery, and desire not the fruit of violence. If riches increase, set not your heart upon them. For all flesh is grass, and all the glory of it as the flower of the grass. The grass withereth, and the flower thereof fadeth away ; but the word of the Lord endureth for ever."

As I have written, William I was more than the greatest of the Normans. He had no peer among his other contemporaries. In his strength, his persistence, his statecraft, his sincerity, and the decency of his personal life, he stands alone in the story of the eleventh century.

His eldest son, the " vicious and unruly " Robert, whom his father detested, succeeded him as Duke of Normandy, and, under his rule, the country fell into anarchy and disorder. The second son, William Rufus, became King of England and was crowned by Lanfranc in Westminster Abbey. William Rufus inherited some of his father's alertness and inflexibility, and some of his shrewdness. But he had none of his vision and none of his piety. An austere Puritanism had been the note of the Conqueror's court. Rufus lived in an atmosphere of boisterous and unbridled licence. He was entirely without firmness of purpose. He started enterprises with enthusiasm, soon to become wearied and bored. He was utterly immoral, contemptuous of religion, entirely without a sense of responsibility. His one idea was to have a crudely good time, which he secured with the limit of brutality and oppression. He had courage, he was not without a measure of Norman acuteness but he was too impetuous always to secure even his own ends.

Thanks to the support of Lanfranc, who knew that his father had chosen Rufus as heir to the English throne, his succession was generally recognised. An attempt by a section of the Norman barons to secure the crown for his elder brother Robert was easily suppressed by levies of the native English, to whom Rufus made promises of the abolition of harassing taxation and the abrogation of the hated forestry laws, promises which he never attempted to fulfil. Rufus had no further trouble in England though he was constantly fighting with Robert for dominance in Normandy.

Lanfranc died in 1088, and with his restraint removed, Rufus let himself go with a vengeance. His chief minister was Ralph Flambard, the son of a Norman secular priest, who had been one of the clerks employed in the Domesday survey. As Lanfranc and St. Anselm represent early mediæval clericalism at its best, so Flambard stands for it at its worst. He was an unscrupulous and most ingenious scoundrel.

His task was to provide the king with money and at the same time to fill his own pockets and he went about it with audacious chicanery. He tampered with the measurements and valuations of Domesday Book. He ignored the accepted rents of the royal estates. He harried and robbed the laity, both the nobles and the simple. But it was in his exactions from the Church that Flambard has some historic importance since he established a precedent that was followed in worthier reigns. It was a recognised custom that the revenues of vacant sees and benefices should revert to the crown and Flambard deliberately refrained from filling such vacancies for the benefit of the royal treasury. This, says, Dean Church, was his " great financial invention." His reward from a grateful king was the rich bishopric of Durham.

The king's seizure of the revenues of Canterbury and his refusal to fill the primatial see aroused intense popular indignation. Each year Rufus " put up the Church of Christ for sale " and each year the highest bidder obtained the over-lordship with a free hand to squeeze the last possible penny out of the church tenants. The monks were dispersed or left half starved, the services were neglected. The Norman barons, turbulent and self-seeking as they might be, shared the Conqueror's regard for the ministers of religion. To them, as to the native English, Canterbury was the object of veneration and the fact that, for nearly five years, there was no Archbishop of Canterbury to govern the Church and to be heard in the counsels of the state became intolerable. The trouble was to find a man brave enough and distinguished enough to succeed Lanfranc and then to force the king to nominate him, and men began to think of the good and learned Abbot of Bec.

Anselm was pressed to visit England, but he had heard that his name was being widely mentioned for the Archbishopric and, dreading the troubles and responsibilities of the position, for some time he refused to take the journey. But he was urged by his brethren at Bec to visit the monastery's English property, which doubtless badly needed looking after. He crossed from Boulogne to Dover and at Canterbury he was acclaimed by the people as the future Archbishop, a reception that made him very uncomfortable, and on his way to Chester he had an interview with the king, whom he boldly upbraided. " Openly or secretly," he told Rufus, " things were daily said of him by nearly all the men of his realm which were not seemly for the king's dignity."

Anselm had finished his business in five months and was ready to return but for obscure reasons the king refused his permission.

On their part, eager to make the fullest use of the Abbot's presence, the bishops and barons petitioned the king to permit prayers in the churches that God " would put it into the king's heart to raise up the widowed see from its scandalous and unprecedented desolation " and Rufus, who cared for none of these things, cynically agreed, adding that " the Church might ask what it liked but he would not give up doing what he chose," and that " neither Anselm nor anyone else at this time shall be Archbishop except myself."

Early in 1093, Rufus was seriously ill, and, with fear of

death, he suffered a temporary repentance. He felt the need for ghostly counsel and Anselm was summoned to the royal sick-bed. As the result of his advice, " the king, when he thought himself soon to die, promised to God, as his barons recommended to him, to correct his life, to sell no more churches, nor put them out to farm, but to defend them by his kingly power, to take away unrighteous laws, and to establish righteous ones." The king was further urged to name the new Archbishop and he named St. Anselm.

There is no question that St. Anselm was genuinely reluctant to accept the nomination. To suggest that he was play-acting in the scenes that followed the king's decision is to show an entire failure to understand a character of appealing modesty and of a man with no sort of desire for personal distinction. St. Anselm was urged to go to the sick king and receive from him the pastoral staff. He refused. He was accused of preferring his own peace to hard labour for his brethren. He replied : " I am old and unfit for work. I am a monk and I have always shunned all worldly business. Do not entangle me in what I am unfit for." He was a foreigner and he had ties that could not be broken with his monastery. Then he was dragged by force to the bedside and the king bade his attendants to kneel and beg St. Anselm's assent. He still refused, and the pastoral staff was pressed against his clenched hand. Then, with the singing of the *Te Deum*, he was bodily carried to a neighbouring church. He has himself described this strange scene. " It would have been difficult to make out whether madmen were dragging a man in his senses or sane men a madman, save that they were chanting and I, pale with amazement and pain, looked more like dead than alive."

Afterwards St. Anselm went back to the king, assured him that he would get well and that if that were then his will, the nomination might be withdrawn. Then he addressed the bishops. They were endeavouring to yoke together an untamable bull and an old and feeble sheep. Lanfranc had been a strong ox. In his place they would place a poor sheep. " who in his own place might furnish milk and wool and lambs for the service of the Lord, but now could only be the victim of violence which he would be powerless to prevent." He knew full well what would happen. He would have to bear the brunt of the king's savage temper. They would not have the courage to stand by his side and when he was crushed they would be worse off than ever.

But Rufus had now made up his mind. If he had to have an Archbishop, he should be St. Anselm. The necessary consent from the Duke of Normandy and the Archbishop of Rouen were at once obtained, but the monks of Bec, who also had to consent, were naturally unwilling to lose their beloved Abbot. St. Anselm explained his position to them in a characteristic letter.

" I have lived for thirty-three years in the monastic habit; three without office, fifteen as prior, as many as abbot; and those who have known me have loved me, not from care of my own about it, but by God's mercy; and those the more, who knew me the most intimately and familiarly; and no one saw in me anything from which he could gather that I took delight in promotion. What shall I do then? How shall I drive away and quench this false and hateful suspicion, that it may not hurt the souls of those who once loved me for God's sake, by chilling their charity; or of those to whom my advice or example, be it worth what it may, might be of use, by making them think me worse than I really am; or of those who do not know me and hear this, by setting before them an evil example? . . . Thou God seest me; be thou my witness, that I know not, as my conscience tells me, why the love of anything, which thy servant as a despiser of the world ought to despise, should drag and bind me to the archbishopric to which I am suddenly hurried." " Here," he proceeds, " is my conscience, about my wish for the archbishopric or my dislike to it. If I deliberately lie to God, I don't know to whom I can speak the truth." He goes on, after warning those who were busy in fostering suspicion, " whether many or one," to notice some of the forms in which the claim of the monastery to keep him was put. " Some of you say that I might have reasonably held out against the election; they say, ' When he was compelled to be an abbot, he delivered himself as a servant to us in *the name of the Lord.*' . . . But what did I give you in *the name of the Lord?* ' Surely this : that I would not of my own will withdraw myself from your service, nor seek to withdraw myself, except under the obligation of that order and obedience of which I was before, according to God's will, the servant." . . . " I trusted to my strength and wit to keep myself where I wished to be; God has been stronger and craftier than I, and my confidence has come to nothing." . . .

" For myself I pray that you will not love me less, because God does His will with me; that I may not lose my reward with you, if I have ever wished to do your will, because now I dare not and ought not and cannot resist the will of God, nor up to this time see how I can withdraw myself from the Church of the English, except by resisting God. Show that you have loved me, not only for yourselves, but for God's sake and my own."

As St. Anselm had anticipated, Rufus got well. " The devil was well, the devil a monk was he." He revoked all the concessions that he made and, where he had before chastised with whips he now chastised with scorpions. " There arose such misery and suffering through the whole realm that, whoever remembers it, cannot remember anything like it in England. All the evil which the king had done before he was sick seemed good in comparison with the evils which he did when restored to health." But he made no attempt to get rid of St. Anselm.

St. Anselm, however, laid down specific conditions before he consented to be consecrated. All the possessions of the see in Lanfranc's time must be restored. He must be regarded by the king as " his spiritual father and ghostly adviser." And he insisted that the king should recognise Urban II as the rightful Pope, though the Emperor still supported the anti-Pope Clement. Rufus asked, as a personal favour, that his gifts of ecclesiastical lands for military service should be recognised. But St. Anselm flatly refused. He would not be a party to the robbery of the church. And, at the eleventh hour, he hoped to escape the responsibility that he dreaded. It was pressure from the harassed Canterbury monks that at last convinced him of his duty to compromise. He was consecrated by the Archbishop of York on December 4th, 1093, in the presence of nearly all the English bishops. And it was characteristic of Rufus that Ralph Flambard was at once sent to Canterbury to launch a suit in the king's name against certain of the Primate's tenants.

I have said that St. Anselm was a scholar and a saint. I have summarised the philosophy which gives him a high place among European thinkers. The saintliness of his character is made evident in his relations with his brethren at Bec, where his administration was characterised by sympathy, understanding and common sense. As Abbot, Lanfranc had, though with kindness, to establish order and discipline. When St. Anselm took over from Lanfranc, he was able to rule with even greater gentleness. He was, indeed, incapable of severity.

The philosopher, concerned with the eternal problems of living, must often have found the routine duties of administration tiring and irksome, but he fulfilled them all with smiling cheerfulness. His days were spent in listening to difficulties and to trivial complaints, in giving wise advice, in discussions with the brethren in the cloisters, in tending the sick in the infirmary, in shriving and comforting the dying. Then the long day's work done, the Abbot would spend half the night writing his treatises or, may be, correcting the ill-written manuscripts in the monastery library.

To us St. Anselm is curiously modern. He was more or less a Hegelian centuries before Hegel, and he had what are even now sometimes regarded as new fangled ideas of the right treatment of the young. He had a particular interest in young minds, " not yet dulled to the wonders and great ends of living." He invited their questions. He took immense pains to find satisfactory answers. He was all for persuasion ; he set little store on punishment. On one occasion, a brother Abbot complained of his failure with the boys in his care. The more they were beaten, the duller they became. And St. Anselm wrote to him :

"Tell me, my lord abbot, if you planted a tree in your garden, and tied it up on all sides so that it could not stretch forth its branches, what sort of tree would it turn out when, after some years, you gave it room to spread ? Would it not be good for nothing, full of tangled and crooked boughs ? And whose fault would this be but yours, who had put such constant restraint upon it ? And this is just what you do with your boys you plant them in the garden of the Church, that they may grow and bear fruit to God. But you cramp them round to such a degree with terrors and threats and blows, that they are utterly debarred from the enjoyment of any freedom. And thus injudiciously kept down, they collect in their minds evil thoughts, tangled like thorns ; they cherish and feed them and with dogged temper elude all that might help to correct them. And hence it comes that they see nothing in you of love, or kindness, or goodwill, or tenderness towards them ; they cannot believe that you mean any good by them, and put down all you do to dislike and ill-nature. Hatred and mistrust grow with them as they grow ; and they go about with downcast eyes, and cannot look you in the face. But, for the love of God, I wish you would tell me why you are so harsh with them ? Are they not human beings ? Are they not of the same nature as you are ? Would you like if you were what they are to be treated as you treat

22

them ? You try by blows and stripes alone to fashion them to good : did you ever see a craftsman fashion a fair image out of a plate of gold or silver by blows alone ? Does he not with his tools now gently press and strike it, now with wise art still more gently raise and shape it ? So if you would mould your boys to good you must, along with the stripes which are to bow them down, lift them up and assist them by fatherly kindness and gentleness " . . . " But," the abbot insisted, " what we try to do is to force them into seriousness and sturdiness of character ; what are we to do ? " " You do well," said Anselm ; " but if you give an infant solid food you will choke it. For every soul, its proportionate food. The strong soul delights in strong meat, in patience, and tribulations, not to wish forwhat is another's, to offer the other cheek, to pray for enemies, to love those that hate. The weak and tender in God's service need milk : gentleness from others, kindness, mercy, cheerful encouragement, charitable forbearance. If you will thus suit yourselves both to your weak and your strong ones, by God's grace you shall, as far as lies in you, win them all for God."

The kindliness and the quaint humour of the philosopher-saint are both evident in a letter pleading for forgiveness for a repentant runaway monk :

" He does not yet judge himself worthy to be called a son or a brother ; he desires to be as one of the hired servants among you. And for his sevant, whom he tempted away to content to obey him, out of attachment to himself, he fears even more than for his own person, inasmuch as if the servant is, as would be his just doom, punished with a heavy sentence, he sees that punishment will be exacted from his own soul for this. The money borrowed under a pledge to restore it, he has, through his own want of care and the cheating of another, entirely spent : and he is most anxious about it, for, unless by your generosity, and your permission for him to get help wherever he can, he can be freed from that debt, he can never hope that his heart will be comforted for that disgrace. He perceives that fo so many and such grave shortcomings no prayers of his own either may, or ought, to suffice ; and therefore he asks me, your servant, thinking that he will find no one more devoted to you, or more likely to obtain favour from you, to intercede for him. There is no greater intercession than yielding up skin for skin, life for life, according to the Lord's saying ' *Greater love hath no man than this, that he lay down his life for his friends.*' My beloved, let brother Moses be to you as if clothed from head to foot in the skin of brother Anselm, and let his mouth be mine. If there is any one among you whom I have formerly wronged of my own will, let him be the first to punish my skin in him, and condemn my mouth to abstinence. But after this fault, I most earnestly commend my skin to brother Moses, to be kept as he loves his own ; and to you— I do not say to be spared. For if through his fault my skin is hurt or severely punished, I will require it from him, being thankful, however, to whoever spares him. As to his servant, I have no other skin ; for his salvation is mine, his soul is mine. As to the request about money, the thing is easy to do, and will not, I think be hard to obtain through your mercifulness. About all this, he would wish to know your will by letter before he begins his journey to you, nor that he refuses to hasten even to torment if you command him : but he desires to return with good hope and joyfully to those for whom he longs. Farewell."

He knew, of course, that the Marys had chosen the better part, but he did not fail to recognise the importance of the Marthas. To an aged monk, weary of the humble duties of a cellarer, he wrote :

" It is, therefore, for your soul's good, brother and son most dear, that you should persevere in the office (' obedience ') which to the best of your power you have held, according to God's pleasure as far as we know, and the pleasure of your abbot and brethren, as long as life is in you, and your abbot bids you : with a good and glad mind, with no bitterness, no murmuring, so that you may even yield your breath speaking and giving directions about what concerns your office. So shall that promise be yours which is made to those who endure to the end. And do not let it frighten you that, from bodily weakness, you cannot do and look after the business of your office as you used to do in health and youth. For God requires nothing from you beyond your powers. Nor let any troubles disturb you, wherever they come from, by which the enemy of your soul seeks to annoy and weary you, that so you may faint before the end and lose the prize of perseverance. I exhort, therefore, and beseech you to resolve and settle in your heart that the good work which you have hitherto by God's help held fast, you will never give up while you live, unless your abbot and your brethren—not from your importunity, but of their free will—bid you leave it."

To another of his brethren, who complained that he had to spend time looking after the monastery's accounts when he would have been at his prayers, St. Anselm wrote :

" You complain that what you are doing now keeps you from being earnest in study and prayer : but let this be your not trifling consolation, that charity covereth a multitude of sins. For while in that work you are drawn away, another is attracted ; where you are bent down, another is set upright ; when you are oppressed, and the burden is heavy on you, you are carrying another's burden. And remember, that it is the servant who returns home empty who runs quickest ; but the servant who comes home loaded, is he whom the whole household welcomes with gladness. No one will blame him for having been so long in coming : but as he is tired to good purpose, he is told to take his rest. If you tell me that you have not the energy nor activity sufficient for the task enjoined you, let me answer, assuming your own estimate of yourself, which is not mine. A diseased eye, or but one eye in the head, cannot, of course, *adequately* discharge the office of seeing ; but as this imperfect eye is the only organ in the body which can see at all, in what it *can* do it is not a failure."

He insisted on thoroughness, persistence and humility. He, himself, was notably humble. But he could be very subtle, and was quite capable of outwitting opponents. Eadmer gives an account of his conduct in a law suit that he had to defend :

" So it happened that, sitting among the contending pleaders, while his opponents were taking counsel by what skill or by what trick they might hold their own cause or damage his, he, not minding it, was conversing with any one who wished to address him, either about the Gospel or some other divine Scripture, or some point of right conduct. And often, when he had no one to listen of this kind, quietly at peace in the purity of his heart, he would close his eyes and sleep. And often it came to pass that the cunning devices against him, when they came to his hearing, were at once exposed and torn to pieces, not as if he had been asleep all the while, but as if he had been fully awake and keenly watching. For charity, ' which envieth not, vaunteth not itself, seeketh not her own,' was strong in him, by which he saw at a glance the things that he ought to see ; for the truth was his guide."

This was the man who was enthroned at Canterbury.

He had confessed that he was handicapped by the fact that he was a foreigner, but his attitude to the English, whose language he did not speak and whose customs were hard for him to understand, is shown in a letter that he wrote, while he was still at Bec, to a Norman monk, who had been appointed Abbot of St. Albans :

" Though your Holiness is placed over barbarians, whom you cannot teach on account of difference of language, still you will never be able to excuse yourself before the awful Judge if you neglect to win others to God. For what you cannot say in words, you can show in life. For good is so much the more effectively recommended by example than by word, as goodness is loved in the silent, and loud talk despised in the slothful. Try, therefore, more to be loved by all for mercy and gentleness than feared for too austere and unsparing justice. Let men of all sorts who are committed to you rejoice that they are given to the care of a father and pastor, not tremble at being handed over to a tyrant and oppressor. Let your neighbours be glad that an adviser and helper has come to them from God, not deplore that an invader has arrived of other men's property, or a persecutor on evil pretexts."

From the Domesday survey, completed seven years before St. Anselm's enthronement, Dr. Seebohm calculates that at the end of the eleventh century, some five million acres of the land of England were under the plough. Of these half were small holdings, varying from thirty to three or four acres, held under various forms of tenure by freemen, " half-freemen," and " cottier tenants," most of whom had to work on their lord's demesne for a specified number of days of a year. In addition, there were rural townships which Professor Vinogradoff has described as " unions of peasant shareholders."

During the reign of the Conqueror, the small man may have had a tolerable life with the assurance of a fair return for his labour. During the thirteen years of the reign of Rufus, his lot must have been progressively miserable. Rufus was an expert blackmailer. The exactions, imposed on bishops and barons, were passed on to their tenants and dependents, and the recorded plight of the tenants of the Archbishopric of Canterbury suggests the general conditions of the country.

In the long contest between the spiritual and temporal powers, " the lowest rabble, poor artisans and ass-drivers " only rarely had the chance for any direct intervention. But they always stood to gain from the dominance of the spiritual authority. The Church was often their friend and protector. They had no other.

St. Anselm's first clash with the King after he became the Primate was concerned with his consideration for the poor and distressed. Rufus was preparing to invade Normandy and he needed money. In accordance with custom, St. Anselm offered him a gift of 500 marks, but it was not regarded as enough and was refused, and St. Anselm used the money as a Christmas present to the poor. Rufus was furious and the Archbishop was advised to buy back his favour. " Give him the 500 marks you offered," urged his suffragans, " and promise as much more, and he will give you back his friendship." Again St. Anselm refused. His tenants had been sufficiently oppressed, it was not for him " to strip them in their nakedness or rather flay them alive." The refusal earned him the king's open enmity. " Yesterday," said Rufus, " I hated him much, to-day still more ; to-morrow and ever after he may be sure that I shall hate

him with more bitter hatred." The quarrel developed after
the king's return from the continent.

According to the established rule, St. Anselm asked permission to go to Rome to receive the Pallium of his office
from the Pope. For all his jealousy for what he regarded as
his prerogatives, the Conqueror had agreed to Lanfranc
making this journey. But Rufus, desiring to weaken St.
Anselm's position, refused his permission on the ground
that there were two Popes in Rome and that England had
not acknowledged either. St. Anselm demanded that the
question should be referred to the Great Council of England,
and a meeting was summoned at Rockingham in Derbyshire
in Lent, 1095.

St. Anselm put his case with straightforward simplicity.
He reminded the Council that he had done all in his power
to avoid preferment. " But," he went on, " seeing that
you were importunate, I have trusted myself to you, and
have taken up the load you put on me, relying on your
promised assistance." He owed fealty to both the Pope
and the king. The two loyalties were not incompatible.

The bishops, many of whom had bought their sees from
the king, tried hard not to take sides. The lay nobles were
inclined to support the Archbishop. The common folk,
who had come to Rockingham to listen, were enthusiastically
on his side.

St. Anselm was unmoved by cajoling and by threats. He
accepted Urban as the rightful head of Christendom and he
declared : " Know ye therefore, all of you, that in the
things that are God's, I will render obedience to the Vicar
of St. Peter ; and in those which belong to the earthly
dignity of my lord the King, I will render him both faithful
counsel and service, to the best of my understanding and
power."

His serenity and his astuteness, were embarrassing. It was
complained that he listened to the arguments of the negotia-
tors and " with one breath of his lips he breaks them as if
they were cobwebs." The bishops were terrified, the nobles,
welcoming the attempt to curb the king's arrogance were
cynically amused. Finally the Council declined to obey the
king.

St. Anselm, realised the consequences of the King's anger and asked for a safe conduct to quit the kingdom. But Rufus would not let him go while the Archbishopric was still his and, prevented for the moment from destroying the shepherd, he revenged himself on his flock. More exactions were imposed on the unfortunate people of Canterbury and the result was that for which Rufus had hoped. " Every one agreed that it would be better to be without a pastor at all as they had been than to have a pastor such as this."

Rufus did not lack persistence and his next move was to endeavour, with lavish promises, to enlist Urban against St. Anselm. But the attempt was a failure and, with a rebellion threatening in the north, Rufus concluded that it would be wise to patch up some sort of peace with the obstinate cleric. They met at Windsor, and the King agreed that St. Anselm should be accepted as the spiritual father of the realm, but this concession did not secure an agreement from the Archbishop to receive the Pallium from the royal hands. Then Rufus made a further concession. The Pallium was laid on the high altar at Canterbury, from which it was taken by the Archbishop.

1096 was the year of the First Crusade. The First Crusade was part of, perhaps it would be more accurate to say the culmination of, the religious revival of the eleventh century. Hildebrand had contemplated an expedition of the Christian nations to drive the Moslems out of Asia Minor. But it was Urban who, in a famous sermon at Clermont, in 1095, called for a truce of God in Europe and for all Christians to unite to rescue Jerusalem, the expedition to be counted as a full penance. Urban was a Frenchman, always influenced by his training at Cluny, and his appeal was mainly answered by Frenchmen. Peter the Hermit, a priest of Amiens, went from Clermont to stir the mass of the people, much in the manner of a modern revivalist preacher, and it was French and Norman knights who, attracted by the call to military adventure, sanctified by religious zeal and the benediction of the Church, were the backbone of the force that eventually captured the Holy City.

Dr. Ernest Barker has suggested that the hordes of the

commonalty who followed Peter the Hermit, Walter the
Penniless, William the Carpenter and the other popular
leaders were really emigrants, escaping from the famine and
pestilence that ravaged Europe in 1094 and 1095, and eager
to find new homes in the East. Dr. Barker describes them
as " tramps and bankrupts, camp-followers and hucksters,
fugitive monks and escaped villeins." But it is surely per-
missible to believe that " the motley crowd " which treked
across Europe, was influenced by religious fervour at least
as much as by hunger. Indeed, there is far more interest in
the Crusade of the people that was a complete and pitiful
failure, than in the crusade of the Franco-Norman princes,
who, backed by the money of the Italian cities anxious for
new markets, achieved a considerable measure of success.

There were few English recruits among the Crusaders, but
the Crusade had its effect on the course of English history.
Robert of Normandy was an enthusiastic Crusader, and to
provide for the equipment of his army he sold his duchy
for three years to his brother Rufus. To raise the money,
Rufus commandeered the treasure of the churches which in
the circumstances could not well be refused.

In 1097, St. Anselm was again in trouble with the king.
Under feudal law, he had had to supply a contingent to
the forces with which Rufus attempted to subdue a rising
in Wales. The King complained that the Archbishop's
soldiers were badly equipped, and St. Anselm was summoned
to appear before the King's Court. Eadmer wrote :

> " Knowing that all judgments of the King's Court depended on the
> king's word, and that nothing was considered there but what he willed,
> Anselm thought it an unbecoming farce to strive as litigants do about a
> verbal charge, and to submit the truth of his cause to the judgment of a
> court, of which neither law, nor equity, nor reason were the warrant.
> He held his peace therefore, and gave no answer to the messenger, looking
> on this kind of summons as belonging to that class of annoyances which
> he well remembered ; and this only he earnestly prayed, that God would
> claim them."

St. Anselm then asked permission to leave the country,
and, after months of negotiation, the King consented and
the two men parted, the Archbishop with " a cheerful and
bright countenance," the King with a show of good feeling.

But the Archbishop's baggage was rudely searched before he was allowed to embark at Dover. Before leaving, he said to the King :

> " My lord, I go. If it could have been with your good will, it would have better become you, and been more agreeable to all good people. But as things have gone contrary, though on your behalf I am sorry, yet as far as I am concerned, I will bear it with an even mind, and not for this will I give up, by God's mercy, my love for your soul's health. And now, not knowing when I shall see you again, I commend you to God ; and as a spiritual father to his beloved son, as the Archbishop of Canterbury to the King of England, I would fain before I go, if you refuse it not, give God's blessing and my own."

St. Anselm landed on the continent in November, 1097, and in the long winter journey across Europe, he was everywhere received with honour and regard. In his appeal to Rome, St. Anselm was not as Dean Church suggests, " inviting foreign interference in our home concerns." The modern idea of nationalism and of the rights of sovereign states was not to appear in Europe for another five hundred years. Rufus, the king of England, was a Norman, St. Anselm was an Italian, who had for years lived in Normandy, the Pope was a Frenchman. St. Anselm appealed to the guardian of the moral and religious life of Europe against the lawliness, oppression and corruption that existed in one of the provinces of Christendom, for the spiritual well-being of which the Pope was responsible to God. Dean Church correctly says : " When others acquiesced in the evil state, he refused ; and further, he taught a lesson which England has since largely learned, though in a very different way. He taught his generation to appeal from arbitrary will and force to law." That is enough to secure for him a high place in the history of his adopted country.

St. Anselm, now a man of sixty-four, found the summer heat in Rome very trying, and the Pope was in no hurry to make any pronouncement. So, in perfect content, he retired to a small monastery in the hills and wrote his *Cur Deus Homo*, in which he dealt with the mysteries of the Incarnation and the Atonement and, once more to quote Dean Church, " moulded the character of all Christian doctrine since."

St. Anselm had to travel to Capua for his first meeting with the Pope, whom he met in the camp of his Norman allies. He begged to be canonically relieved of his Archbishopric, but Urban was anxious to keep on good terms with all the Normans and he hesitated openly to flout Rufus and St. Anselm was advised to state his case at a Council to be held at Bari, but which did not meet until the late autumn of 1098. Here St. Anselm was received with the honour due to his learning and his character. He took a leading part in defending against the Greeks the inclusion of the *ex filioque* clause in the creed and he so impressed the council that there was a unanimous vote for the excommunication of the King of England. But the Pope took no action.

St. Anselm, however, had vastly impressed the bishops and another council, held in Rome at the following Easter, was opened by a sermon by an Italian bishop in which he dramatically exclaimed :

" Hither are brought the complaints of the oppressed and the spoiled ; from hence, as from the head of all, counsel and help are asked for. And with what result all the world knows and sees. One is sitting among us from the ends of the earth, in modest silence, still and meek. But his silence is a loud cry. The deeper and gentler his humility and patience, the higher it rises before God, the more should it kindle us. This one man, I say, has come here in his cruel afflictions and wrongs, to ask for the judgment and equity of the Apostolic See. And this is the second year and what help has he found ? "

This honest outburst greatly annoyed the Pope, who ordered the preacher to bring his sermon to an end. And the next day St. Anselm left Rome for Lyons, having gained nothing.

St. Anselm remained in France for nearly another two years, and " there grew up an extraordinary and incredible affection for him among all the people and his goodness was spoken of far and wide."

Rufus was killed in the New Forest in August, 1100, and was succeeded by his brother, Henry I, the Conqueror's fourth son, who at once solemnly promised before the altar at Westminster to govern according to law. Henry inherited much of his father's statecraft. He was well educated—he once said that an unlettered king was a crowned ass—; he could read and write Latin, and he could speak English and knew something of English law. He realised that to make his position secure he must placate both the Church and the English population. To attain the first end, he promptly arrested the rascally Ralph Flambard and sent a deputation to beg St. Anselm to return to England. To attain the second end, he married Edith, the daughter of the King of Scotland and through her mother the last representative of the Saxon kings.

St. Anselm landed at Dover on September 23rd and met the king at Salisbury. There had been objections to Henry's marriage on the ground that Princess Edith had taken the vows as a nun, which she denied, and St. Anselm's first duty after his return was to make a full enquiry into the charge which he found unsubstantiated and the Archbishop blessed the marriage.

For thirteen years Henry had suffered many things at the hands of his older brothers. He had been kept in obscurity and little was known of his character. But it was soon made clear that while, unlike Rufus, he had inherited their father's love of order, he had all the masterfulness of his father and his brother. " I will have all the croziers in my hand," the Conqueror had declared and Henry was equally determined. His position was not too secure. He needed the Church not as an independent ally, but as a loyal vassal.

He insisted that the position should be made quite clear, and, to that end, he demanded that St. Anselm should be re-invested in his Archbishopric. This demand was entirely unprecedented. It implied that the highest ecclesiastical offices automatically became vacant with the death of one king and the accession of another.

St. Anselm was bound to refuse. He regretted that he had come back to England. It was evident that he could not work with the King for the good of the people. He asked that he might be allowed to go again. But to this Henry could not agree. " It was a grave matter to lose the investiture of churches and the homages of prelates ; it was a grave matter, too, to let Anselm take his departure, while he himself was not fully confirmed in his kingdom. For on one side it seemed to him to be losing, as it were, half of his kingdom ; on the other he feared lest Anselm should make his brother Robert, who would most easily be brought into subjection to the Apostolic see, King of England."

So there was another compromise and yet another appeal to Rome. Meanwhile the King and the Archbishop remained on good terms and St. Anselm was very useful in his support of Henry in a quarrel with the Norman barons. " The English and the common soldiers were also true."

After a long delay the answer came from Rome, from Urban's successor, Paschal II, also a Cluny monk. As was expected, the Pope was unable to accede to the King's latest demand and there followed the old business of persuasion, threats and intrigues, which St. Anselm must have found infinitely wearisome.

A second embassy was sent to Rome and this time the answer was indefinite. Paschal had his own troubles with rival claimants for the Papal throne and he had no stomach for further complications. But St. Anselm wanted a straight answer to a straight question. " I am not afraid," he wrote to Rome, " of banishment or torments or death ; for all these, God strengthening me, my heart is ready in obedience to the apostolic see, and for the liberty of my mother, the Church ; all I ask is certainty that I may know, without doubt, what course I ought to hold by your authority."

In 1102 a Council was held at Westminster to tighten clerical discipline and to deal with increasing sex perversion, and the Archbishop threatened excommunication in the case of blatant sin.

Throughout this year the contest with the king went on, but Henry, with all the rest of the world, had a deep admiration and real affection for St. Anselm and his violent reproaches were generally followed by kindliness. It was suggested that it would be wise if the Archbishop himself went to Rome and in the early summer of 1103, St. Anselm started on a third journey to Italy, glad enough to be out of the ceaseless turmoil.

On his way he spent pleasant, restful days at his old home at Bec. After his interviews with the Pope yet another conciliatory letter was written to Henry, but St. Anselm was formally confirmed in his Primacy, which was the snub direct to the King. Word was sent to St. Anselm not to return to England, and following the example of Rufus, the King seized the Canterbury revenues, though this time the receivers were the Archbishop's men "who, as they were bound by fealty and oaths to Anselm, would exercise their office less vexatiously to the tenants." According to the chronicler, this anticipation was disappointed.

Henry and St. Anselm wrote friendly letters to each other. The Queen sent the Archbishop affectionate messages. The Canterbury monks implored him to give way and to save them from further persecution. But this he could not do.

He was bored by the whole question of the investitures. Had it been a personal matter, he would have met the wishes of the King. But it was for the Pope to command and for him to obey and, without precise instructions from Rome, he would not submit to what was a revolutionary demand. At last, in March, 1105, St. Anselm was convinced that it was hopeless to expect a clear lead from Rome and he decided that it was his duty himself to excommunicate the King. The threat was enough. Henry was always prudent and knew when it was policy to give way. Through the good offices of the King's sister, Adela, the two men met at Chartres. The King promised to restore the revenues of St. Anselm's see, but he repeated his demand for the investiture. Further, to provide funds for a war in Normandy he had heavily taxed the clergy as a punishment, so he explained for the clerical marriages that continued to be a scandal, the innocent being mulcted as well as the guilty. This naturally antagonised even those bishops who had hitherto sided with the King and strengthened St. Anselm's position.

Permission came at last from Rome to Anselm to release the prelates from the excommunication imposed for submitting to the King's demand and this made it possible for the Archbishop to return home. But he was feeling the weight of his seventy-three years, he was tired and ill and for the last time he found peace at Bec, where the King once more visited him. Henry had decisively defeated his brother, his throne was now secure, and he acted with a statesmanlike magnanimity, withdrawing many of his claims, conceding all for which St. Anselm on his side had contended, and the Archbishop crossed to England to be warmly welcomed by the Queen and the people. Eadmer, the chronicler, says :

" On the first of August (1107)—it would have been at Whitsuntide but for Anselm's illness—an assembly of bishops, abbots and chief men of the realm was held in London, in the king's palace, and for three days continuously the matter of the investitures of churches was fully discussed between the king and the bishops, Anselm being absent ; some of them urging that the king should perform them after the custom of his father and brother, and not according to the command of the Pope. For the Pope, standing firm in the decision which had been promulgated thereupon, had allowed the homage which Pope Urban had forbidden equally with investitures ; and by this had made the king inclinable to him on the point of investitures. Then, in the presence of Anselm, the multitude standing by, the king granted and decreed that from that time forth for ever no one should be invested in England with bishoprics or abbey by staff and ring, either by the king or by any lay hand ; Anselm also allowing that no one elected to a prelacy should be refused consecration on account of homage done to the king. This, then, having been settled, fathers were appointed by the king, by the counsel of Anselm and the chief men of the realm, without any investiture of the pastoral staff and ring, in nearly all the churches in England, which had long been widowed of their pastors."

The long contest was over and the victory was St. Anselm's. His triumph was the triumph of conviction and still more of character. It was said, indeed, at one of the councils in Italy, that he attended, that his silence was more difficult to answer than his words.

The decision of 1107 completed what had been begun by the Conqueror and by strengthening the ties with Rome it brought England definitely into Europe, where she remained until the Reformation. Dean Church says that the fact that St. Anselm's victory made Rome more powerful in England " did not recommend it to the sympathy of Englishmen." I cannot find the smallest justification for this suggestion of the mind of Englishmen at the beginning of the twelfth century. It is, indeed, an example of prejudice that is unexpected in the great Dean of St. Paul's.

The trouble was not that the Pope was too strong, but that he was not strong enough. Even under Hildebrand, Rome could be successfully defied by ruthless temporal sovereigns.

In England St. Anselm compelled the recognition that the bishop has a supernatural authority, and that, while he may pay homage to the King, he remains more than the King's man.

In the last two years of his life, St. Anselm, whose many worries never killed his absorption in philosophic and theological speculations, wrote a treatise *Concerning the Agreement of Foreknowledge, Predestination, and the Grace of God with Free Will*. On Palm Sunday, 1109, it was evident that he was dying. Eadmer, his faithful attendant and biographer, has related the events of his last days :

> " On the following Tuesday, towards evening he was no longer able to speak intelligently. Ralph, Bishop of Rochester, asked him to bestow his absolution and blessing on us who were present, and on his other children, and the people of the land who had kept themselves under God in his obedience. He raised his right hand, as if he was suffering nothing, and made the sign of the Holy Cross ; and then dropped his head and sank down. The congregation of the brethren were already chanting Matins in the great church, when one of those who watched about our Father took the book of the Gospels and read before him the history of the Passion, which was to be read that day at the Mass. But when he came to our Lord's words, ' Ye are they which have continued with me in my temptations, and I appoint unto you a kingdom, as my Father hath appointed unto me, that ye may eat and drink at my table," he began to draw his breath more slowly. We saw that he was just going, so he was removed from his bed, and laid upon sackcloth and ashes. And thus, the whole family of his children being collected round him, he gave up his last breath into the hands of his Creator, and slept in peace.

> " He passed away, as morning was breaking, on the Wednesday before the day of our Lord's Supper, the 21st April, in the year of Our Lord's Incarnation, 1109—the sixteenth of his pontificate and the seventy-sixth of his life."

Chapter II

THE SAINT

AS Freeman pointed out, of few of the great figures of
English history is there so vast an amount of contemporary information as there is of St. Thomas of London.
" We have original materials of every sort—chronicles, biographies, private letters, state-papers ; we have the panegyrics of friends, the invectives of enemies, the correspondence of the man himself." But with all this material for
judging his character, the estimates of St. Thomas are almost
grotesquely divergent. To Froude he is an unqualified
villain, violent, overbearing, ambitious and unscrupulous,
as venal as Flambard, a man whose piety was hypocrisy,
whose charity was dictated by policy, who fought viciously
for a bad cause. And though Froude himself would hardly
have claimed to be a master of restraint, he seems to have
been particularly shocked by the fact that St. Thomas was
" not select in his language." Freeman agrees with Froude
in believing that St. Thomas contended for " principles
which we must all rejoice did not ultimately prevail " ; but
Freeman adds he was " a great and heroic Englishman."

" His great qualities were an ardent and impetuous spirit,
a practical energy that carried everything before him, an
admirable versatility which could adapt itself to all circumstances and all people, and a lofty sense of duty which could
support him under any amount of adversity and disappointment. His faults were chiefly the exaggeration of his virtues."

This is the balanced judgment of an historian striving to
be impartial. But generally St. Thomas has been eulogised
or condemned according to the conviction of his biographers.
To the " sound Protestant " he is an ignoble self-seeker. To
the Catholic, whether of the Roman or the Anglican obedience, St. Thomas is a martyr and a saint.

I make no claim to any inhuman impartialities. I have
already written of St. Thomas at some length in a volume
published seventeen years ago and my admiration remains
for the first great Englishman of the Middle Ages. It is

true that his father was born in Rouen and his mother in Caen. But he, himself, was English born and his qualities were those that have come to be regarded as typically English. He could never do anything by halves. He went from one extreme to another. He had a tremendous capacity for personal enjoyment and the complementary capacity for personal sacrifice. Again, as Freeman has insisted, he was "a muscular Christian," the sort of man that the English have always loved. He fought the King, he was often opposed by the barons and nearly as often at loggerheads with the bishops, but from the day that he was enthroned at Canterbury until his martyrdom, he was the hero of the common people.

St. Anselm died in 1109. St. Thomas was born in Cheapside on December 21st, 1118, and was consecrated Archbishop of Canterbury on June 3rd, 1162, the first Englishman to occupy the throne of St. Augustine for over one hundred years. After the death of St. Anselm, Henry I, following the Flambard precedent, contrived to keep the see of Canterbury vacant for five years and from 1114 to 1136 (Henry died in 1135) there were two more Norman primates, both nonenities. In 1139, in the early years of the anarchic reign of Stephen of Blois, Theobald became Archbishop. He was the spiritual successor of Lanfranc and St. Anselm. Like them he had been a monk at Bec. Like St. Anselm he was a scholar, asking for nothing but peace and the company of learned men, and also like St. Anselm, he could be courageous and astute, demonstrating that the children of light are sometimes a match for the children of this world.

In Rome, Paschal II died in 1118, and, between that year and the beginning of St. Thomas's English Primacy, nine Popes and several anti-Popes reigned or strove to reign as supreme heads of Christendom. The last was Adrian IV, the one Englishman in the long line of Roman pontiffs. Alexander III became Pope in 1159, destined to carry on a protracted struggle with the Emperor Frederick Barbarossa, similar to the struggle in the century before between Hildebrand and the Emperor Henry IV.

The reign of law established in England by the Conqueror and re-established by Henry I came to an end when

Stephen ascended the throne and, for fourteen years, the country was ravaged by civil war. It was inevitable that the prevailing lawlessness should have affected the Church, but the spiritual decadence has been grossly exaggerated by Froude. He says in his *Life and Times of Becket* :

> " Speaking generally, at the time when Becket declared war against the State, the Church, from the Vatican to the smallest archdeaconry, was saturated with venality. The bishops were mere men of the world. The Church benefices were publicly bought and sold, given away as a provision to children, or held in indefinite numbers by ambitious men who cared only for wealth and power. Very many of the common clergy were ignorant, dissolute, and lawless, unable to be legally married, and living with concubines in contempt or evasion of their own rules. In character and conduct the laity were superior to the clergy."

The truth is that the religious revival of the eleventh century continued into the twelfth. This was owing, to some extent, to the influence of the Crusades. Rahere, for example, the light-hearted courtier of Henry I, returned from the Holy Land to found St. Bartholomew's Hospital and to devote the rest of his life to the service of God. The building of St. Paul's Cathedral was begun and other great churches were built, and Green says that the churchmen of the twelfth century " derived whatever might they possessed from sheer holiness of life and unselfishness of aim " ; and H. G. Wells, certainly no lover of the Church, has written : " The period from the time of Gregory VII onward for a century and a half was the great period of ambition and effort of the Church. There was a real sustained attempt to unite all Christendom under a purified and re-organised Church." The Church was constructive, while the secular powers were merely destructive.

To the student whose main interest is the condition of the common people the greatest religious achievement of the century was the birth of the Cistercian Order, " the great preachers of labour." The Cistercians fasted and prayed and spent long hours in contemplation and they found time to teach the English peasantry better methods of cultivating the land, tending sheep and breeding horses. They were agricultural experts and pioneers, and these Cistercian monks were the fathers of English overseas trade. The first wool exported from these shores came from the Cistercian farms. They drained swamps, they dug channels and ditches, they built barns and mills, they made roads. And this transformation of the countryside was effected in the name of the Lord. Never was faith expressed in more practical or more valuable works, and the Cistercians could certainly have counted on the special patronage of St. James. Their first English home was established at Furness in 1127. A hundred others were in existence when St. Thomas became Archbishop of Canterbury.

In the eleventh century, St. Anselm had lived years of peaceful life at Bec, apparently unaware of the constant fighting almost outside the monastery walls and of the portentous struggle between the Pope and the Emperor; so in the twelfth century, the Cistercians in England went on ploughing and reaping, too busy with the things that mattered most to bother about the contest between Stephen and the Empress Mathilda.

The common land of England was held in common by the common people and the common sense leadership of the Cistercians must have made for the common good. Where the monks were landlords, as Cobbett insisted, they were generally good landlords. They never evicted their tenants and they never demanded a rack rent.

While the Cistercians were revolutionising English rural life, the craft guilds, definitely religious in their constitution, were systematising the life of the towns. They were the forerunners of the nineteenth century skilled workers' Trade Unions. In his *The Parish Guilds of Rural Mediæval England*, Canon Westlake describes one of these guilds :

"The craft-gild weavers at Lincoln, which received a charter from Henry II in 1157, was in its religious aspect a fraternity of the Exultation of the Cross, though it does not appear as such till 1346. It provided a great candle before the ' high cross in the body of the mother church of Lincoln,' which was renewed yearly, brought thereto in a solemn procession. Like most of the gilds of Lincoln, it made ordinances for such brethren as desired to go on pilgrimage. Such ordinances may be illustrated from the Rule of the gild of St. Anne in the parish of St. Peter at the Skinmarket. A brother who would make pilgrimage to the Holy Land, Rome or St. James, must first of all surrender any gild property he may have in his hands. On his setting out the brethren lead him as far as the Cross on Lincoln Green, and there the Graceman, as the masters of the gilds of Lincoln were called, gives him 2d., the two wardens 1d., and every gild brother ½d. On his return he is met at the same place and conducted with joy and honour to the cathedral church and thence to his home."

St. Thomas's father was a well-to-do *bourgeois* with aristocratic connections. Thomas was sent to school at Merton and afterwards at Paris and he spent his holidays at Pevensey, where he lived the life of a Norman country gentleman. When he was twenty-two, his father lost most of his money and Thomas was employed for a time in the office of a kinsman who was Sheriff of London. This gave him his first experience of public affairs. There is a contemporary description of St. Thomas as a young man :

"Slim of growth and pale of hue, dark of hair, with a long nose and straightly featured face ; blithe of countenance was he, winning and lovable in all conversation, frank of speech in his discourse, but slightly stuttering in his talk, so keen of discernment and understanding that he could always make difficult questions plain after a wise manner. Of such wondrously strong memory was he that whatsoever he had heard of sentences and law awards he could cite it at any time he chose to give it forth. By reason of these great gifts of God which we have told of even now it was easily understood by wise men that he was predestined to a high station in the church of God."

In the twelfth century, the Church was the obvious career for a young man of outstanding ability and small means, and when he was twenty-four, St. Thomas secured a position in the household of Theobald, Archbishop of Canterbury. The Canterbury cathedral school was, as Stubbs says, " a substitute for the as yet undeveloped universities." The scholarly atmosphere was more than congenial to St. Thomas and, as one of the Archbishop's secretaries, he was extremely useful and widely interested in the tangle of ecclesiastical politics. Theobald recognised his capacity. He had a paternal affection for him, he learned to trust his judgment, and when St. Thomas was twenty-six, he was sent on a confidential mission to Rome to protest against the appointment of Henry of Blois, Bishop of Winchester, the brother of Stephen and incidentally an admirable prelate, as Papal Legate. As such his authority in England was greater than that of the Archbishop, who had no love for his family and

Theobald, easy-going as he generally was, found the position intolerable. St. Thomas's first diplomatic experience was a complete success and Theobald, not Henry, became the legate in England of the Apostolic See.

In 1148, when he was thirty, St. Thomas had his first contact with the contest between Church and King, which was to cost him his life. He went with the Archbishop to a council at Rheims called by Pope Eugenius III, at which the appointment by Stephen of his nephew as Archbishop of York was declared invalid. Stephen retaliated in usual way by confiscating Theobald's property and forcing him to a short exile. But Stephen, well intentioned and weak willed, was no match for the might of Rome. At Theobald's suggestion, the Pope formally recognised Henry of Anjou, the Conqueror's great-grandson, as the heir to the English throne, Theobald insisting on the Hildebrandian claim that to the Church " it principally belongs to elect the king."

Stephen naturally wished to secure the succession for his son and refused to recognise the Papal decision. But he was promptly excommunicated and brought to heel, and, on Stephen's death, Henry was crowned King of England at Winchester in 1154.

The Council at Rheims, in 1148, was mainly concerned with doctrinal questions and it was dominated by the great Cistercian, St. Bernard of Clairvaux, Pope Eugenius being himself a Cistercian monk. It is a significant commentary on Froude's distorted description of the state of the Church that so many of the Popes in the early Middle Ages were monks of Cluny or Bec or Clairvaux, men of outstanding piety and devotion.

I have said in the preceding essay that William of Normandy, Hildebrand and Lanfranc were the greatest figures of the eleventh century. It is unquestionable that St. Bernard was the most influential figure of the twelfth, and it says a good deal for the spirit of his age that he owed his influence to his sheer goodness. St. Bernard was a Bible Christian. He was saturated in its language and its spirit. A man of great parts he was as kind as he was wise. His austerity was unqualified and being as practical as he was pious he was the most influential inspirer of the Cistercians in their work of genuine social Christianity. St. Bernard had no patience with the unrealities of the schoolmen. He possessed a Christlike tenderness, but on occasion he showed an equally Christlike scorn for folly and pretence. His faith was clear and definite and he followed with indomitable courage and persistence where his faith led him. He was a zealot, but he was neither a bigot nor a persecutor. On one occasion, he saved the Jews from persecution, and he taught that heretics should be taken " not by force of arms but by force of argument." Humble without servility, determined without offence, there is no nobler figure in the pageant of Christian history than St. Bernard of Clairvaux.

This was the man whom Thomas met at Rheims when he was thirty. No man could come into contact with St. Bernard without being affected by him, and the influence of the noble Cistercian is very evident in many of the characteristics of St. Thomas's troubled later life.

When Henry II was crowned at Winchester, St. Thomas was still only a deacon. Thanks to the favour of Theobald, he held a number of lucrative clerical offices that might well have filled the most successful of eighteenth-century pluralists with envy. He had the livings of St. Mary-le-Strand and of Otford in Kent. He was a Prebendary of St. Paul's and of Lincoln, and he was Archdeacon of Canterbury. Clerical pluralism is always scandalous (the Reformation did nothing to discredit the scandal), but Thomas appointed competent deputies for the duties which he could obviously not perform himself. As Archdeacon, he was responsible for the administration of the canon law and, to fit him for this office, Theobald had sent him for a course of study at the university of Bologna.

Henry owed his crown to the backing of the Church. He knew little or nothing of England. He was never primarily the King of England. Nominally the vassal of the King of France, he was politically and militarily far more powerful in France than his suzerain. From his father, the incompetent Geoffrey of Anjou, he had inherited Anjou, Maine and Touraine. Through his mother, the masterful Mathilda, daughter of Henry I, he was Duke of Normandy and suzerain of Brittany. Through his marriage, he had become Duke of Aquitaine. He controlled the western seaboard of France from Calais to the Pyrenees and his possessions extended eastward to Tours. He was, that is, master of nearly half modern France.

Henry was his mother's son. He was a true Norman in his firmness of purpose, his capacity for rule and his love of discipline and order.

Henry never spoke a word of English. He spent a very short time during his reign in England. But he was determined that in his long absences England should be efficiently governed and to that end he needed a capable minister who knew the country. He consulted Theobald, who suggested his favourite subordinate, and in 1155 St. Thomas became Chancellor of England. He was then thirty-seven and the King was twenty-two. It has been suggested by his enemies that St. Thomas bought this high position. But, remembering the character of the King, this is most unlikely. It was essential for Henry to have a thoroughly competent Chancellor ; he was not the man to be bribed into the appointment of an incompetent. Moreover, there is evidence that St. Thomas had no desire for the position. His life was bound up with the Church. He was devoted to Theobald and had listened to St. Bernard. He had an intimate knowledge of the inevitable hostility of the secular and spiritual authorities. He feared that, in serving the King, he might be compelled into strife with the Church. A contemporary writer says :

> " Hence it is written that he prayed the archbishop Theobald, often times with tears, that he might be taken back into his service so as to withdraw his neck from under the yoke of the thraldom of standing between the Church and the King's men. This, however, the archbishop could not grant him, saying that, by the spiritual reward which awaited him, he was the more needed for the Church the heavier the trials were that he must needs endure."

Immediately after his accession, Henry made a progress through his new dominions and St. Thomas travelled with him. Henry was tireless. He never stayed more than a week in one place. He talked with all sorts and conditions of men. He listened to complaints and investigated grievances.

After the royal progress, the King went back to France and St. Thomas was left to govern the country and to work out the reforms that the King had initiated. He was the chief judge of the King's courts. He was the Chancellor of the Exchequer. He was frequently sent on diplomatic missions outside the kingdom. On occasion, the churchman became the eager and not too scrupulous soldier. In 1159, he was with the expedition sent by Henry against Toulouse and he took a contingent of 6,000 men to fight with the King in a campaign on the Norman frontier. This martial enthusiasm in a man, soon to be called to the highest ecclesiastical office, is only to be understood if it is remembered that St. Thomas just had to be thorough. When he was a soldier, he was nothing but a soldier, fierce, energetic, intent on gaining military advantage, just as during the years when he was an archbishop, he was nothing but an archbishop, austere, devoted, caring for nothing but the Church that had been committed to his care.

As Chancellor, St. Thomas lived in an atmosphere of magnificent pomp, but the magnificence had a political intention. Henry had no party manners. When he was in England he was abrupt and inhospitable, and St. Thomas's lavish hospitality, as the King's representative, had a definite political value.

When he was sent as ambassador to Paris, his ostentation was the reminder that his master, the nominal vassal, was at least as rich and as powerful as his suzerain, while the gifts that the Chancellor made to the University of Paris and his help to the poorer English students were in accord with his never-failing consideration for both learning and the needy.

Robert Cricklade says that " to needy folk and foreigners he yielded them in their hardships unstinted comfort in gifts of money, although it were hidden from the knowledge of the multitude." And Edward Grim, his faithful Saxon secretary, records : " The poor and the oppressed found ready access to him ; the cause of the widow did not come before him in vain ; he gave justice and protection to the weak and needy." Froude refers scornfully to " the crowd of mendicants " that followed St. Thomas—Froude is as fond of the term " mendicant " as Mrs. Wilfer was—and suggests that the charity was a mere bid for popularity. In fact it was the natural expression of a kindly heart.

St. Thomas had retained all his ecclesiastical positions with their considerable incomes. In later years he was charged with appropriating the revenues of vacant bishoprics and abbeys, but there is contemporary evidence that this is another false charge. Fitzalan wrote :

> " He might have had all the parochial churches that were vacant, both in the towns and castles, for no one would deny him, if he would only ask ; but he showed such greatness of mind in repressing all views of interest, that he disdained to forestall the poor priests or clerks, or take from them the opportunity of gaining those churches for themselves."

His income as Chancellor was inconsiderable, but, in addition to his ecclesiastical appointment he was custodian of the Tower of London, which he restored at his own expense, like the good Londoner that he was, and of the castles of Eye and Berkhampstead.

The trappings of the Chancellor's life were ornate. His personal life was austere. Of this there is ample and reliable witness. His chastity is admitted even by Froude, who appears to regard it as another proof of his rascality. He was by common assent " a man of pure life and good manners." His biographer says :

> " The holy fathers have made plain that a chaste monk is like unto a knight who keepeth his wealth and life in a close stronghold. But he who liveth chastely in the world signifieth a knight who fighteth with sword and shield in open field and receiveth a great reward the more glorious victory he gaineth ; for that indeed is a more wondrous art to stand on the embers being unburnt than to shun the fire and be unscathed. Both these signs point to that laudable man the blessed Thomas. He was placed by the Lord king in the way of such a good hap and fulness of this world's bliss, as hath been before told, and yet he wore over his breast, nevertheless, such a trusty hauberk of virtue through God's abiding with him that he never departed from a life of purity and holy endeavour ; for if in the daytime the fulfilment of many duties hindered he would get up anight-tide to worship his Creator."

It is important to remember the asceticism of his life, while he was a great secular personage, in the attempt to understand a man of many apparent contradictions. It is sometimes suggested that he was converted by the grace of the episcopacy. Mgr. Knox has suggested that St. Thomas would not have become a saint if he had not become Archbishop, but it is surely dangerous to suppose that saintliness is secured or even encouraged by preferment. It is truer to say of St. Thomas that, while he was in the world, in matters of vast import he was not of the world.

Theobald died in 1161, and Henry determined that St. Thomas should be his successor. Theobald had crowned him and had subsequently opposed him. Experience had taught him not to underestimate the power of the Church. He needed the Church but it must be a Church subservient to his will. He believed that the man who had already proved himself an entirely dependable and highly efficient servant and who was his intimate friend as well as his servant, would secure for the royal decisions the Church's unswerving approval. So to Canterbury the Chancellor must go !

Thomas honestly admired the King's intelligent and far-sighted statesmanship. He had enjoyed working for him and with him. He had enjoyed playing with him, for sovereign and minister hunted together, hawked together and even romped together like two schoolboys. He appreciated the King's confidence. But he knew the King through and through, and it is not to be supposed that he did not fully realise why the King was determined that he should be Archbishop.

It is claimed that Thomas was guilty of treachery in resisting the King's purpose from the day of his consecration. This is another malicious suggestion. St. Thomas may not have made it clear to Henry that the Archbishop could have none of the pliancy of the Chancellor, but he did his utmost to avoid a change from which he had nothing material to gain and which he knew must mean for him persistent trial and trouble. St. Thomas's reluctance made the King more determined. His mother, to whom he nearly always listened, warned him again against the appointment, but he could not believe that the faithful Chancellor could be a rebellious Primate. A conversation at Falaise, between St. Thomas and the Cardinal Henry of Pisa, has been recorded.

" The King is planning an attack on the rights of the Church. If I am made Archbishop I must resist it at all costs."

" If your fears are justified, there is the greater reason for you, the Church's ablest son, to accept the call to her service."

" But, Eminence, I shall earn the King's enmity and lose the friendship that has been the best thing of my life."

" That, my son, is the sacrifice demanded of you."

" But above all I am not worthy. I have lived in the world. I have fought in the army of the King. Who am I that I should lead the hosts of the Lord ? "

" In serving the Church, my son, you will save your own soul."

The Cardinal was speaking for Rome and the aged Henry of Blois, Bishop of Winchester, was among the others who urged Thomas to obey the royal wishes. But Gilbert Foliot, the Cluniac Bishop of London, bitterly opposed the nomination, declaring that Thomas was " entering into the sheepfold not by the door but by climbing up another way " and the Canterbury chapter was with difficulty persuaded to elect him. The men most concerned for the preservation of the rights of the Church, were as little prepared as the King was for St. Thomas's championship of those rights. St. Thomas was ordained priest on June 22nd, 1162, and on the next day was consecrated Archbishop by Henry of Winchester. He had put off the old Adam and now he put on the new. Henceforth he always wore the habit of a canon regular, and he lived according to the strict Augustinian rule. He " mortified his flesh by spare diet and his general drink was water."

St. Thomas had never failed in charity and now his care for the needy became systematic and part of his daily routine. In his *History of the Holy Eucharist in Great Britain*, Fr. Bridgett says that " the Blessed Sacrament was the strength of the saint in all his combats," and Herbert of Bosham wrote :

" He himself did not celebrate every day, and this was, as he himself said, not through negligence but reverence. . . . When he received the sacred vestments from the ministers, his countenance changed, and he was so affected that tears burst from his eyes. And when he stood at the altar praying for his sins and those of his people, his heart was so humbled and contrite, that he rather sobbed than spoke the words of intercession. During the early part of the Mass which is called the Mass of Catechumens, to preserve himself from distractions, while the ministers were singing, he would read some devout book, most frequently the book of prayers composed by his predecessor, St. Anselm. He generally said one collect, and sometimes three, but rarely if ever more. But all who witnessed his Mass attest that he wept and sobbed as if he saw and touched the wounds of Christ."

Early in 1163, Henry returned to England after an absence of nearly four and a half years. The Archbishop met him at Southampton, but the meeting was anything but cordial. News had been carried to Normandy of the Archbishop's new mood, and particularly that he had compelled the return to the see of Canterbury of properties filched from it by certain barons. In May, St. Thomas himself crossed the Channel to attend a Council at Tours, within Henry's French dominions, called by Pope Alexander III. He had been driven from Italy by Frederick Barbarossa, who had established a rival Pope in Rome. Alexander had been a professor at Bologna when St. Thomas was a student there and was an heir of the Hildebrandian tradition. Froude says that the Pope disliked the Archbishop—I can find no authority for the suggestion—but the two men must have discussed the situation in England, and Alexander, who was suffering from the anti-clerical claims of the Emperor, could hardly have failed to sympathise with St. Thomas's intention to resist the similar claims of the King of England.

The Archbishop was back at the end of June and at once trouble flared up. Henry desired to establish one judicial system in England, and to abolish the ecclesiastical courts, established by his great-grandfather or radically to reduce their jurisdiction. The pretence was that these courts were misused to protect " criminous clerks " from just punishment. That this was untrue is proved by the popularity of the courts with the laity. Dean Hutton says : " Men brought suits where they could procure a rapid and probably a just decision and where on the whole the forms were less complicated and the proceedings more intelligent."

To prove his charges against the courts, Henry selected the case of one Philip of Blois, described by Froude as " a young gentleman who held a canonry at Bedford." Here is Edward Grim's account of what followed :

" A new method of attacking a clerk, Philip of Blois by name, was resorted to by the resuscitation of a charge that had long been forgotten. He had been accused of the murder of a certain knight, but when the case had been heard in the audience of the Bishop of Lincoln, he was acquitted by ecclesiastical law, and, the matter ended, he was claimed as free by his kinsfolk. Later on, however, one of the king's officers to whom that duty belonged, wishing, from an ancient grudge he bore him, that the clerk should be ruined, brought forward the case again, and repeated the charge of murder. But the clerk, being a man of high birth, overwhelmed with grief and indignation, attacked the sheriff with abuse. The sheriff reported this contumelious language to the king, who, glad (as it was thought) to have an occasion of venting his spleen on a clerk, poured upon Philip the wrath that he had conceived.

" When the question was raised about the clerk in the presence of the archbishop, the king protested that full justice should be done both about the homicide and about the insult, and that the acquittal would not stand. But the archbishop received the clerk into his court under the protection of the Church that he might there answer for himself and reply to the charge. Bishops and others of either order were accordingly sent by the king to judge the clerk. He denied the charge of homicide, asserting that he ought not to be compelled to make any further answer to it, and that there was no legal right to try a case over again, a case which had been ended by the solemn purgation and which the peace he had made with his opponents had buried.

" ' I confess,' he said, ' that in the bitterness of my heart I have abused the king's officer, but I promise a full amendment for my misdeeds, yet let not the correction exceed the bounds of reason.' 'And we decree,' said they, ' that your prebend remain under the king's hand for two years, and your possessions and all your incomings to be distributed at his will and pleasure to the poor.' They added that he was to stand naked before the king's official, just as a layman might, and offer him his arms for the injury he had done him and live in subjection to him. The clerk submitted to the judgment, glad to have escaped the sentence of death which the king threatened.

" The king, on the other hand, wishing to condemn the man to death, contended that an injury had been done to himself and to the prejudice of his court. He exclaimed that the bishops had had respect of the person because of the archbishop, and had not judged according to equity, and he added, ' By the eyes of God, you shall swear to me that you judged a just judgment and did not spare the man because he was a clerk.' "

According to Grim, the alleged crime had been committed some time before, the accused had been tried and acquitted, though he admitted that he had lost his temper and had behaved in a manner unseemly in a clerk, and while finding that the acquittal on the capital charge was just, the Archbishop severely punished Philip for his misconduct.

The decision seems an admirable example of justice tempered with common sense mercy. Henry had demanded that the accused man should be executed for an unproved offence. St. Thomas carefully considered the verdict of the ecclesiastical judges, and came to a judicial decision. Tyranny on the one side, fair play on the other.

In this same year Henry discovered two other cases in which the ecclesiastical courts were said to have showed partiality to clerical offenders and St. Thomas agreed that, if clerks had been found guilty by their peers of manslaughter or robbery they should be excommunicated and should then be " amenable to lay folk law." But this was not enough for Henry. He wanted to destroy the ecclesiastical courts. He could count on the support of certain of the bishops, and St. Thomas felt obliged to seek the support of the Pope. But Alexander, still in exile, was in no mood to antagonise Henry and the King, believing that now that he was standing almost alone, the Archbishop would be forced to submit to his will, ordered him to come to Northampton. The interview has been fully reported. St. Thomas was respectful but unshaken. In answer to the royal unbraiding, he said :

" I trust and lean upon God, for cursed is the man that putteth his hope in man. Nevertheless, whatever you may say and may answer, as of old so now, I am ready for your honour and good pleasure, saving my order. But on these things which concern your honour and the salvation of your soul you should rather have consulted one whom you have ever found faithful and useful in your counsel rather than those who, under pretence of your honour, have kindled this flame of envy, and strive to take vengeance on me, who never hurt them. You will not deny that I was ever your faithful servant though below the sacred order ; how much more then ought you to believe me faithful in all things when you raised me to the office of the priesthood ? "

With this they parted, the King being still further angered by the " many wholesome words." For a time St. Thomas weakened, thanks mainly to repeated pressure from Pope Alexander. In January he attended a royal council near Salisbury and, with his episcopal brethren, pledged obedience to what were called the royal " customs." The pledge was apparently vague, but as soon as it was given, Henry produced the famous and very definite Constitutions of Clarendon, which he demanded should be approved and accepted.

The Constitutions consist of sixteen clauses. The first two clauses were of no great importance. The third was :

" Clerks accused of any crime shall be summoned by the king's justice into the king's court to answer there for whatever the king's court shall determine they ought to answer there ; and in the ecclesiastical court for whatever it shall be determined that they ought to answer there ; yet so that the king's justice shall send into the court of Holy Church to see in what way the matter shall there be handled ; and if the clerk shall confess or be convicted, the Church for the future shall not protect him."

This clause suggests that the accused clerk could be tried twice for the same offence ; it makes the ecclesiastical courts subservient to the king's courts and deprives them of any real jurisdiction. The fourth clause, which forbade English bishops to leave the country without the consent of the King, was intended to prevent consultations with the Pope. The seventh clause, which forbade the excommunication of the King's tenants, was another surrender of spiritual authority. The twelfth clause, which enacted that the revenues of vacant bishoprics should revert to the crown, regularised established if evil custom.

The last clause ran : " The sons of rustics shall not be ordained without the consent of the lord in whose land they are known to have been born." This implies that the sons of the poor were frequently admitted into the priesthood, and is one more proof that the mediæval Church was the protector of the humble.

In drawing up the Constitutions, the intention of Henry II was exactly the intention of Henry VIII. He wanted to create a national Church, cut off from the rest of Christendom, and over which he should be the supreme authority.

The Church was to be financially weakened and, in consequence, more or less dependent on the royal bounty and subservient to the royal will. Its attachment to the see of Rome was to become little more than nominal. The spiritual authority of the clergy was not challenged, but their ordination was not to affect their *status* as subjects, amenable to the secular laws.

St. Thomas was horrified when he read the document and deeply humiliated that it should have been supposed that he would submit to such intolerable demands. When he was asked to set his seal to the document he declared : " Never while life is in this earthly vessel," and still unmolested, he left the royal court, for a few months' respite, while Henry, who was rarely in a hurry, planned his next move. The Archbishop spent his time in the administration of his diocese. Herbert of Bosham records :

" The archbishop, supported by apostolic authority and exhortation, being fervent in spirit soon shook himself out and with the prophet's mattock he plucked up, pulled down, scattered, and rooted out whatsoever he found planted amiss in the garden of the Lord. His hand rested not, his eye spared not ; whatsoever was naughty, whatsoever rough, whatsoever crooked, he not only assailed with the prophet's mattock, but with the axe of the Gospel he cut it down. Of the royal and ecclesiastical customs, he observed such as were good : but those which had been brought in for the dishonour of the clergy, he pruned away as bastard slips, that they might not strike their roots deep."

In September, 1164, St. Thomas was summoned to appear at the royal court in Westminster to defend a suit entered against him by one John FitzGilbert. He ignored the summons and he was then ordered to attend a council at Northampton, not as Primate of England but as a breaker of the secular law. At Northampton he was subjected to every sort of mean humiliation. He was fined for failing to go to Westminster and then, without warning, he was accused of appropriating public revenues while he was Chancellor. St. Thomas was ill. The knights in his suite left him, and Froude pleasantly remarks that " their place had been taken by a swarm of mendicants." He went, still a strong, vigorous man, in his simple habit, to the King's castle. The streets were lined with the kneeling poor, asking for his blessing. Within the castle his old enemy, Gilbert Foliot, tried to snatch away the processional cross that the Archbishop was carrying and was roughly thrust aside. St. Thomas remained a muscular Christian. A deputation came to him from the King asking if he had appealed to the Pope, and he answered : " I place my person and the Church of Canterbury under the protection of God and of my lord the Pope." A long list of charges against him was then read by the Justiciar, a group of bishops standing shamefaced and studiously apart from the Primate. St. Thomas refused to listen. There had been no trial, there could be no sentence. " Now will I depart for the hour is past."

Again bearing the cross, and accompanied only by Herbert of Bosham, he pushed his way through the threatening barons and the trembling bishops to be welcomed with loudly expressed affection by the crowds outside the castle gates. He smiled as he raised his hand in blessings. Then he mounted his horse and rode away alone, " comforted and fortified by the trust of the poor."

On All Saints' Day he sailed from Sandwich in a small boat, accompanied only by two priests, the King not daring to prevent him, and in the early hours of All Souls' Day he landed in France.

St. Thomas remained in exile for six years. He first stayed at the Cistercian Abbey of Clairmarais near St. Omer, where he was joined by Herbert of Bosham, who brought him money and luggage and from there he wrote to the Pope. He had, he said, been fighting the battle of the Church against the indefensible demands of the secular power. With characteristic scorn he denounced the bishops who had encouraged the King. " Put forth your severity and coerce those who have stirred up this persecution, but lay it not at the King's door ; he is the instrument rather than the author of these machinations."

Pope Alexander was at Sens and he received the letter, carried to him by Herbert of Bosham before the arrival there of the Archbishop of York and the Bishop of London, Thomas's bitterest enemies, who had been sent by Henry to endeavour to secure the Pope's neutrality if not his support. Herbert reported his interview with Alexander.

" He listened with paternal compassion as we told of his son the archbishop's hardships, dangers and griefs, perils in that fight with beasts at Northampton, perils among false brethren, perils in flights, perils in the way, perils in the sea and even in the harbour, his labour, want and distress, and his change of garment and name to avoid the snares of his enemies. And when he heard these things the father of all fathers was moved with compassion towards his son, and could not restrain his paternal love, but wept and said to us, ' Your lord yet lives in the flesh, as ye say ; yet while still living in the flesh he can claim the privilege of martyrdom.' ''

But if the Pope was lukewarm, Louis VII of France, on whose support the Pope depended, was more than friendly. Louis had been greatly influenced by St. Bernard and an American historian has said that " his religiosity developed to such an extent as to make him utterly inefficient," another " sound Protestant " judgment. Louis had good reason to dislike and to fear Henry of Anjou, and his comment on Henry's claim to have the right to depose the Archbishop was : " I, at least as great a King as Henry, have not the power to depose the least of the clerks in my realm."

Alexander still had a peck of troubles of his own, and was anxious not definitely to condemn Henry, but the King's envoys played their cards badly, the Bishop of London in particular was offensive, and despite a bribe in the shape of a handsome contribution to Peter's pence, the royal envoys were sent empty away.

Four days after their departure, St. Thomas arrived at Sens. He brought with him a copy of the Constitutions of Clarendon. He put the case against them with admirable skill. "As if he were Solomon, he pleadeth forth his cause with many fair reasons." And the Pope formally condemned all but six of the Constitutions, approving, however, that ' the sons of rustics should not be ordained without the consent of their lord." With this condemnation St. Thomas was told that he must be content and it was hinted to him that his continued presence at Sens was an embarrassment.

He went to another Cistercian house, this time at Pontigny, where he stayed for eighteen months. St. Thomas was angry, disillusioned and disappointed, sick of the world and of contest and intrigue. For a while he lived according to the hard Cistercian rule, with the result of a severe illness. Then he took to the systematic study of canon law which brought a protest from the pious John of Salisbury.

" Whoever arose with a feeling of contrition from a study of the laws or even of canons ? The exercises of the schools, too, are far more likely to puff us up with the pride of science than to kindle within us any feeling of devotion. I would far rather see your lordship's thoughts employed upon the Psalms or on sermons of the Blessed Gregory than intent upon the philosophy of the schools."

With St. Thomas out of the way, Henry proceeded to consolidate the power of the crown and to grind the faces of both the rich and the poor. The ecclesiastical courts, always anxious when possible to forgive, were practically abolished and the royal courts ruthlessly administered the codified royal law. It was money that the King needed and his judges found it for him.

"Fines were imposed on individuals and on communities for all manner of fantastic offences and with perfectly uncanny ingenuity. The rich were relieved of their money, the poor of their eggs and their fowls. So great was the popular terror that whole villages fled for refuge to the woods, when news came to them of the approach of the royal judge. The system was orderly, intelligent and terribly harsh."

In the spring of 1166, St. Thomas wrote to the King demanding the return of the possessions of the Church of Canterbury, "otherwise know for certain that you shall feel the divine severity and vengeance." Henry's answer to this was to threaten the Abbot of Pontigny and St. Thomas was obliged to leave his retreat and to go to Vezelay. But his position was, for the moment, far stronger. The rival Pope had been forced to leave Rome and Alexander was back in the Eternal City, no longer fearful of the King of England and ready now to back St. Thomas. With this assurance, at Whitsuntide St. Thomas excommunicated certain of the English bishops who had opposed him, published the Pope's condemnation of the Constitutions of Clarendon, and once more warned the King of what might befall him. This time Henry was shaken. He realised the political consequences of excommunication and the bishops were in terror. A curious and often acrimonious correspondence followed between the Archbishop and his suffragans, who charged him with ingratitude to the King and vulgarly taunted him for his humble birth. There is a significant passage in one of the early letters. "Suppose," the bishops wrote, "that by your means and by your exasperation our lord the King (which God forbid) with so many nations and kingdoms which God has given him, should desert our lord the Pope and refuse for the future to follow him, because perchance he may not aid him against you." This suggests that as early as the twelfth century a section of the English episcopate was ready, in certain circumstances, to repudiate the Papal supremacy.

St. Thomas soon discovered that he was not so strong as he had supposed. Alexander, "a holy and retired man" as John of Salisbury called him, was again in danger from the Emperor and was again endeavouring to secure Henry's support without, however, making any definite promises, and, once more driven from Rome, in June, 1167, he agreed that the Archbishop of York should crown the King's son. But once more the tide swiftly turned. A plague broke out in Rome, the German soldiers died in hundreds, the Emperor's army was withdrawn, and Alexander, restored to power, appointed legates to meet both the King and the Archbishop and to endeavour to patch up a peace.

The negotiations were a waste of time. Henry was now determined to get rid of St. Thomas once and for all, and St. Thomas was equally determined that the King should be broken. On the Feast of the Epiphany, 1169—nothing much happened in 1168—St. Thomas met both Henry and Louis at Montmirail, and in studied language begged forgiveness. "On the whole subject, therefore, which lies between us, my lord the King, I throw myself on your mercy and on your pleasure, here, in the presence of our lord the King of France, and of the archbishops, bishops, princes and others who stand round us—saving the honour of God." As St. Thomas must have anticipated, the concluding ambiguous words infuriated Henry, who had unjustly warned Louis that "whatever his lordship of Canterbury disapproves he will say is contrary to God's honour, and so he will on all occasions get the advantage of me." Louis agreed and St. Thomas was urged by him to withdraw the *Salvo honore Dei*, and St. Thomas refused.

He went back to Sens, where he was then living as the honoured guest of the Archbishop, and on Palm Sunday he formally excommunicated the Bishops of London and

Salisbury, with the approval of the Pope. This only added to the hardness of Henry's heart. On Michaelmas Day he issued decrees that any person carrying to England any letters from the Pope or a mandate from the Archbishop, imposing an interdict on the country, should be arrested as a traitor, that if such an interdict were imposed all persons obeying it should be exiled and their goods confiscated, that no appeals should be made either to the Pope or the Archbishop, that no one should be allowed to leave the country without the royal licence, and that in future Peter's pence should be paid into the royal treasury.

This virtual break with Rome was too much for the hitherto complaisant clergy, and the Archbishop of York warned the King that they could not surrender their allegiance to the Pope or ignore the excommunication of the two bishops. Henry's temper never for long had the better of his judgment. He knew that he had blundered and he agreed to yet another meeting with the Archbishop. This took place at Monmartre, now crowned with the church of the Sacre Cœur. The two men were studiously polite. There was no mention of the *salvo honore Dei* but Louis felt that " under the honeyed words which had hitherto passed between them, they had perhaps been made to drink poison." Henry was no humbug and he refused to give the kiss of peace, and St. Thomas knew that, without this symbol, there could be no peace.

So the war went on, the Pope under pressure absolving the excommunication of the Bishop of London on Easter Day, 1170. This was for St. Thomas the last straw. " I know now," he wrote, " how it is that in the court of Rome the Lord's side is always sacrificed, that Barabbas escapes and Christ is slain." In March, Henry was in England, intent on restoring order, removing incompetent officials, insisting on respect for the law and in June, the Pope now agreeing, his son was crowned as heir apparent in Westminister by Roger of York.

This reasonable step to ensure the succession roused the country as nothing before in Henry's reign had done. The French King protested, the whole episcopacy was antagonised, the people were furious, and Henry was advised that to save his throne he must somehow or other persuade St. Thomas to return to Canterbury. There was a final meeting at Chartres. The King was deferential and there was the pretence of forgetting and forgiving. But St. Thomas knew his man. He was weary of the struggle and his English heart was longing for England, though he had no doubt of what awaited him there, when he would have no protector against the royal anger. " I go into England to die," he said to the Bishop of Paris when they said good-bye, and when he parted from the King at Tours he said : " My lord, it seems that I depart from you as from him who in this life I shall see no more."

St. Thomas landed at Sandwich on December 1st. He had left England in a small boat manned by a couple of priests. He returned with the semblance of authority, with the primatial cross flying at the masthead of the ship and accompanied by a representative of the sovereign. But before he landed, it was made clear to him that, for all the honeyed words at Chartres, the King's purpose remained. On the beach were the sheriff of Kent and Ranulf de Broc, who had seized the arch-episcopal lands, with an armed guard, and the demand that, before he put his foot on English soil he should absolve the excommunicated bishops. But the people intervened.

" The Kentish peasants, who loved him, crowded the beach and hustled the sheriff's guards ; fishermen ran into the water to have the honour of drawing the boat to land ; men and women and children knelt on the shingle begging his blessing as he landed. The great crowd pressed round him, throwing their cloaks on to the beach that his feet might not be made wet, and with tears in their eyes shouted together : ' Blessed is the father of orphans, the judge of widows, blessed is he that cometh in the name of the Lord.' And as Becket stood there with his own people with him, blessing them left and right, noting with ironic amusement the angry faces of robber Ranulf and the king's sheriff, he must have felt that the death to which he was going was a death worth dying.

" The journey from Sandwich to Canterbury was one long triumph. In every village Thomas was met by priest and people begging his blessing and repeating the cry ' Blessed is he that cometh in the name of the Lord.' It is only twelve miles from Sandwich to Canterbury, but the journey took a whole day, and the enthusiasm of the countryside was merely a suggestion of the happy rejoicing that awaited him in his cathedral city. The cathedral itself had been decorated, the people crowded the streets, wearing their best clothes, ' silk and costly array,' as was meet on the feast of reunion, and, remembering the Archbishop's sympathy, a great banquet had been prepared for the poor."

" Christ's poor received him as the Lord's anointed, it seemed as though his heart aflame showed also in his face." He gave his clergy his blessing from his throne in the Cathedral, he preached a sermon from the text, " Here we have no abiding city but we seek one to come," and thus finished " that joyful and solemn day."

On the next day the sheriff and Ranulf de Broc repeated the demand for the removal of the excommunications, warning St. Thomas that if he still refused " marvellous and stupendous things " would happen to him. The King had no intention of restoring the arch-episcopal possessions, and St. Thomas learned that Henry had ordered a picked number of the clergy of London and Salisbury to go to Normandy and there to elect the royal nominees to the vacant sees. He determined to go to London to endeavour to arrive at some understanding with the young Prince Henry, now his father's English representative. The journey from Canterbury was another royal progress and the enthusiasm of the countryside was redoubled when he reached London.

"At Southwark the streets were again packed with enthusiastic crowds. Thomas was Thomas of London, and in this his last visit to his native city his fellow-citizens received him with affectionate acclaim. Hundreds of the clergy, with thousands of boys from the London schools, lined his path, and as he dismounted from his horse, raising his hands to bless the people, they burst out into a great ' Te Deum,' which they followed with the hymn ' Blessed be the Lord God of Israel.' "

Prince Henry refused to receive the Archbishop and though he was pressed to spend Christmas at St. Albans in the Abbey of the first English martyr, he made his way slowly back to Canterbury, " attended by a mighty concourse but only of the poor, who came to ask his blessing and who brought their children in hundreds for Confirmation the Archbishop continually dismounting and administering the Sacrament in fields and on the roads."

So Thomas went home to die.

In his *Murder in the Cathedral*, T. S. Eliot has made vivid all the grim grandeur of St. Thomas's martyrdom, preceded by the simple Christmas Day sermon from the text " On earth peace and good will towards men." The sermon was his farewell to his people, and the congregation wept while they listened. " These were no wolves," wrote Herbert of Bosham, " but sheep who knew the voice of their shepherd and grieved when they heard that he would soon leave this world, knowing neither when nor wherefore this should come to pass."

After the Christmas Mass came for the English saint the Christmas dinner, and he " who had shown himself so devout at the Lord's Table showed himself happy, as was his wont, at the table of this world." On St. Stephen's Day, he sent Herbert to France. The mission was a pretext. St. Thomas knew what was coming to him. He was determined that his faithful secretary should not share his fate. Herbert was most reluctant to go, but the Archbishop was insistent and they parted on St. John the Evangelist's Day, Herbert writing : " With this I end my history. I pray with my whole heart, with all my soul and with all my strength that him, whom I may not see again in time, I may be worthy to see in eternity, and may be his partner in the crown as I was his companion in the battle." Herbert knew St. Thomas better than any other man could have known him, and he loved him as no other man loved him.

The death sentence had been pronounced before the Christmas feast. Henry was at Bayeux. With him were the excommunicated bishops and St. Thomas's lay enemies, intent on adding to the King's wrath, and quite beside himself, Henry burst out with the words that were to ensure St. Thomas the martyr's crown and were to cost the King dear :

" ' A fellow,' he exclaimed, ' that has eaten my bread has lifted up his heel against me—a fellow that I loaded with benefits dares insult the king and the whole royal family, and tramples on the whole kingdom—a fellow that came to court on a lame horse, with a cloak for a saddle, sits without hindrance on the throne itself.' ' What sluggard wretches,' he burst forth again and again, ' what cowards have I brought up in my court who care nothing for their allegiance to their master ! Not one will deliver me from this low-born priest ! ' "

The words did not fall on deaf ears. There were ruthless men at Bayeux eager for the royal favour and the next day, with money supplied by the Archbishop of York, Reginald Fitz-Urse, William de Tracy, Hugh de Morville and Richard le Bret, four sorry fellows to live in history because they killed a saint, started for England. It is said that Henry heard of their going and guessed their intention, and, his rage having cooled and his shrewd political judgment again prevailing, that he tried to prevent them from crossing the Channel, but it was too late. On December 28th they were at Saltwood Castle consulting with their fellow rascal, Ranulf de Broc, and on the 29th they rode, with a troop of soldiers, to Canterbury. Rumour of their coming had reached the city and there was a crowd of terrified citizens outside the Cathedral. The four knights found St. Thomas with pious and timid John of Salisbury and it is significant to remember the Saxon monk, Edward Grim, who was to show far greater courage than John. The Archbishop greeted the knights courteously, and Grim recorded : " The wretches, who made a treaty with death, answered his greetings with curses and ironically prayed that God might help him." Fitz-Urse was the spokesman :

> " The king, when peace was made between you and all disputes were ended, sent you back free to your own see, as you demanded ; but you, on the other hand, adding insult to your former injuries, have broken the peace and wrought evil in yourself against your lord. For those by whose ministry the king's son was crowned and invested with the honours of sovereignty, you, with obstinate pride, have condemned by sentence of suspension, and you have also bound with the chain of anathema those servants of the king by whose prudent counsel the business of the kingdom is transacted ; from which it is manifest that you would take away the crown from the king's son if you were able. Now your plots and designs against the king are known to all. Say, therefore, are you ready to answer in the king's presence for these things ? : for therefore are we sent."

The Archbishop answered with unruffled dignity. " When the rights of the Church are violated I shall wait for no man's permission to avenge them. I will give to the King the things that are the King's but to God the things that are God's." The knights shouted and threatened, the Archbishop's servants rushed into the room. Fitz-Urse declared that the King ordered that the Archbishop should leave the kingdom. And now, inspired to show defiance by the danger that he was in, St. Thomas replied :

> " Never shall the sea again come between me and my Church unless I am dragged thence by the feet. You threaten me in vain ; were all the swords in England hanging over my head you could not terrify me from my obedience to God and my lord the Pope. Foot to foot shall you find me in the battle of the Lord. Whoso shall presume to violate the decrees of the sacred Roman See or the laws of Christ's Church and shall refuse to make satisfaction, whosoever he be, I will not spare him nor will I delay to inflict ecclesiastical censures on the delinquents."

The knights went for their arms, which they had left in the courtyard, the gates of the palace were shut and guarded. It was five o'clock, the hour of Vespers, and with the crozier carried before him, St. Thomas went into the cathedral, as was his wont. His calmness added to the terror of the monks. They urged that the cathedral doors should be shut, but that was forbidden. " It is not meet to make a fortress of the house of prayer." Before the service could begin, the murderers made their way into the south aisle and the monks, John of Salisbury among them, bolted. Only Robert of Merton, William Fitz-Stephen and Edward Grim the Saxon remained. St. Thomas, wearing a white rochet, stood in the Lady Chapel near the altar of St. Benedict. The story of the brutal murder is too familiar to be repeated in any detail. St. Thomas died as he had lived, boldly and consistently. He was scornful of the timidity of his followers (" I wonder why monks should all be cowards "), but he was intent on saving them. " In the name of Almighty God I forbid you to hurt my people whether clerk or lay." He was still the muscular Christian and, facing unarmed four armed men, he picked up the miserable Tracy and pitched him off the altar steps. And, bruised and bleeding and unbroken, he whispered his last words : " For the name of Jesus and for the defence of the Church I am willing to die."

Leaving his body on the altar steps, the assassins proceeded to sack the arch-episcopal palace. They piled up the vestments, the pictures, the silver and the furniture on waggons and went their way, leaving nothing behind but two hair shirts ! When the trembling monks stole back to the Cathedral to tend the maimed body of the saint they discovered the extent of the austerity to which he had subjected himself. St. Thomas had always worn a rough hair shirt and a pair of close-fitting hair drawers, which he never took off, and which inevitably abounded with vermin, " boiling over with them like water in a simmering cauldron." To a generation that counts cleanliness as of far greater importance than godliness, this is revolting. It will be remembered that Dr. Barnes once scornfully referred to St. Francis as " verminous," that fact apparently causing the eminent Birmingham mathematician to be completely untouched by the much more important fact that St. Francis was the most lovable man who ever lived.

I am one of the great majority incapable of the deliberate mortifying of the flesh. But I can understand why better and far more useful men than I am have subjected their bodies to what to me would be intolerable discipline. The hair shirt and drawers of the twelfth century Archbishop and the self-inflicted tortures of the twentieth century Father Doyle, a Jesuit and another very masculine Christian, were clearly not examples of crazy masochism. They had a definite and perfectly rational purpose, and they were endured with a persistent courage that commands wondering admiration. I have already written of St. Thomas's discipline :

> " The method adopted by the saint for making his body subject to his soul may be denounced as revolting, but it was at least effective. There was a thoroughness about the mediæval mind. Becket knew the certain consequences when he put off the habit of the Chancellor to put on the habit of the Archbishop. He knew exactly the character of the task that he had to fulfil. In his early days in the palace at Canterbury he concluded knowing himself so well, that it was only by persistently keeping the body under, that he could attain the strength and serenity necessary to fight the king and to maintain the rights of the Church. It is easy to say that the flagellations, the hair shirt and the fleas could have no sort of connection with the persistence of the years of exile, and with the courage of the death in the cathedral. Thomas believed they had, and perhaps he knew better than his modern critics, who regard abstention from meat on Fridays as the limit of defensible bodily sacrifice."

St. Thomas had carefully concealed, even from his intimates, the daily agony that he imposed on himself. Over the hair shirt and drawers he wore white linen garments and it was only when they had stripped his dead body that the Canterbury monks learned " what a true monk he had been." No Requiem for the murdered Archbishop could be said in his desecrated Cathedral, and secretly and silently he was buried in the crypt.

The story of the murder in the Cathedral spread through Europe with amazing swiftness, remembering the difficulties of travel and communication, and everywhere it caused profound indignation. With characteristic Victorian old-maidishness Dean Stanley wrote of " the violence, the obstinacy, the furious words and acts which deformed even the dignity of his last hour and well-nigh turned the solemnity of his martyrdom into an unseemly brawl." The Dean would have had St. Thomas die with the meek propriety of the lamb. Being St. Thomas, he died with the courage of the lion and even Froude admitted that " he had fallen with a dignity and even grandeur that his bitterest enemies were obliged to admit."

" Miracles come when they are needed," according to Froude. That is unfortunately not true. If it were, there would be many miracles in our time. But there is abundant contemporary evidence that miracles began to occur at the tomb of St. Thomas immediately after his death. Pilgrims flocked to Canterbury from every part of Western Europe, some to pray for their souls, some to pray for bodily cures, and in many cases their prayers were answered. Dr. Abbot, who cannot be dismissed as over-credulous, says that the poor " persisted so to speak in being cured at a time when such cure was unfashionable or even dangerous," and it seems to me merely absurd to suppose that the pilgrimages would have gone on if the cures had not taken place as, indeed, it seems to me absurd to regard the cures at Lourdes as untrue.

Non discredo quia impossibile. I learned years ago, from George Saintsbury, that this is the attitude of the true rationalist. One of the few things of which I am certain is that I do not know and that I can never know what is and what is not impossible.

For Henry the murder was a political catastrophe. He

realised that excommunication and an interdict would probably follow with rebellions in both England and Normandy.
Something had to be done at once to placate the Pope and
to prove that the King was a faithful son of the Church.
Emissaries were sent to Rome to assure the Pope that Henry
was ready to submit to any penance that was imposed on
him and at once to obey the command sent to him by the
English Pope Adrian, sixteen years before, to restore order
in Ireland and to compel the Irish Church, that had given
Christendom so many saints and missionaries, to recover
Catholic discipline and to return to the Papal obedience.
Henry landed in Waterford in October, 1171, and, in the
following spring, he reported to Rome that he had fulfilled
his mission. Back in Normandy he met the representatives
of the Pope at Avranches in September and confessed that
he had been indirectly responsible for the murder in the
cathedral. He was ordered to equip an expedition to fight
against the Saracens in the Holy Land and, if required to
do so, to send another expedition against the Moors in
Spain, to renounce the Constitutions of Clarendon, and to
restore all the possessions that had been filched from the
Church. Henry agreed to this surrender, but it was not
enough. The Pope was satisfied, the people were not.

Popular indignation was exploited by the barons and there
were risings against the royal authority. It was clear that
the dead saint himself must be placated. Henry was no
fool, but, unlike Froude and Dean Stanley and even Dean
Hook, he believed in the reality of the Canterbury miracles.
Froude sadly comments that " his piety was a check upon
his intellect." His penance had to be personal, public and
dramatic. So he hurried to England.

He landed at Southampton, and made his way to Canterbury, making handsome gifts to the churches in the villages
and towns through which he passed. On the outskirts of
Canterbury he put on the hair shirt of the penitent and, with
bare feet soon made to bleed by the cobble stones, he walked
to the Cathedral, where, prostrate on the steps of the altar
where St. Thomas had died, he confessed his responsibility
for the martyrdom. His penance was expensive, for so
thrifty a monarch. To the Cathedral chapter he gave lands

and " rich silks and wedges of gold." But still not enough. So great a sin demanded an equally great humiliation. Throwing off his cloak, the King lay on the altar steps and the bishops and abbots and the eighty monks, who were present, struck him with a whip. And then the great King sat through the night by the martyr's tomb, bruised and bleeding and without food, while a crowd of St. Thomas's Canterbury poor stood within the Cathedral doors, in silent wonder.

" So deep a humiliation," says Dean Stanley, " of so great a Prince was unparalleled within the memory of that generation." And it had its reward. When Henry returned to London, news came to him that the King of Scotland had been taken prisoner, and, a few months later, the rebellions had been suppressed, and, thanks to the mediation of the Pope, Henry had been reconciled to Louis of France.

St. Thomas was canonised in 1173. In 1179, a house for the care of the sick poor was built on the south of the Thames, opposite Westminster," in honour of God and the blessed martyr St. Thomas of London," and, at the dissolution, the citizens of St. Thomas's city built St. Thomas's Hospital on the site. During his lifetime St. Thomas never failed in his care for the unfortunate ; it is fitting that nearly eight hundred years after his death his memory should be preserved in a place of healing and mercy.

It is the common Protestant suggestion that St. Thomas fought obstinately and died bravely for a thoroughly bad cause and that the victory, that was bought with his life, was a national misfortune. Froude concludes his *Life and Times of Thomas Becket* with the assertion : " The English laity were for three centuries condemned to writhe under the yoke which their own credulous folly had imposed on them, till the spirit of Henry II at length revived, and the aged iniquity was brought to judgment at the Reformation." This is unhistoric nonsense.

Henry was determined that the Church in England should be the King's church. St. Thomas was determined that it should be God's church, a loyal part of a supra-national institution, to which rulers as well as ruled should be subject and which should be powerful enough to protect the ruled from the tyranny of the rulers. St. Thomas fought and won for the cause for which Hildebrand had fought and lost a hundred years before.

In England it was the Church, led by the great Archbishop, Stephen Langton, who specially venerated St. Thomas, that compelled King John to sign Magna Charta. Unless the Church had established its authority in the twelfth century it is impossible to believe that the secular princes would have tolerated the revolutionary teaching of St. Francis in the thirteenth and the mediæval world would never have learned the gaiety of goodness.

It is clear, even from Froude's jaundiced pages, that St. Thomas was loved and trusted by the people, and it was for the people that he died as Laud was to die. St. Thomas loved England and, because he loved England, he was concerned that his country should be a great power in the real sense of the term, a strong nation within a united Christendom, not a servile colony of a foreign king. And it was the English who remembered and venerated him. The pilgrims who journeyed to his shrine from the Tabard Inn, in Southwark, were typically English in their love of fun and their hatred of pride. Their pilgrimage was, as every pilgrimage should be, a religious beanfeast. Happily the spirit of St. Thomas continues in England. How England would applaud to-day if a sturdy priest threw a blustering ruffian out of his church ! And on his Feast Day, December 29th, English men and women may well pray :

" O God, Who for Thy Church's sake didst suffer Thy Bishop St. Thomas gloriously to be slain by the swords of wicked men, grant we beseech Thee, that all who call upon him for succour may be profited by the obtaining of all that they desire."

CHAPTER III

THE REFORMER

IT is impossible to determine how far the man makes the occasion and how far the occasion makes the man. It is commonly said to-day that, without the genius of Lenin, the Russian revolution, the most portentous event of our time, would never have occurred. It is also true that, unless the Czarist regime had been hopelessly weakened and discredited by military defeat, Lenin would not have been able, in 1917, to put into practice his carefully thought out political and economic philosophy. But Lenin's philosophy would certainly have sooner or later affected social and political history. On the other hand, the moral and material chaos of the years between the wars gave the demagogic genius of Hitler and Mussolini the opportunity to secure their dominant positions. In normal conditions neither of them would have emerged from obscurity.

There have been men whose names are written large in human history, whose characters and qualities would have secured them influence and distinction, if the circumstances of their lives had been entirely different. Napoleon would not have been Emperor of the French if there had been no Rousseau and no Revolution. But if the Bourbon rulers had continued and France had been involved in war, which she almost certainly would have been, Bonaparte's military genius must have given him pre-eminence. St. Thomas of London was another such great man. He was born for greatness, and greatness would have been his even if he had not worn the martyr's crown. On the other hand, there have been men, with little strength of character and moderate gifts on whom greatness has been thrust by the chance of circumstance. Such a man was Thomas Cranmer, Lord Archbishop of Canterbury from 1533 to 1556. St. Anselm was a Catholic saint, St. Thomas was a Catholic saint and martyr, Cranmer was a Protestant martyr, but his apologists have never claimed him as a saint. He was born on July 2nd, 1489, thirty-six years after the fall of Constantinople, when the Middle Ages are commonly regarded as having come to an end and the Renaissance to have begun.

The authority of the Church, strengthened by the martyrdom of St. Thomas, was at its zenith during the Papacy of Innocent III, a man of supreme character and high moral earnestness, as learned as he was determined, who reigned in Rome from 1198 to 1216. Innocent believed that "the Lord left to Peter the governance not of the Church but of the whole world," and he succeeded in imposing his will on the whole of Europe. Incidentally, it is interesting in these days that it was his purpose "as Pope to shake off the Imperial yoke and as Italian prince to clear the land of the hated Germans."

Innocent's masterfulness was a blessing to Europe and particularly to England. In 1207, he insisted that Stephen Langton should be consecrated as Archbishop of Canterbury. King John had his own candidate and the Canterbury monks had theirs, but the Pope over-ruled them and undoubtedly chose the best man. John refused the Pope's nomination, and in March, 1208, Innocent imposed an interdict on England. The churches were closed, the Holy Sacrifice was not offered. The King replied by seizing the temporalities and for a while he waxed fat, but in 1212 the Pope declared that he was deposed from his throne and ordered the King of France to carry out the deposition. And John grovelled. He agreed to recognise Langton as Archbishop, to compensate the clergy for his robberies and to hold the kingdom as the vassal of the Pope.

Though he was the Pope's nominee, Langton was a patriotic Englishman who never regarded himself merely as a Papal delegate. It was he who summoned the barons to Runnymede and he was the author of Magna Charta, that was signed there. The Church was thus the founder of English political liberty.

One of the sixty-three clauses of Magna Charta declares that "the English Church shall be free," but it is not clear whether Langton had in mind freedom from the arbitrary enactments of the King or of the Pope. Possibly the intention was freedom from both and a national church governed by its own sacred synod.

Henry III, who reigned for fifty-six years, from 1216 to 1272, was an entirely futile monarch, the constant victim of unworthy foreign favourites, one of whom, Boniface of Savoy, described as " illiterate and unclerical in his habits," the King made Archbishop of Canterbury. But, despite the futility of the King, there was vivid material, cultural and religious life in the England of the thirteenth century.

In the middle of the century, St. Edmund of Abingdon was Archbishop of Canterbury, the third and last canonised saint to sit on the throne of St. Augustine. Anticipating St. Thomas Aquinas, he was an Aristotelian, a scholar of acknowledged eminence, whose humility and charity were as outstanding as his learning. St. Edmund had no desire for preferment to the Primacy. Mgr. Knox has written that he would have been " a far happier man if he had never worn a mitre ; his archbishopric was only an addition to his mortifications." On occasion, he was bold enough to rebuke the King, but Henry could always count on the support of the Pope, and St. Edmund found the clash between Rome and Canterbury intolerable and he died in voluntary exile.

A far more effective ecclesiastic was Roger Grosseteste, Bishop of Lincoln, a man of humble Suffolk birth, a clerical reformer, an English churchman who resolutely opposed Papal exactions and " not merely a great ecclesiastical who patronised learning in his leisure hours, but the first mathematician and physicist of his age." Gorsseteste was the intimate of Simon de Montfort, the greatest English statesman of the century, known to his contemporaries as " Earl Simon the Righteous " and he was the friend and patron of the Franciscans, whose coming to England in 1220 was the most important incident in its religious history of the thirteenth century.

The noblest act in the great pontificate of Innocent III was his instant recognition of the saintliness of St. Francis and his approval of the foundation of the Franciscans. With inspired gaiety the friars preached the gospel to the poor and their own poverty, their sincerity and their laughter gave religion a new reality. St. Francis himself cared nothing for learning, but it is not to be forgotten that the Oxford scholar Roger Bacon, " a man vastly ahead of his time both in the methods of his research and the results of it," was a Franciscan friar.

Many of the loveliest of the English cathedrals were built while Henry III was king, among them Salisbury, Wells and the new Westminster Abbey. The Church was very much alive.

Edward I came to the throne in 1272 ; a strong, wise and far-seeing statesman followed a fool. Early in his long reign, Edward determined to check the accumulation of real property by the religious houses, and he persuaded Parliament to pass the Statute of Mortmain, which forbade any man to alienate property to the Church without the royal licence. The reason for the statute was that ecclesiastical property was not subject to royal taxation. Twenty years later, the clergy refused to make a grant to the King for the war he was planning against France. This was in obedience to a bull of Pope Boniface VIII specifically forbidding the Church in any circumstance to contribute to the secular revenue. Edward promptly sequestered the Canterbury revenues, and the Archbishop threatened excommunication, but Edward was a diplomat and the quarrel was patched up, the King graciously accepting a " voluntary gift " which was not to be regarded as a tax.

The reign of Edward I has been described as " the culmination and crowning point of the middle ages."

The fourteenth century in England was dominated by Edward III, a capable prince with insane ambitions that burdened the country with the Hundred Years' War. The most important domestic event of the century was the Black Death, which reduced the population by a third, compelled the initiation of a new system of land tenure and was the reason for the Statute of Labourers, enacted in 1351, which made it a penal offence for the workers to demand any advance in rural wages. But the Statute was rendered largely inoperative by the growth of urban industries with the increasing demand for labour. The general condition of the people—it is suggested in *The Canterbury Tales*—seems to have been at least tolerable. Their piety and good humour are both emphasised by Chaucer, and the stamina of the English yeomen was proved at Crecy.

In the middle years of the reign of Edward III the Statutes of Praemunire and Provisors were passed to check the Pope's influence in England, and, in its last years, John Wycliffe, sometime Master of Balliol and afterwards Rector of Lutterworth in Leicestershire, was denouncing the corruption of the clergy and demanding repudiation of the Papal jurisdiction.

It is difficult to estimate Wycliffe's influence in the history of the English Church, as difficult as it is to estimate the later influence of Wesley. It has, indeed, been suggested that through his Czech follower, John Huss, he had a greater influence on the continent than he had in his own country. His translation of the Bible justifies the claim that he was the founder of English prose. In his insistence that the Bible must be the foundation of a Christian's religion, he anticipated the Sixteenth Century Reformers. It is interesting that in the fourteenth century there was no interference by the ecclesiastical authorities with the circulation of the Scriptures in the vernacular. Wycliffe has been described as the last of the great English scholastics, with more links with mediæval than with Reformation thought. He was a strong nationalist, but his anti-Papalism was little more, at the beginning, than the anti-Papalism of the English kings.

In his attacks on the higher clergy, Wycliffe was supported, for his own political ends, by John of Gaunt, popularly hated as " the insolent Duke." The particular target was the famous William of Wykeham, the Chancellor and a shameless clerical pluralist, who used part of the fortune he accumulated—he was the son of a carpenter—to endow Winchester College and New College, Oxford.

Wycliffe's loyalty to John of Gaunt was so thorough that he hotly defended the duke when he violated the sanctuary of Westminster by sending armed men into the Abbey to arrest two of his squires who had taken refuge there, a crime that infuriated the people of London. Wycliffe frequently preached in London, but Londoners had no love for him or for his teaching. It is true that in his anti-Papalism Wycliffe had the support of a considerable part of the nation, the traditional national resentment of foreign interference being intensified by the Popes' residence for nearly a hundred years in Avignon where they were inevitably under the influence of the French kings with whom England was constantly at war.

On the other hand, Wycliffe's repudiation late in his life of Catholic doctrine had comparatively little popular response. His followers, the Lollards, were mainly Oxford scholars, with a section of the country gentry and some of the poorer class, who were affected by Wycliffe's itinerant preachers. He had considerable admiration for the early Franciscans and in his early days he was intimate with many of the friars.

It was unfortunately true that the simplicity and sincerity of St. Francis had been largely lost. His followers had become self indulgent. They were no longer regarded as the friends of the humble. Piers Plowman, in 1394, described " the fat friar with his double chin shaking about as big as a goose's egg, and the ploughman with his hood full of holes, his mittens made of patches, and his poor wife going barefoot on the ice so that her blood followed."

Wycliffe hoped that his preachers would recover the Franciscan evangelical poverty of the twelfth century and their mission was to preach the Franciscan " plain and homely doctrine." The Lollards have been described as mediæval Socialists. Dean Hook says that Wycliffe " left behind him not a religious party, but only a violent political faction which in his name propogated what would now be called the principles of Socialism ; this so alarmed the conservatism of Europe as to delay an effectual reformation for more than a century."

This suggestion has little foundation. The Lollard Conclusions are for the most part the denunciation of Catholic doctrine and practice with the condemnation of all wars as " but the murdering and plundering the poor to win glory for kings." The only suggestion of " Socialism " is the condemnation of luxury trades " such as those of goldsmiths and armourers."

It has been also suggested that the Wycliffe preachers were largely responsible for the resentment that led to the Great Revolt of 1381. John Ball, the famous hedge priest, certainly claimed to be one of Wycliffe's disciples, but

Lollardy did not spread until after Wycliffe's death and there is nothing to show that he had any sympathy with Wat Tyler and John Ball. The revolt was a proletarian movement caused by the imposition by Archbishop Sudbury of an iniquitous poll tax and of the Statute of Labourers. The peasants had the support of the humbler priests, but Wat Tyler was sufficienty anti-clerical to demand the confiscation of all church lands. Before the end of the fourteenth century the Church was no longer generally regarded as the protector of the poor.

Lollardy continued in England until the Reformation, a small persecuted sect. Its existence was the excuse for the passing, in 1399, of the Statute *De heretico comburendo*, which legalised the torturing of the pre-Reformation martyrs. For this another Archbishop, Thomas Arundel, was responsible.

The fifteenth century opened with the reign of Henry V, a picturesque adventurer whom the genius of Shakespeare has made a national hero. The victory of Agincourt and Henry's other successes in France were not of the smallest benefit to the English people, and his only historic importance is that his temporary conquests inspired the zeal and military competence of St. Joan of Arc and caused the birth of popular nationalism, first in France and afterwards in this country.

Henry Chicheley was Archbishop of Canterbury from 1414 to 1443. He persecuted the Lollards but he was in constant conflict with Rome, having been, before his consecration as Archbishop, a party in a case in which the Court of King's Bench decided that a papal bull could not overrule the law of the land.

Chicheley was educated at Winchester and New College and, following the tradition of William of Wykeham, he founded St. John's and All Souls at Oxford and a college at Higham Ferrers and he persuaded Henry VI to found Eton and King's College, Cambridge. The Church remained the patron of learning, after it had ceased to be the protector of the poor.

Jack Cade's rebellion, in 1450, has sometimes been compared to Wat Tyler's rising. As a matter of fact Cade was an unemployed mercenary who was out for loot and the rebellion had no popular backing. The Wars of the Roses filled thirty years of the century. They were, in effect, the struggle between two aristocratic factions, though the merchant class, growing in importance through the development of woollen manufactures and of the shipping trade, were steadily on the side of the Yorkists.

The country was still mainly cultivated by more or less prosperous small holders. There was no lack of employment in the towns. But the Church was in a bad way. It has been said : " It is difficult to find a single bishop in the whole period who was respected for his piety or virtue. The best of them were capable statesmen, the worst were mean time-servers." The intellectual life and the philanthropic activity of the monasteries had come to an end. Pluralism was rampant and absenteeism in the parishes almost the rule. But men still built beautiful new churches. The fifteenth century bequeathed to us the nave of Winchester, the Lady Chapel at Gloucester, the central tower of Canterbury and many fine churches in East Anglia and Somersetshire. While the barons were destroying, the Church went on building.

John Addington Symonds says that the Renaissance, " a period and a process of transition, fusion, preparation, tentative endeavour," began with the capture of Constantinople by the Turks in 1453, with the consequent recovery of classic learning from the Greek scholars, who found refuge in Italy, and that it continued until 1530, when the Emperor Charles V pacified Italy. After 1530, with the Reformation and the Counter-reformation, the history of the modern world begins.

The Renaissance in Italy was a pagan revolt against Christianity. The new learning bred contempt for the old religion. The magnificent luxury of the Florentine Medicis was imitated by the Renaissance Popes. Blatant immorality became a convention. " Adultery, simony, usury defiled the sanctuary." Renaissance Italy gave many lovely things to the world even though there was justification for Savanorola's charge that love of art was " really nothing but the shameful appetite for vice." But it also gave posterity the amoral political philosophy of Macchiavelli, which has inspired the statecraft of every tyrant from Cesare Borgia to Hitler.

Among other things the Reformation was a reaction to the Renaissance.

The political opposition to a foreign pontiff, as I have shown, endemic in England since the Conquest, was strengthened by righteous disgust at the lives of the Borgias. Men, like Savanorola, who never wavered in their adherence to the orthodox faith, were moved to scornful indignation by the character of the men who were, for the time, the chief custodians of the faith, and men, doubtful of Catholic doctrine, had their doubts strengthened by Renaissance Rome.

But the claim that the Reformation was a moral reformation as well as a religious revolution is hard to maintain. It would be folly not to admit the gross wickedness of Rome at the beginning of the sixteenth century, but, though it is true that in Renaissance Italy, as John Addington Symonds has said, " the Christian virtues were scorned by the foremost actors and the ablest thinkers of the times," it has to be remembered that Cesare Borgia, for all his cardinal's hat, never professed to be a Christian and that Machiavelli was a professed pagan. Nor can it be forgotten that great art flourished in Italy in these years ann many lovely things were bequeathed to posterity. The decadent era was short and it was followed by the counter-reformation with its saints and its scholars and its practical recognition of the social gospel.

The Reformation had its great men, but none of them had a suggestion of the lovableness of St. Thomas More or of the abounding selfless charity of St. Philip Neri and St. Vincent de Paul. Luther caused, if he did not incite, the peasant murders in Germany ; Calvin was one of the mos-terrifying figures in modern history. It is not for me td judge the comparative heinousness of different sins, but I confess that I find the boorish brutality of Knox and the lying savagery of Prynne as detestable as the wickedness of Alexander VI. Protestantism brought with it, too, an unctuous hypocrisy that made religion ridiculous and repellent to the common Englishman, with his traditional instinct for recognising humbug.

The revival of learning had a different effect in Germany and England to that which it had in Italy. Its spirit was " pugnacious and polemical, eager to beat down the arrogance of monks and theologians rather than to pursue an ideal of æsthetic self-culture."

The Renaissance was most pugnacious in Germany when Luther nailed his thesis to the church door at Wittenburg. It was at its sweetest in England when Colet and Erasmus and More met and gossiped at Oxford and in the Deanery of St. Paul's. Rarely has there been a group of men so learned, so single minded, so truly religious. Colet had listened to Savanorola thundering from his pulpit in Florence, and when he came back to Oxford to deliver a famous series of lectures, in which, incidentally, he showed sound Liberal learning as when he described the first chapter of Genesis as a summary written " after the manner of a popular poet," he must have reported to Thomas More what he had heard. During the short time that the Dominican monk had established a benevolent theocracy in Florence, he had contrived to find work for the unemployed, and to secure adequate wages, and equal justice for all men. All these things exist in More's *Utopia*. Colet was a rather dour and very serious man. More was the whimsical saint. Erasmus was the laughing philosopher. They were all genuine reformers ; they wanted to reform, not to destroy.

In a letter to Archbishop Warham, another friend of the new learning, Erasmus said : " I admit that the corruption of the Church requires a drastic medicine, but drugs wrongly given make the sick man worse." That was the view, too, of Colet, of More, of Warham, as it was of Fisher of Cambridge. It never occurred to any of them that Christendom should be split into a number of independent national churches. They realised the supreme importance that the Catholic Church should remain supra-national. Erasmus, indeed, was a complete cosmopolitan. He passed frontiers without knowing it. It was perhaps, too, his abounding sense of humour that made him suspect Luther. When he heard that Luther had married an ex-nun, he said :

" Some call Lutheranism a tragedy, I call it a comedy, where the trouble ends in a wedding."

Henry VIII succeeded his father in 1509. He, too, was affected by the new learning. He was young and cultured. He made Linacre, another friend of More and Colet, his physician. Men in England may well have believed that these early years of the century were to be the beginning of a golden age.

In 1498, Thomas Cranmer, the second son of a small landowner, was entered by his widowed mother at Jesus College, Cambridge. He was then fourteen. John Fisher, scholar, humanist and one day to be martyr, was the Vice-Chancellor of the University. He had established the Lady Margaret Professorship of Divinity and the Lady Margaret Preachership, and in 1511, after Cranmer had graduated, Erasmus was appointed Lady Margaret Professor and Cranmer attended his lectures.

In 1512 Cranmer married an innkeeper's daughter—the admiring Professor Bollard unctuously comments : " Inns had not then degenerated into mere drinking-shops ; they were rather hotels and clubs, and the hosts were in better social estimation than the publican of to-day "—and he had to resign his Fellowship. His wife, however, died within a year, and the Fellowship was restored. Cambridge was, of course, influenced by Erasmus towards new learning and in particular to the study of the Scriptures, and Cranmer was a keen and industrious student. A contemporary admirer recorded :

> " Then he, considering what great controversy was in matters of religion (not only in trifles, but in the chiefest articles of our salvation), bent himself to try out the truth herein ; and, forasmuch as he perceived that he could not judge indifferently in so weighty matters without the know-ledge of the Holy Scriptures (before he were infected with any man's opinions or errors) he applied his whole study three years to the said Scriptures. After this he gave his mind to good writers, both new and old, not rashly running over them, for he was a slow reader, but a diligent marker of whatsoever he read ; for he seldom read without pen in hand, and whatsoever made either for one part or the other of things being in controversy, he wrote it out if it were short, or at the least, noted the author and the place, that he might find it and write it out by leisure ; which was a great help to him in debating of matters ever after. This kind of study he used till he was made Doctor of Divinity, which was about the thirty-fourth of his age."

His friends at Cambridge at this time included Coverdale, Tyndale and Latimer, and, with some others, they regularly met to discuss Luther's theses, and the meetings were forbidden by Thomas More as High Steward of Cambridge.

Cranmer was ordained in 1523 and soon after he proceeded to the degree of Doctor of Divinity. In 1528 he had a meeting with Stephen Gardiner; this was his first step towards distinction.

Gardiner was another Cambridge man who had been influenced by Erasmus. He was a far more distinguished scholar than Cranmer, a canonist of recognised authority, and, as one of Wolsey's secretaries, he had, when he met Cranmer, been concerned with the early negotiations with Rome for the annulment of the King's marriage with Katharine.

The question was discussed by the two Cambridge men and Gardiner was impressed by Cranmer's suggestion that, for the time at least, Rome should be disregarded and that the matter should be referred to the doctors of the English universities.

For political reasons, Henry had married his brother's widow in 1509. Such a marriage was canonically forbidden and a Papal dispensation had been granted only after considerable hesitation. There was indeed grave doubts whether the Pope had authority to over-ride the decisions of a General Council.

Henry, a lusty sensualist, never pretended to have any love for his dull, plain wife, who was some years his senior Before the birth of the Princess Mary in 1516, the Queen had had a series of miscarriages and of still-born babies Other miscarriages followed the birth of the Princess and it was clear that Katharine could never be the mother of the male heir, who, Henry believed, was necessary for the continuance of his dynasty. Political expediency was therefore, the main reason for his endeavour to have the marriage formally declared invalid. Another reason was that Anne Boleyn, the King's mistress, was pressing for marriage, and, in addition to his natural desire for a son Henry had, for a prince of his time, a strange dislike of irregular unions.

Whatever may have been the King's motives, the fact that Stephen Gardiner supported the royal demand is the proof that it could be canonically and politically justified, for Gardiner was one of the finest of contemporary figures, a man of courage, honesty and consistency.

It was hopeless to expect an unbiased decision from Rome, for Clement VII was absolutely dependent on the support of the powerful Charles V of Spain, Queen Katharine's nephew. Gardiner, therefore, felt justified in repeating to the King Cranmer's advice that appeal should be made to the universities, and Cranmer was ordered to put his opinion into writing, citing what authority he could find for such procedure. While he was doing this it was significant that he was lodged in Durham Place, the London palace of the Earl of Wiltshire, Anne's father, which stood on the site of what was afterwards the Adelphi. This was a dramatic change for a poor, obscure Cambridge don.

Cranmer was then a man of forty. For twenty-six years he had lived a placid life at Cambridge. He was to spend twenty-seven years in the turmoil of public affairs. He must have congratulated himself on the chance that had brought him the royal favour. As a matter of fact, it was a tragedy for him and for the English Church. He was without any of the qualities demanded by the high office to which he was soon to be called. He had no real convictions. If he were not driven hither and thither by every wind of doctrine, he changed his mind with amazing celerity when the change of mind was dictated by prudence. What he professed to believe to-day he was ready to repudiate to-morrow. Until the end of his life, having no conviction, he had no courage. Men never willingly suffer for what they only half believe. Had he remained in comfortable obscurity in Cambridge, his scholarship would have secured him mild academic distinction, his amiability would have assured him pleasant friends and his pliability would have enabled him, without difficulty, to change his theological opinions to suit the changing views of authority with the same happy result as that attained by the Vicar of Bray. At Lambeth and Canterbury he was inconsistent and unhappy and a terrible death was the end of a pitiful life.

In 1529, England was predominantly anti-Papal and almost entirely Catholic. Lutheranism had made few converts in this country, practically none outside the universities. Henry, a man of genuine intellect and a considerable lay theologian, had earned from the Pope the title of Defender of the Faith for his attack on Luther's teaching, and the great majority of his subjects were in religious agreement with him. The clergy and in particular the monks and the friars were the objects of popular gibes, but it would be as absurd to regard these jests as evidence of widespread anti-clericalism as it would be to quote Gilbert's " mild young curate " as proof that the Victorians regarded the Church with contempt. It has always been the virtue of the English to see the joke, even in people whom they regard and in institutions which they value. Replying in 1528 to the attacks on the clergy Thomas More wrote a comment that might well have been written four hundred years later.

> " In reproach of them we be so studious that neither good nor bad passeth unreproved. If they be sad, we call them solemn, if they be merry, we call them mad. If they keep few servants, we call them niggards. If they keep many, we call them pompous. If a lewd priest do a lewd deed, then we say, lo see what sample the clergy giveth us as though that priest were the clergy. But then forget we to look what good men be therein, and what good counsel they give us, and what good ensample they show us. But we fare as do the ravens and the carrion crows, that never meddle with any quick flesh, but where they may find a dead dog in a ditch, thereto they flee and thereon they feed apace. Let a good man preach, a short tale shall serve us thereof, and we shall neither regard his exhortation nor his good examples. But let a lewd friar be taken with a wench, we will jest and rail upon the whole order all the year after."

Canon Deane says that the King's determination to get rid of Katharine and to marry Anne was " odious to all Englishmen," but I very much doubt whether the mass of the people were in the least outraged by a proposal, justified by political expediency and certainly not without precedent.

The year that saw the beginning of Cranmer's public career, also saw the fall of Wolsey, who had been the real ruler of England since the King's accession. In his magnificence, his ability and his love of learning, Wolsey was a typical figure of the Renaissance. He was, wrote the Venetian Ambassador in London, " very handsome, learned, extremely eloquent and indefatigable." And in addition, " he favours the people exceedingly, and especially the poor, hearing their suits and seeking to despatch them instantly." Henry had grown tired of Wolsey's tutelage ; he resented his wealth and magnificence ; he was incensed by his minister's failure to secure the annulment of his marriage. So Wolsey " fell, never to rise again," and St. Thomas More was appointed Chancellor in his place, to hold office only for three years.

In view of what was to happen it is worth while to remember that Wolsey endowed Christ Church, Oxford, with the property of twenty-four monasteries and that St. John Fisher obtained the dissolution of certain monasteries for the endowment of the professorships that he founded at Oxford and Cambridge.

In 1529 Thomas Cromwell, with whom Cranmer was to be closely associated, passed from the service of Wolsey to the service of the King. Most men—great men as well as little men—are a compound of good and evil. Cromwell was an unmitigated and rather sordid rascal. In Italy he had learned the principles of unscrupulous statescraft taught by Macchiavelli. He was exceedingly able, cruel, greedy, mean, a 16th century Nazi. Cromwell was told of Cranmer's suggestion of an appeal to the universities, but he proposed to the King a more drastic policy. Let him take this opportunity to repudiate the Papal jurisdiction and to declare that the English King is the Head of the English Church. Such a claim could not be unpopular. It had been made by more than one of Henry's predecessors. Parliament could be cajoled or threatened into agreement. But Henry hesitated. He was proud of the title Defender of the Faith. He was determined to have his own way, but he had no wish for a break with the Pope. He would first make the appeal to the universities suggested by the Cambridge doctor, and at the same time he would send another mission to Rome. With insolent folly he ensured the failure of this mission by appointing Anne's father as his ambassador with Cranmer as his canonical expert. The replies, too, received from

Oxford and Cambridge were not encouraging, and it was clear that coercion would be necessary before the authoritative English doctors of the Church would agree that the marriage with Katharine was canonically invalid. With Cromwell whispering at his elbow, the opposition of Rome and the hesitancy of the English scholars made Henry more obstinately bent on getting rid of one wife and securing another, who might be expected to provide him with an heir.

Wolsey died in November, 1530, and Henry made his first move. It was alleged that, in accepting the office of legate from the Pope, Wolsey had broken the Praemuraire Act and that in recognising him as legate, the bishops had been his accomplices and were liable to heavy penalties. But the King would pardon the offence on the payment of considerable fines by the two Provinces and the acknowledgment by Convocation that he was " sole protector and Supreme Head of the Church and clergy of England." This step was suggested by Cromwell, and taken without consultation with the Chancellor. Convocation agreed and Parliament approved and, as Dean Hook insists, it is important to remember that the lords spiritual were a majority in the House of Lords.

Cranmer was not a member of Convocation, but after his return home he was still busy with the annulment. In Italy, he had almost certainly met Cardinal Pole, another of the gracious figures of the times, and he was bidden to examine Pole's book on the proposed divorce. Cranmer loved good writing and he paid honest tribute to Pole's skill, but his judgment was that the book was dangerous and that its circulation in England should be forbidden.

Henry was now openly living with Anne and, in a letter to her father, Cranmer said : " The King and my lady Anne rode yesterday to Windsor, and this night they be looked for again at Hampton Court ; God be their guide." It was for a man and woman living in open adultery that the pliant Cranmer invoked the Divine blessing.

In 1532, Cranmer was sent by the King to Germany on a second futile mission, this time to discuss " the king's matter " with Charles V. In Germany he met the Lutheran leaders for the first time, and was definitely drawn to their teaching. Incidentally—and suggestively—he married the young daughter of a Lutheran pastor, a woman twenty years his junior. Canonically, the clergy were forbidden to marry, but the law was generally disregarded in Germany and in England as it had been in Italy. Margaret Cranmer does not seem to have played any great part in her husband's life.

In 1532, Convocation agreed to what was afterwards the Clergy Submission Act, St. Thomas More was permitted to resign the Chancellorship and William Warham, Archbishop of Canterbury, died. Warham, a man of ability and character, had grown weary of ceaseless trouble and controversy. He had always lived simply and charitably and he died—he was eighty-two—with a gentle jest on his lips and empty coffers.

It had been expected that Stephen Gardiner would succeed. But Henry was a shrewd judge of men. He was not going to make the blunder that Henry II made when he sent St. Thomas to Canterbury. Gardiner was not sufficiently pliable. He had conviction and courage. Henry wanted an Archbishop who would be first and always his man, and word was sent to Cranmer in Germany that the King had chosen him as Warham's successor. In effect, he was Thomas Cromwell's nominee. Professor Pollard, Cranmer's apologist, says that the nomination was a "somewhat unpleasant surprise." That is possible. Cranmer knew that he was to be made Archbishop for the primary purpose of arranging the marriage of Henry and Anne, and, though he probably quite honestly regarded the marriage with Katharine as invalid, he might well have preferred to have had the case decided by another judge.

Henry wasted no time. The Pope was persuaded to issue the necessary bull and Cranmer was consecrated on March 30, 1533, formally taking the oath of obedience to the Pope, and at the same time declaring before a notary that he should not regard the oath as binding if it conflicted with his duty to the King.

It is an unhistoric exaggeration to say that the English Church would not have broken with Rome but for the carnal desires of an adulterous monarch, but it is abundantly clear that Cranmer would never have been Archbishop of Canter-

D

bury unless Henry had been certain that he would contrive the royal divorce. His real talents were unknown. Cromwell vouched for his readiness to obey. So, by the will of the King, he was consecrated as the successor of St. Thomas, who, by his death, had humbled a greater King.

As I have said, Cranmer knew what was expected of him and he submitted himself to the royal will with abject servility. He would do what the King bade him to do ; he would believe what the King bade him to believe. He sent the King a statement of his sacramental beliefs, adding : " This is my opinion and sentence at present, which, nevertheless, I do not temerariously define, but refer the judgment thereof to Your Majesty."

On May 11, Cranmer held his court at Dunstable Priory, having begged Cromwell to keep his intention secret, since " if the Lady Katharine be counselled or persuaded to appear before me, I shall thereby be greatly stayed in the process." But he need not have feared. Katharine ignored his court.

On May 23rd, the Archbishop declared the marriage with Katharine null and void. On the 28th, at another secret court, he declared that the marriage, which had already taken place with Anne, was lawful, and on June 1st he crowned Anne at Westminster. Whatever may have been the excuses, the whole business was mean and cruel, and Cranmer's part in it was despicable.

Having obediently obeyed the King, and served the royal purpose, Cranmer was left to his own devices. Cromwell had, for the moment, no further use for him. He spent his time in an elaborate provincial visitation, which was bitterly resented by his suffragans, and in particular by Gardiner, the Bishop of Winchester and the Bishop of London. The avowed object of the visitation was the restoration of discipline and order. The real reason was that the visiting Archbishop always demanded heavy fees from the dioceses, religious houses and parishes that he visited, and Cranmer was badly in need of money. Canon Deane has pointed out the interesting fact that in the injunctions that the Archbishop afterwards sent to the religious houses, there is no reference to the immorality that was soon to be charged against them as the excuse for the dissolution.

Having flouted Rome, and got rid of Katharine, Henry was now determined to regularise his position as Supreme Head of the Church by Acts of Parliament and forcibly to suppress any resistance to his authority. Cromwell was his confidant, his adviser and his instrument. Willing as he might have been to help, Cranmer was rarely, if ever, consulted. Cromwell packed the House of Commons with his creatures and warned possible recalcitrant spiritual peers not to attend the sittings of the House of Lords. In 1534, the subservient Parliament humbly begged the King to confiscate a portion of clerical incomes for his own use, and the authority of Rome was specifically repudiated, and in 1534 the Act of Supremacy and Succession, with its enforcement of an oath for its acceptance, was passed. The result was the arrest, the mock trial and the execution of John Fisher and Thomas More, one the high-minded, scholarly ecclesiastic, the other statesman, great lawyer and wit—both among the greatest and best of Englishmen. Centuries ago they were numbered with the saints, and it is a matter for congratulation to all Englishmen that Rome has belatedly recognised their sainthood.

Fisher and More were willing to recognise Anne's daughter as heiress to the English throne, but they would not recognise Henry as Head of the English Church. Cranmer made a very timid effort to save their lives, but was warned by Cromwell to mind his own business and, fearing for himself, with characteristic servility, he arrested humbler persons accused of " speaking well of the Pope or slightingly of the Queen."

Cranmer had aided Henry to get rid of Katharine, and in 1536, after being ignored for years, he was sent for to aid the King to get rid of Anne. Cranmer was the queen breaker. Henry was tired of Anne and wanted yet another wife, and Anne was accused, almost certainly falsely, of adultery. Cranmer was amazed. He was, he wrote, " in such a perplexity that my mind is clean amazed," as well it might be. But his one thought was for the King, for " the deep sorrows of Your Grace's heart." Canon Deane charitably finds this guileless. I find it nauseating.

Without a shred of evidence against her, Anne was condemned and beheaded and Cranmer held a court to declare the marriage that, three years before, he had solemnly declared valid, was really entirely invalid.

Anne was executed on May 19th, 1536, and on the 20th Henry married Jane Seymour. Jane gave birth to the future Edward VI on October 12th, 1537, and died ten days later.

It has become the fashion to argue that the peculiarly unpleasant character of the King had very little to do with the revolutionary changes in England during his reign, but there is no question that the uncontrollable sexuality of a determined monarch fundamentally affected his public policy. His two most capable ministers, Wolsey and Cromwell, both owed their falls from power to the King's matrimonial adventures. The quarrel with the Emperor was due to, and the break with Rome was, at least, hastened by the discarding of Katharine.

Professor Pollard, a staunch Protestant and an unconscious humourist, says of the King, for whom Cranmer had such unbounded admiration : " his morals, it is true, left much to be desired." As is proved by the many miscarriages of both Katharine and Anne, the early death of Jane, and the physical disabilities of Mary, Elizabeth and Edward, the truth is that Henry was a syphlitic as well as a debauchee. If he had been able to be the father of healthy children, the course of English history must have been vastly different.

But while the repudiation of Papal jurisdiction was hastened by the royal lust, it was the culmination of the long and bitter struggle between the two authorities to which the English Church admitted allegiance, and the Act of Supremacy gave the King little more than his predecessors had claimed. This has to be kept in mind if the character of the protagonists of the Reformation drama, of Gardiner as well as of Cranmer, are to be justly estimated.

In the spring of 1534, the Convocations of the two Provinces agreed that " the Pope of Rome hath no greater jurisdiction conferred on him by God in Holy Scripture in this kingdom of England than any other foreign bishop.'

Much earlier, in the Statute of Praemunire, it was asserted that the crown of England is subject " to God in all things touching its regality and to no other ; and ought not to be submitted to the Pope." These declarations were the preliminaries to the Act of Supremacy which decreed that the monarch was the Supreme Head of the Church " so far as the law of Christ permits." Both Henry and Elizabeth after him disclaimed any right of interference with the ghostly authority of priests or bishops, and Dean Hook declares that after the Act of Supremacy Henry was " a Catholic king, resuming in the national Church right and authority which his Catholic ancestors had claimed." While More and Fisher died rather than subscribe to the Act, Gardiner emphatically and the pious and conservative Bishop Tunstal, of Durham, with some hesitation, supported it.

The Act of Supremacy did not, as Gladstone pointed out in his " Remarks on the Royal Supremacy," establish the complete royal mastery of Convocation that Henry succeeded in establishing over Parliament. Gladstone wrote :

> " The Reformation statutes did not leave the Convocation in the same condition relatively to the crown as the Parliament. It was under more control ; but its inherent and independent power was thereby more directly recognised. The King was not the head of Convocation ; it was not merely his council. The Archbishop was its head, and summoned and prorogued it. It was not power but leave that this body had to seek from the Crown in order to make canons. A canon without the royal assent was already a canon though without the force of law ; but a bill which had passed the two houses is without force of any kind until that assent is given. . . . In the one case the Crown is the fountain of the whole authority of the law ; the lords and commons are its advisers. In the other, the Convocation decrees and ordains ; the King gives legal sanction and currency to that which without such sanction would have remained a simple appeal to conscience. In statutes the King enacts with the advice and assent of Parliament ; in canons the Convocation enacts with the licence and assent of the Crown."

But Henry did not recognise the limitation of his authority, and, without the smallest legal justification, he at once claimed the right as Supreme Head to create a new office of Vicar-General, to which he appointed Thomas Cromwell. The Vicar-General was to preside at the meetings of Convocation, ousting the Archbishop from that position, and he was commissioned officially to visit the universities and the religious houses. The occasional interference of the Pope was no longer possible, but the Church found itself under the hard heel of the King, and the Archbishop, betraying the obligations of his office, accepted the humiliation without any protest, writing, indeed, to Cromwell a series of abjectly fulsome letters.

Cromwell always planned ahead. He did not bother to visit the universities, and his visitation of the monasteries was the prelude to the dissolution and despoilment which he and the King had decided. There had been a serious deterioration in the quality of monastic life and in the public usefulness of the monasteries. That is made sufficiently clear in the writings of Rabelais and Erasmus. On the whole, the monks remained good landlords and kindly neighbours. But some of the smaller houses were nearly empty. The rule had grown lax. With the foundation of lay schools the educational value of the religious houses had largely come to an end. The charges of evil living were almost entirely untrue inventions to excuse barefaced robbery. But there is no doubt that the monastic system was crying out for the reform that a few years later was on the continent one of the many good results of the counter-reformation.

There had always been trouble between the regular clergy and the monasteries, most of which were outside episcopal jurisdiction, and the scholastic foundations of William of Wykeham, Archbishop Chicheley, Wolsey and Fisher were endowed from the sequestration of monastic properties. Cromwell had precedents, therefore, for his seizures, but the one real object was to benefit the royal exchequer and to fill his own pockets and the pockets of the lying ruffians who supplied the false evidence of monkish wrongdoing. In 1536, seventy-six of the smaller religious houses were suppressed and the King's income was increased by £32,000. Then came the turn of the larger foundations and, in all, more than a million pounds was stolen from the Church. Three abbots were hanged for resisting the robberies, 8,000 religious were evicted, and over 60,000 of the monastery tenantry lost their homes and their livelihoods. The dissolution was accompanied by an orgy of destruction of beautiful buildings, ancient manuscripts and altar ornaments.

Part of the confiscated wealth was paid in bribes to the members of the servile Parliament and was the beginning of the fortunes of the class that was to be dominant in England from the Puritan revolution until our own day.

Cranmer made no protest against proceedings that, Canon Deane says, " shook England from one end to the other." On the contrary, he tried (one is glad to know in vain) to secure a portion of the swag. He wrote to Cromwell :

> My singular good lord, in my most hearty wise I commend me unto your lordship. And whereas I perceive that your lordship, not without urgent and godly considerations, hath suppressed already divers friars' houses, and bestowed them on honest men, as I am informed, which your godly proveeding, as I trust, shall as well extend unto Canterbury as in other places, to the intent that the irreligious religion there may be extincted with other ; and forasmuch as the Gray Friars in Canterbury lieth very commodiously for this bearer, Thomas Cobham . . . these shall be to beseech your lordship to be so good lord until him as to help him unto the said house of the Gray Friars. Thus, my lord, right heartily fare you well."

It is good to know that there were among the opponents of monasticism men more religious than the Archbishop who protested against the spoliation and defended the character of Cromwell's victims. Hugh Latimer, a far more fervent Protestant than Cranmer, wrote to the Vicar-General on behalf of the prior of the Benedictine house at Great Malvern, asking : " for the upstanding of his aforesaid house and continuance of the same to many good purposes—not in monkery, he meaneth not so, God forbid !—but any other ways, as should be thought and seem good to the king's majesty, as to maintain teaching, preaching, study, with praying and (to which he is much given) good house-keeping, for to the virtue of hospitality he hath been greatly inclined from the beginning and is very commended in these parts for the same. . . He feedeth many, and that daily, for the country is poor and full of penury. And, alas, my good lord, shall we not see two or three (sc. monasteries) in every shire changed to such remedy ? "

The popular resentment of the dissolution found expression in the Pilgrimage of Grace, a rising in Yorkshire and Lincolnshire, and it is notable that Cranmer was counted with Cromwell as one of the enemies of the people. The leader was Roger Aske, and one of the rebels' songs ran

> Crim, Cran and Riche
> With three L's and their liche.
> As some men teach,
> > God amend them.
>
> And that Aske may,
> Without delay
> Here make a stay
> > And well to end.

Riche was a tame lawyer of Cromwell's and one of the L's was Latimer.

The rebellion was suppressed mainly by promises that the King never intended to keep, followed by savage punishments. But it was in the Pilgrimage of Grace that the people of England made one of their rare interventions in public affairs.

Close friendship with the German Protestant princes was the objective of Cromwell's foreign policy. But Henry was still determined not even to let it appear that he favoured continental Protestantism. It was equally dangerous in the England of 1540 to deny the doctrine of transubstantiation as it was to acclaim the authority of the Pope. By the King's orders the bishops drew up a profession of faith in Ten Articles which were to define the position of the Church of England. The Articles were unanimously approved by the bishops, who included Gardiner and Latimer, and they probably expressed Cranmer's own position at this time. They are a notable example of the Church of England's genius for compromise. Professor Pollard has summarised the Articles :

> Three sacraments, baptism, penance and the Eucharist, were strongly upheld ; works of charity were declared to be necessary to salvation; auricular confession was not to be condemned, and justification could only be attained ' by contrition and faith, joined with charity.' Images were to stand in the churches, saints to be invoked as intercessors, the usual Catholic ceremonies to be observed, and prayers to be offered for the departed. On the other hand, the Bible and the three Creeds were to be regarded as the standard of orthodoxy, a position from which the Reformed

Church of England has never varied ; amendment of life was pronounced a necessary part of penance, faith was joined with charity as necessary to justification, and the article on the Eucharist did not go beyond an assertion of the Real Presence ; there was to be no censing, kneeling or offering to images, the invocation of the saints was ' to be done without any vain superstition, as to think that any saint is more merciful, or will hear us sooner than Christ,' ceremonies were declared to have no power to remit sin " nor masses to deliver souls from purgatory."

With all his inconsistences, his pettiness and his time serving, Cranmer showed real courage in his persistent urging that the circulation of Holy Scripture in English would strengthen both religion and the national spirit. As is shown in the prayers in the Book of Common Prayer, he, himself, wrote beautiful English and he had a real love for the language. Tyndale's translation of the Bible was marred by its violently Protestant introduction and Henry had ordered it to be publicly burned. Cranmer urged that the bishops should undertake another version and Gardiner translated two of the Gospels, and in 1536, with the authority of the Archbishop, Coverdale's unsatisfactory version was printed. In 1539 the Great Bible, which was largely Tyndale's (its versions of the Psalms are retained in the Prayer Book), was issued, and Cromwell ordered that a copy of it should be placed in every parish church. This was a great event in the history of England, and because of his responsibility for it, Cranmer has his place among English worthies.

The Bible in the Authorised Version, published seventy years after the Great Bible, was to be the basis of English popular culture. It gave the nation its imagery, its phraseology, its poetry and its stories. The English were to become, in a real sense, Bible Christians, and there is nothing more lamentable in the England of our times than the fact that our children no longer " know their Bibles."

In 1537 Cranmer persuaded Convocation to reduce the number of holy days. Holy days were holidays, and it is a curious and suggestive fact that the opponents of the Catholic religion have always itched to restrict the playtime of the common people. It seems certain that Cromwell, whose greed was never satisfied, was behind this proposal. The observance of saints' days meant the bringing of gifts to the saints' shrines, and, having despoiled the monasteries, Cromwell was now eager to rob the shrines.

Henry had a particular aversion for the memory of St. Thomas, whose murder had compelled a proud king to an uncomfortable penance, and it was with unusual satisfaction that he received from Cromwell the gold and jewels stolen from the shrine in Canterbury Cathedral, the most magnificent as it had been the most cherished shrine in England. It was characteristic of Cranmer that he found a petty way of showing his contempt for his martyred predecessor. It is recorded in a contemporary journal that " the same year the Archbishop of Canterbury did not fast on St. Thomas's eve, but did eat flesh and did sup in his parlour with his family, which was never seen before."

The shrines were destroyed, but the saints were not forgotten, and Cranmer complained to Cromwell that the common people were still " very obstinately given to observe and keep with solemnity the holy days lately abrogated."

Sheer greed had led Henry to approve the dissolution of the monasteries and the despoilment of the shrines, but both Cranmer and Cromwell seem to have believed that the King was at least beginning to sympathise with the theological teaching of the continental reformers, which he had vehemently and effectively attacked. So Cromwell urged more strenuously than ever the alliance with the German princes and Cranmer invited three Lutherans to visit England. But these poor men came too soon and they had a very chilly reception. The King would not receive them and the lodging provided by Cromwell was miserably uncomfortable, over-run with rats and, as they complained, " the kitchen standeth directly against their parlour where they daily dine and sup, and by reason thereof the house savoureth so ill that it offendeth all men that come into it."

This visit convinced Henry that it was necessary to make it quite clear what he believed and what he was determined that his subjects should believe, and, by a personal appearance at the debates, he forced the notorious Statute of Six Articles through Parliament, Cranmer once again plucking up sufficient temporary courage to speak against it in the

House of Lords. The Statute demanded acceptance of transubstantiation, communion in one kind, clerical celibacy, religious vows, auricular confession and private masses, and it enacted that to repudiate any one of them was to risk being burned as a heretic. Latimer at once resigned his see of Worcester, but Cranmer was content to send his wife back to Germany, where she was to stay for seven years.

It is very difficult to be sure what Cranmer's doctrinal position really was. While Henry lived, he was ready to subscribe to any doctrine that had the royal approval, and this can only mean that he had no genuine faith of his own. He had opposed the Six Articles, but he was afterwards personally concerned in the arrest of clerks and lay people who refuse to subscribe to them.

By 1539, Henry had grown weary of Cromwell as he had grown weary of Wolsey, and the Vicar-General, who had bored his master by his insistence on the German alliance, sealed his doom when he provided him with an ugly German wife. When Henry saw the plain and stupid Anne of Cleves at Greenwich, Cromwell's ascendancy finished. He was arrested on a trumped up charge and promptly beheaded, a fate which he richly deserved, and the German princess was left to live in peace in England on a comfortable pension. A fortnight after Cromwell's death Henry married the pretty, flighty Katharine Howard.

Canon Deane suggests that Cranmer was probably the only man in England who did not rejoice at Cromwell's execution. He was stunned and terrified for himself, and he hastened to write to the King, expressing thankfulness that his patron's treason had been " discovered in time ! " After the death of Cromwell and for the last seven years of Henry's reign, there was a persistent contest between the semi-Protestant Archbishop and the anti-Papal Catholic Gardiner.

Henry soon tired of Katharine Howard and she was executed for immorality in 1541, and in 1543 Henry married the elderly Catherine Parr, a lady of definite Protestant sympathies, whom Cranmer expected to count as an ally, but who was far too cautious to annoy her husband by taking sides. Henry never lost his interest in theology. He was in a sense a religious man as he was a cruel, greedy and sensual tyrant. He was eager for order and conformity and he still felt that his subjects should be told with greater definiteness what he expected them to believe. Accordingly, in 1543, he caused to be published " A Necessary Erudition for any Christian man, set forth by the King's Majesty of England," commonly known as " the King's Book." Originally largely written by Henry himself, it was improved and sub-edited by the Archbishop. It contained articles on the faith, the creed, the sacraments, the Lord's Prayer and the Ave Maria, free will and prayers for the dead. It insisted on the doctrine of Transubstantiation and it was definitely anti-Protestant.

Henry died in 1547. His son Edward was a boy of nine, and Henry had in his will nominated a Council of Regency with limited powers. His wishes were ignored when he could no longer enforce them and the Council appointed a Protector with all the powers in Church and State which the old King had assumed.

The six and a half years of the reign of the sickly Edward VI were a period of greedy tyranny, political ineptitude, social misery and religious innovations imposed by foreign influence on an unwilling Church and nation. Nevertheless, the reign began well. Somerset, chosen as Protector because he was the King's nearest male relative, was definitely sympathetic to the Protestant doctrines, but he was a tolerant liberal-minded man with a developed social conscience, and the worst that can be said of him is that he was praised by the unspeakable John Knox.

In 1543, in obedience to King Henry, Cranmer had subscribed to the Six Articles. Four years later, owing to the influence of his chaplain Nicholas Ridley, a sincere and honest Lutheran, he rejected all that he had professed to believe, and having no longer to fear his old master, he collaborated with Somerset and the Council, from which Gardiner had been excluded, in securing drastic changes in the Church's teaching and practice. The first step was an order for the removal from the churches and cathedrals of all images and pictures. Cranmer was at least partially responsible for a campaign of iconoclastic vandalism that robbed the Church of many lovely possessions and was to be imitated by the Puritans of the next century. The English churches had glistened with ornaments, the work of inspired artists and craftsmen. In an orgy of godless folly, ancient illustrated missals were burned ; windows were broken ; frescoes were hidden by whitewash. Nothing was to be left to inspire grateful remembrance of the saints or to emphasise the beauty of holiness.

The images of the good and the noble were condemned, but, such was the fantastic mood of this class-directed Protestantism, that it was decreed that there must be no destruction of " the images of any king, prince, nobleman or any other dead person that hath not been commonly reputed and taken as a saint." So, as Canon Deane has recalled, in Worcester Cathedral, the images of St. Oswald and St. Wulfstan were destroyed, but the tomb and figure of the despicable King John remain unto this day.

To me it is one of the evidences of the truth of the Catholic faith that the rejection of Catholic doctrine has filled men with a strange and furious hatred of the beautiful. In the ages of faith men built the great Cathedrals. In the days of the most fervent Protestant piety, they built the Methodist chapels, the ugliest of all the ugly buildings that encumber this fair England. In his many vacillating moods, Cranmer seems for a time to have shared the appalling belief that God is offended by the beautiful works of men's hands.

In addition to the " King's Book," Cranmer also prepared and issued a Book of Homilies, which was badly needed, as the majority of the clergy were incapable of preaching any sort of sermons. The Homilies were anti-Catholic, and Gardiner protested against the publication and was sent to the Tower. Gardiner particularly objected to the exclusion of charity from the works of justification in the Homily on Salvation.

At Cranmer's instance communion in both kinds was first recommended and then commanded, and clerical marriages were permitted, and Mrs. Cranmer came back from Germany to Canterbury. The Statute of Six Articles was repealed and there were no more prosecutions for heresy. Dr. Lindsay, the Presbyterian historian, says that all these changes had been contemplated by Henry, which is manifestly absurd, and, if Cranmer asserted that they had been, he was deliberately lying, which is by no means unlikely.

This " reformation in a hurry " led to endless confusion. " In one parish the old ceremonial would be maintained and the old scheme of fasts and festivals punctiliously observed. In the next parish a reforming incumbent would denounce ceremonial and saints' days alike as inventions of Satan." Much of the same state of affairs exists to-day in the Church of England, as witness the services at All Saints', Margaret Street, and at All Souls, Langham Place, just round the corner. But Cranmer and Somerset were as eager for uniformity as Henry had been, and in 1549 was published The First Prayer Book of Edward VI and after Whit-Sunday of that year the use of any other form of public worship was punishable by imprisonment and deprivation.

This Prayer Book is a very noble national possession. Its teaching is definitely Catholic, being largely based on the Sarum liturgy. The Latin prayers are translated into beautiful sonorous English. It emphasises that, though England had broken with the Pope, there was no break in the historic continuity of the English Church. There have been revisions of this first Prayer Book, all for the worse, but its essential qualities remain. It was Cranmer's great achievement. No Englishman has equalled his genius for the writing of prayers. It is impossible to forget the wobbling meanness of his public career. It would be the grossest ingratitude to forget his one great gift to the Church.

In this same year, 1549, Somerset fell from power. England was in a bad way. Wages were falling and the cost of living was rising. The countryman was finding the new landlords harsh and inconsiderate after the rule of the easy-going monks and the Protector sympathised. He tried to prevent the enclosures, and the majority of the Council, concerned only with feathering their own nests, " scouted Somerset's notions of liberty and deeply resented his championship of the poor against greedy landlords." There were peasant risings easily suppressed by hired German mercenaries, and Somerset was overthrown and arrested by a cabal led by the Duke of Northumberland.

He was another unqualified ruffian, a worthy successor o

Cromwell. He had no sort of personal religion, but he favoured the extreme Protestants because he planned with their help further to rob the Church, and he was acclaimed by them as a hero of the faith. Hooper, who thought that it was wicked to kneel while receiving Holy Communion, declared that the rascally Northumberland was " a most holy and fearless instrument of the Word of God."

Among other things Northumberland offered the bishopric of Rochester to John Knox and it remains a matter for thankfulness that Knox refused. But at Cranmer's invitation, hordes of German reformers settled in the country after Henry's death. Protestantism was under a temporary cloud in Germany and they were safer on this side of the Channel, where they were given livings, comfortably housed and admitted into the Archbishop's confidence. The English peasants had been dragooned by German soldiers and now the English Church was to be dragooned by German theologians.

The Germans were a mixed bag, Lutherans, Zwinglians, Calvinists, Anabaptists and adherents of other fancy religions. But they were all affronted by the Catholic tone of the Edwardian Prayer Book and urged Cranmer to prepare or to let them prepare a revised edition more to the taste of Wittenberg and Geneva. In view of his later views, it is important to emphasise that the 1549 book was almost entirely Cranmer's work. He was an expert liturgiologist and the Book was no hasty compilation, but the result of the work of years. It is probable that Gardiner's unexpected approval of the Book affected Cranmer more than the disapproval of the Germans, and with the help of Peter Martyr, for whom the Archbishop had obtained a Theological Professorship at Oxford, and Martin Bucer, a refugee from Strasbourg, comfortably settled in a similar professorship at Cambridge, Cranmer prepared the Second Prayer Book of Edward VI, which was published in 1552.

The principal alterations were in the Holy Communion service. The doctrine of the Real Presence was definitely taught in the First Book ; the vague wording of the Second Book might justify the Zwinglian teaching that the Sacrament is a mere commemoration, with the denial of any definite Presence of Christ in the Elements. This Second Book was never sanctioned by Convocation, was legally in use for only eight months and was never used at all in the majority of parishes.

Northumberland, Cranmer abetting him, went on with the forcible Protestantisation of the Church. Catholic-minded bishops, including the pious Tunstall of Durham, were ejected from their dioceses, and Lutherans were appointed in their places. Ridley, the Archbishop's chaplain, went to London and at once ordered the altar in every parish church to be replaced by " an honest table, decently covered," and Hooper, who disapproved of all bishops, became Bishop of Gloucester. Many Catholic-minded priests lost their livings, their places remaining unfilled and their incomes appropriated by Northumberland and his friends.

In 1552, Northumberland had Somerset executed, and again Cranmer feared for his own life, and found it politic to live quietly in his own diocese and to keep out of public life. In his retirement, he drew up Forty-two Articles of Religion, hoping that by designedly vague wording he might secure acceptance from both Catholics and Protestants, for it must, in justice, be admitted that Cranmer was honestly desirous of contriving religious agreement in England. But the Articles were still born. Edward signed them on June 12th, 1553, and he died on July 6th.

Northumberland knew, of course, that his tyranny was precarious. The boy King obviously could not live long. It must have been obvious to Northumberland that, on Edward's death, there would be a popular demand that he should be succeeded by his half-sister Mary. Nobody in England, except the small band of Protestant fanatics, regarded her as illegitimate. There had never been a queen regnant in England, but Mary was the daughter of the bluff King, for whom the people had retained a queer and entirely undeserved regard, and they were as weary of upstart political dictators as they were of the Germans who were dictating how they should worship God.

Northumberland decided, however, to keep Mary from the throne. He had married his fourth son to Lady Jane Grey.

the great-grand-daughter of Henry VII, and he persuaded the dying King to name her as his successor as the only way to save England from the Roman Catholics. Cranmer was told to add his signature to the document. Canon Deane says that " he argued, he pleaded, he demurred, he hesitated " and then he signed. That was Cranmer's way.

He hated and feared Northumberland. He knew that he was a ruffian. He knew, too, that if the hapless Lady Jane were the nominal monarch, Northumberland would be the actual ruler. But yet he signed. Afterwards he described his treachery as " heinous folly and offence." It was that and worse. But nothing was gained by the treachery. On July 6th Edward died. On the 10th, Lady Jane Grey was proclaimed Queen. On the 18th she was in the Tower. On the 21st Northumberland was there, too. On August 3rd Mary made a triumphal entry into London, Queen of England, with the whole-hearted support of the majority of her people. England was dead weary of Northumberland, Protestantism—and Cranmer.

To every Englishman, who realises the supreme value of the Catholic religion—and by the Catholic religion I certainly do not mean subservience to Rome—the reign of Mary is the most tragic period in the history of his country. It began in an atmosphere of hope and good will The Queen was called to the throne by the voice of the people. She was a woman of thirty-seven. A well-educated and precociously intelligent child, her girlhood had been made miserable by the troubles of her mother and for more than twenty years she had been subjected to persistent humiliation and persecution, which she had endured with courage and dignity. She had the chance and she may well have seemed to have had the ability to have inaugurated a new era of internal peace and justice. But she failed utterly and pathetically, and the failure was largely due to her miserable physical health, a heritage from her syphilitic father, which warped her judgment. She lives in popular history as " bloody Mary." She was in fact a well-intentioned, bruised and bewildered woman, surrounded for the most part by greedy selfseekers, fanatical in her sincere religion, nearly always ill.

The Spanish marriage and the persecution of the Protestants were major political blunders. They affected not only the course of English history, but the mood of the English people. It was hatred of the Spaniard that inspired Elizabethan nationalism, and Latimer was revered as the victim of Spain.

The Council, that had supported Northumberland and had approved the attempt to make England a Lutheran country, rallied to Mary, when it was clear that the nation was determined that she should be Queen. They were for the most part men who had benefited from the sacking of the monasteries and the pilfering of ecclesiastical possessions, and they were perfectly willing again to go to Mass and to subscribe to the doctrine of transubstantiation and even to the supremacy of the Pope, so long as they were permitted to continue to enjoy their new wealth. William Cecil, afterwards Lord Burghley, was one of them. With Cranmer he had signed the instrument in which Edward had named Jane Grey as his successor, but, immediately after the King's death, he rallied to Mary and was, in a comparatively small way, responsible for the ease with which Northumberland was swept aside. During Mary's reign, Cecil was inconspicuous and, when she died, few of his contemporaries could have foretold his predominant position under Elizabeth. In matters of religious faith, Cecil was as cynical as Elizabeth herself. To him it did not matter very much what a nation believed so long as all the people believed the same things. "That state," he said, " could never be in safety where there was a toleration of two religions. For there is no enmity so great as that for religion ; and therefore they that differ in the service of God can never agree in the service of the country." So Cecil went to Mass with Mary, and was not opposed to her determination to compel all her people to go to Mass.

For the rest, as I have said, Mary was surrounded by men who cared nothing for the state or the Church and were only concerned for their possessions. The rule of Mammon, which has brought to this generation the tragedy of two world wars, began in England with the dissolution of the monasteries.

Mary had one wise and single-minded counsellor. On

her accession Gardiner was released from the Tower and re-appointed Lord Chancellor. In the reign of Henry, Gardiner was an anti-Papal Catholic. During his five years' imprisonment, he had decided that the royal supremacy, usurped first by Somerset and then by Northumberland, was more intolerable than the Papal supremacy, and that the Catholic religion could not be preserved in England if the authority of the Pope were repudiated. However mistaken it may have been, in the circumstances of the times, the conclusion is easy to understand. Gardiner had little responsibility for the Marian persecutions. In that monument of fanatical inaccuracies, Foxe's *Book of Martyrs*, he is called " the bloody bishop " and he was grossly misrepresented by Burnett. The truth is that, while he had as Lord Chancellor to preside at the trial of Hooper and other preachers, he did his best to persuade them to follow the course that he himself had found possible.

He and Cranmer hated each other, but he tried to induce the Archbishop to leave the country and secured the royal consent for his going. It was through his good offices, too, that the more conspicuous of the Germans, whom he certainly had no reason to love, were permitted to go home. He succeeded, with great difficulty, in persuading Mary against the execution of Elizabeth, a criminal blunder urged by the Spaniards. He opposed the Spanish marriage. In 1553, when he was at the zenith of his power, not one single person was burned in England and not one person was burned during his lifetime in his diocese of Winchester.

Here, it may be added, that while the persecutions were detestable and utterly stupid, they have been grotesquely exaggerated. Maitland and Hume agree that in all only two hundred and seventy-seven persons were sent to the stake, fewer than the number of the daily civilian victims of the Nazis, and there were no martyrdoms in nine of the fourteen English dioceses.

Parliament and Convocation were as subservient to Mary as they had been to Henry and Northumberland. All the Edwardian religious legislation was promptly repealed and *De Heretico Comburendo* was again the law. Then came the marriage with the dour Philip of Spain, eleven years the Queen's junior, and the end of Mary's brief popularity. Spanish monks arrived in England to be detested even more than the Lutherans imported by Cranmer. And the persecutions began.

In the last months of his life Cranmer showed a courage which, though it was intermittent, was as admirable as it must have been unexpected. He sent his wife and children to Germany with his Lutheran friends, but he refused to go himself. He realised what would probably happen to him, but he remained at his post. He had admitted that he had been guilty of treason in supporting the succession of Lady Jane Grey, but so had others, who had been pardoned, and he might have supposed that his abject confession of guilt might have secured his own pardon. But he should have known that Mary would never forgive him for the leading part that he had played in the stigmatising of her mother as an adultress and herself as a bastard, or for his zeal in contriving the humiliation that had made her life almost insupportable.

Whatever chance he had of escape, he destroyed by writing a definite confession of Lutheran faith which it is suggested was made public against his will. In it he declared that " the Devil goeth about now by lying to overthrow the Lord's supper again, and to restore his late satisfactory Masses, a thing of his own intention and device," and that " the Mass in many things not only hath no foundation in Christ's Apostles or the primitive Church, but is manifestly contrary to the same and containeth many horrible abuses in it." Cranmer had, indeed, abandoned all the doctrines which he had accepted at Henry's bidding and had become the complete convert of Ridley, Bucer and Peter Martyr.

He was summoned before the Star Chamber and once again Gardiner tried to save him. If he would quietly retire into private life, he would be provided adequately for a dignified scholarly life. But Cranmer refused. He would stay at Lambeth and Mary ordered his detention in the Tower, where Latimer and Ridley were already imprisoned.

The resentment against the Spanish marriage led to a futile popular rising, led by Sir Thomas Wyatt, the object of which was to replace Mary by Jane Grey. The rising was easily suppressed, and Cranmer, with Jane Grey and three of her brothers-in-law, were tried at the Guildhall for treason. They were found guilty and, being attainted of treason, Cranmer was incapable of holding any public office and ceased to be Archbishop of Canterbury. For the time that was all that happened to him, but the young, beautiful and innocent Jane Grey was beheaded in the Tower.

In the statement of belief to which I have referred, Cranmer had demanded the opportunity of publicly defending his sacramental views. He was a skilled debater and he may still have had some small hope that if he were heard he might be justified. Rather surprisingly, the demand was granted, and in April, with Ridley and Latimer, he was taken, with studied discomfort and humiliation to Oxford, to dispute with fourteen carefully selected divines, whose instructions were not patiently to listen and judiciously to decide, but to expose the three bishops as " sons of iniquity and perdition, and seditious innovators of error." The proceedings were an unworthy and vulgar farce. Cranmer himself described them.

> This is to signify your lordships that upon Monday, Tuesday and Wenesday last past were open disputations here in Oxford against me, Master Ridley and Master Latimer, in three matters concerning the Sacrament : first of the Real Presence ; secondly, of transubstantiation ; and thirdly, of the sacrifice of the mass. How the other two were used, I cannot tell ; for we were separated, so that none of us knew what the other said, nor how they were ordered. But as concerning myself, I can report that I never knew nor heard of a more confused disputation in all my life. For albeit there was one appointed to dispute against me, yet every man spake his mind, and brought forth what he liked without order. And such haste was made, that no answer could be suffered to be given fully to any argument before another brought a new argument. And in such weighty and large matters there was no remedy but the disputations must be ended in one day which can scanty well be ended in three months ! "

Finally, the three bishops were declared to be heretics, and for nearly eighteen months they were kept in the gaol at Oxford, waiting for the heresy laws of Henry VIII to be re-enacted. During these months, Cardinal Pole was received in England as Papal Legate, and on November 30th,

1554, he attended Parliament and, in the Pope's name, solemnly absolved the kingdom.

Pole's mother was a daughter of George, Duke of Clarence, and the niece of Edward IV. In his youth he was a friend of Thomas More, who said that he was as learned as he was noble and as virtuous as he was learned. He had wide cosmopolitan experience, he had been one of the outstanding figures at the Council of Trent, where he upheld the doctrine of justification by a living faith that shows itself in good works and he had a high reputation for learning and the devoutness of his personal life.

Shortly after his arrival in England the burnings of heretics began, and it is not unnatural that Pole should have been regarded as partially responsible. Canon Deane, generally so careful in his judgments, says that Pole's " simpering affectations failed to conceal his malicious cruelty." Dr. Lindsay, who always writes as a partisan, says that Pole " sometimes rescued prisoners from the vindictiveness of Bonner ; at other times he seemed to have hounded on the persecutors." There is not the slightest evidence of this hounding on. In his first address to Convocation, he urged the bishops to be gentle with heretics. With obvious honesty, he tried to secure the recantation or, as he would have said, the conversion that would have saved the lives of the accused. But when once the prosecution had begun and the accused had been found guilty, the law demanded the penalty of a horrible death.

The bishops could refuse to prosecute. Most of them did. After the sentence, the Legate had no authority to intervene and the royal intervention was forbidden by the twisted conscience of the Queen.

On September 12th, 1555, Cranmer was tried in the University Church, Oxford, by the Bishop of Gloucester, as the delegate of the Pope. He was charged with violating the law of clerical celibacy, with denying the doctrine of transubstantiation and with breaking his oath of obedience to the Papacy. He defended himself with skill and spirit. He denied the jurisdiction of the Pope and, therefore, the right of his, the Pope's, representative to be his judge. But it was the Papal jurisdiction with which Mary was concerned. That would be clearly established if the Primate of England were executed by order of the Pope of Rome.

Ridley and Latimer were burned at Oxford on October 16th, and with diabolic cruelty Cranmer was compelled to witness their suffering. And not unnaturally Cranmer wavered. He was comfortably housed now in the Deanery of Christ Church ; he was old and broken ; he was pestered by the Spanish friars and he was afraid, as many a bolder man would have been. In January, 1556, he signed the first of a series of submissions. It ran :

> " Forasmuch as the king's and queen's majesties, by consent of their parliament, have received the Pope's authority within this realm, I am content to submit myself to their laws herein, and to take the Pope for chief head of the Church of England, so far as God's laws and the laws and customs of this realm will permit.
> " I, Thomas Cranmer, doctor of divinity, do submit myself to the Catholic Church of Christ, and to the Pope, supreme Head of the same Church, and unto the king's and the queen's majesties, and unto all their laws and ordinances."

In February he was formally degraded by direct order of the Pope from Holy Orders, and was removed from the comfort of the Deanery to the squalor of the common gaol, where he wrote two more submissions. But there was no suggestion of pardon or reprieve, and in March he signed what Canon Deane had called " a revolting document," which was almost certainly prepared for him. In it he pleaded guilty to all the charges made against him and admitted the Papal claims and the doctrines of trans-substantiation and purgatory. Then, having had this last humiliation, he was sent to the stake on March 2nd. He was taken to St. Mary's to listen to a sermon from the Provost of Eton, who bade the crowded congregation listen to the prisoner's last words. He began by exhorting his hearers to love God and to honour the King and Queen. He professed his belief in every word taught by Christ and His Apostles. And then slowly and solemnly to the consternation of the Provost and his gaolers, he went on to refer to his recantations :

> " I renounce and refuse as things written with my hand contrary to the truth I thought in my heart, and writ for fear of death, and to save

my life, if it might be—and that is all such bills as I have written or signed with mine own hand since my degradation, wherein I have written many things untrue. And forasmuch as my hand offended in writing contrary to my heart, therefore my hand shall first be punished ; for if I may come to the fire, it shall be first burned. And as for the Pope, I refuse him, as Christ's enemy and antichrist, with all his false doctrines."

He was dragged from the Church and walked with long striding steps to the stake, the miserable Spanish friars panting after him, and when the faggots were lighted he thrust his right hand into the fire, exclaiming, " This hand hath offended." And so he died, not as fiercely as St. Thomas, but as bravely. The man, who, weak and old, faced an exquisitely painful death with splendid courage, commands admiration and more than lenient judgment. Lord Houghton has described Cranmer as a " most mysterious personage." Professor Pollard says that he was " one of the simplest of characters." The mystery to me is that he should have died so bravely for a faith that for the greater part of his life he had rejected.

His inconsistence is obvious. He is said to have regarded it as a duty to believe as the King bade him. He was, therefore, an anti-Papal Catholic in the reign of Henry and a Protestant in the reign of Edward, and consistency would have demanded that he should have become a Romanist when Mary came to the throne.

Canon Deane is probably right in his estimate of the Archbishop. He was a scholar, a canonist, a liturgiologist and one of the greatest masters of English prose. Fundamentally he was, until his last days, personally uninterested in doctrinal controversy. He could never have had any strong personal convictions or he would not have supposed that formulas could be found to which both earnest Catholics and earnest Calvinists could subscribe. His views, says Canon Deane, " were ever apt to be indeterminate and to shift with the company in which he found himself." He was, indeed, " a very fallible and ill-starred man, of whose story, it may be said with truth that the annals of our Church hold few more interesting and none more pathetic."

Equally pathetic and even more pitiful was the end of Queen Mary. Her husband wearied of her and deserted her.

She was heartbroken at her inability to bear a child. Her marriage landed her country, as the ally of Spain, in a futile war with France, the result of which was the loss of Calais. Worse than all, Pope Paul IV, who was elected in 1555, a man as violent tempered as he was pious, hated "the accursed Spaniards" and sided with France. He quarrelled with Pole, who died twelve hours before Mary and deprived him of his office as Legate and the Papacy, for which the Queen and the Cardinal had fought so consistently, deserted them in their last days.

Mary died friendless and unregretted. As Dr. Gardiner has said, "the worldly-minded joined with the godly heretics in stirring up enmity against her."

With two other Cardinals, all of them influenced by Erasmus, Pole had been responsible for the calling, much against the will of the cultured, easy-going and amoral Pope Paul III, of the famous Council of Trent. The hope was that heresy might be destroyed by the root and branch Church reforms that Erasmus had advocated as earnestly as Luther. The reformers were invited to attend the Council but declined. The Council first met in 1545 to be frequently prorogued, and its sittings were not concluded until 1563, five years after Pole's death.

Dean Hook says that the history of the Roman Catholic Church, as we know it, begins at Trent, where the doctrine of Papal infallibility was for the first time defined and accepted. But much more than that occurred at Trent. It was the birthplace of the Counter-reformation, which was as real and as radical as the Protestant Reformation. The seminary system was instituted for the education and training of secular as well as regular priests. The Order of Jesus was founded by St. Ignatius Loyola, to become, from its discipline, devotion and learning, the greatest of all missionary agents, while it was establishing in Europe grammar schools for the benefit of the laity. Education, too, was spread by the Ursulines and later by the Christian Brothers. St. Philip Neri and St. Vincent Paul preached the social obligations of the Catholic faith. The Sisters of Charity left the sheltered walls of the convents to minister to the poor. And, with all this vigorous new life, Catholic mysticism found its most exalted exponents in St. Teresa and St. John of the Cross.

The result of the Counter-reformation was the extirpation of heresy in the whole of southern and a great part of central Europe, and this was due in some degree to the attraction of a definite and uniform Rule of Faith as compared to the many variations of Protestantism even in its early days. The triumph is certainly not altogether to be attributed to the persecutions of the Inquisition. Lord Acton was entirely justified in his assertion that it was " by honest conviction as well as by calculated but not illegal coercion that the Reformation was driven back."

England was entirely unaffected by the Counter-reformation largely because of Rome's failure to understand Elizabeth. With her accession, her country was separated from the main stream of western Christendom.

Nothing is more untrue than the frequent suggestion that the Protestant reformers were the apostles of freedom of conscience. They were as intolerant as the most fervent Romanists and generally far more vulgar and offensive. In fact, in the sixteenth century, statesmen and churchmen all agreed that uniformity of religious belief and practice was essential for the stability of the national life.

Chapter IV

THE MARTYR

THERE could be no greater proof of the power of the new rich in Tudor England than the fact that while Mary, despite deep popular indignation, was able to burn bishops, who denied the truth of the doctrine of transubstantiation, she never even attempted to compel the disgorging of the wealth filched from the monasteries.

When Elizabeth succeeded, in 1558, with her acute political understanding, she realised her dependence on the plutocracy of whom her minister, William Cecil, was the most distinguished and the least self-seeking representative. Politically she was the heiress of her father, with immeasurably greater vision and imagination. She had no personal religion. With Catherine de Medici, she regarded religion as a matter of political expediency, but she accepted the prevailing conviction of her age that " one nation, one faith " was necessary for secular stability. Like her father, she favoured anti-papal Catholicism. She detested the doctrines of the Calvinists, partly because of her sardonic common sense and partly because she understood the political consequences of the acceptance of those doctrines. She would, if she could, have made terms with Rome and the religious and political developments of her reign were due to the ineptitude of Philip of Spain, the undiplomatic vehemence of Pope Pius V and the paramount influence of the new rich.

In the first year of her reign, Parliament passed the Act of Supremacy and enacted that the Prayer Book of 1559, a revision of the revision of 1552, should be the only legal service book. Henry Wakeman says that the Act of Supremacy put back the Church " to the condition in which Henry VIII left it, except the supreme headship which was abolished." The Act was a protection against anything like a repetition of the Marian persecution, through its provision that what was heresy was to be decided by Scripture, the four first General Councils and the decision of Convocation, approved by Parliament.

To their honour be it remembered that thirteen of the fourteen bishops, who had been appointed by Mary and held to the Papal allegiance, refused to take the oath prescribed by the Act of Supremacy and a number of the clergy followed their example. Pole, the Archbishop of Canterbury, was dead and Elizabeth had to deal with a Church with no Primate, one bishop and hundreds of parishes without a parish priest. She found an admirable Primate in Matthew Parker, who has been described as " learned, amiable, conscientious, moderate, against whose character no breath of suspicion had ever been breathed, whose fidelity the Queen could absolutely trust." Parker was a good churchman, his ecclesiastical position being exactly that of Gardiner before his imprisonment in the Tower.

The continuity of the English Church, the fact that it was not a new society, like the continental Protestant churches, created at the Reformation, is stated in the *congé d'élire* in which Elizabeth ordered the Canterbury chapter to elect Parker. He was elected and enthroned as the successor of Cardinal Pole. The significant words are *Cum Ecclesia praedicta per mortem naturalem reverendissimi in Christo Patris et Domini Reginaldi Pole . . . jam vacat, et pastoris sit solatio destituta.*

Continuity and the validity of English orders were specifically denied by Leo XIII in 1896, largely owing to the pressure of the English Roman Catholics. But popular Roman stories about Parker's consecration have been dismissed as sheer fiction by the Roman Catholic historian Lingard, and the validity of English orders has been admitted by such a distinguished Roman Catholic theologian as the Abbé Duchesne.

It is sufficient for my purpose to accent that Parker certainly regarded himself as a bishop of the one Catholic and Apostolic church and that he was certainly so regarded by Elizabeth.

Unfortunately for the Archbishop, the Queen and England, circumstances compelled the consecration to the vacant sees of men exiled during the reign of Mary, who were impreg-

nated with Swiss Calvinist heresies and were eager to bring
the English church, that had broken its allegiance with Rome,
into the thraldom of Geneva. These men, the first of the
clerical Puritans had brought from Switzerland the terrible
doctrine that the sacrifice of the Cross was not made for the
salvation of all mankind, but only of a pre-ordained minority.
They repudiated the doctrine of the Real Presence and they
taught that the Church was not the divine society, created
by the Holy Spirit in Jerusalem on the Day of Pentecost,
but the congregations of the elect. They regarded the claim
of the continuity of the English Church as contrary to the
Protestant theory that true Christianity dates from the sixteenth and not from the first century. To them the Elizabethan Prayer Book was objectionable and Romanist. Its
concessions to Protestant sentiment were inconsiderable, and
the Ornaments Rubric definitely ordered the use of the
mass vestments, that the Calvinists denounced as the
trappings of Satan. Moreover, the words of administration
implied belief in the Real Presence. The Calvinists disliked
the surplice because it suggested continuity with the pre-
reformation Church ; they declined to make the sign of the
Cross in the baptismal rite because that implies the doctrine
of baptismal regeneration ; they regarded confirmation as
meaningless ; they even objected to the wedding ring
because that suggests that marriage is a sacrament. They
were intent on destroying the authority of the episcopate.

This was the faith of some of the men who, hating episcopacy, were raised to the episcopate in the early years of
Elizabeth. They accepted the Prayer Book as a temporary
compromise, with the avowed intention of destroying the
Catholic teaching and practice of the Church. To an extent,
the Queen and the Archbishop were too strong for the
innovators. Further destruction of monuments and glass
windows was prevented, the use of the surplice and of the
font for baptisms was made obligatory and worshippers were
required to kneel when receiving Holy Communion, kneeling
being particularly hated by the Puritans. But the Calvinist
divines had strong lay support in Parliament, and the magnificent Leicester was regarded as their leader. Many of
the charges made against Leicester by the Jesuit Parsons

were probably untrue, but the real character of Puritanism is indicated by the character of its most prominent lay adherent.

In 1576, Parker was succeeded by Edmund Grindal, who angered the Queen by his Calvinism and, in consequence spent most of his Primacy in retirement. Elizabeth saved the English Church from becoming completely Puritanised ; the mass of the English people were never Puritans. The events of the Queen's reign, however, made the nation fiercely anti-Roman. The war with Spain, with the stories that came to England of the cruelties of the Inquisitions, and the enflament of national sentiment by the defeat of the Armada, the excommunication of Elizabeth and the plots against her life, in which the Jesuit missionaries were concerned, not only increased the general anti-Roman sentiment but caused, for the first time, something like popular anti-Catholic prejudice. This was exploited by the Calvinist preachers, who suggested that there was some mystic connection between the wearing of surplices by English priests and decorum at Holy Communion with the brutalities of Alva in the Netherlands, as it has been suggested even in our day by Protestants of the sillier kind that the use of the Eucharistic vestments in English churches is the prelude to the re-lighting of the Smithfield fires.

The Pope called on Elizabeth's Roman Catholic subjects to rebel against her. The answer was a series of penal statutes under which approximately as many Roman Catholics were tortured and executed as the number of Protestants who were put to death by Mary. But Elizabeth would not journey to Geneva. Cecil and Bacon, as well as Leicester and Essex, urged the Queen to strengthen her political position by agreeing to the Calvinists' demands. But she refused, and the refusal infuriated the sectarians. The less astute of the Calvinists lost their heads. Whitgift, who had followed Grindal as Archbishop, was denounced as " Beelzebub of Canterbury," the bishops were described as " incarnate devils, cozening knaves and enemies of God," and the clergy who submitted to authority were " dolts, hogs, drunkards, foxes, dogs, desperate and forlorn atheists." The result of these outbursts was that some of the Puritan leaders were quite properly executed for criminal libel, others were imprisoned and many more went into voluntary exile, settling in Holland, where they joined the Family of Love, the Mennonite Baptists, and others of the then almost countless Protestant sects.

In the last years of Elizabeth, Whitgift was able to give his mind to the restoration of order in the Church and the badly needed improvement of clerical education. But, when Elizabeth died, in 1603, Calvinism was dominant at the universities. " The divinity professorships were in the hands of strong Calvinists ; and the Genevan doctrines were the regular authorised teaching and standard," wrote Dr. Mozley. Of the Regius Professor who was also President of Magdalen, a contemporary wrote : " He sowed in the Divinity Schools such seeds of Calvinism and laboured to create in the younger man such hate against the Papists, as if nothing but divine truths were to be found in the one and nothing but abominations to be seen in the other." The Calvinists had powerful political friends and at Oxford they had it all their own way. Those who thought differently from them kept their opinions to themselves, rather than face the storm of censure and vituperation which they would have encountered by expressing them.

Abbot, the Master of University College, and afterwards Archbishop of Canterbury, was the ruling spirit of the university. A. C. Benson says of this strange divine : " His favourite tenent was the descent of the visible Church, not through the main unmistakable channel, but through by-waters and side-streams. That a man should have gravely held the truth to have passed through Berengarians, Albigenses, Wicklifites, Hussites to Luther and Calvin is nearly incredible ; yet this was the text of Abbot."

The Calvinists at Oxford, as everywhere else, were intent to destroy the beauty, the romance and the humour of mediæval religion. A. C. Benson says : " They forgot that the capacity for beauty in natural things was after all God's work as well. It escaped them that when they cried for the Bible and nothing but the Bible, all they meant was texts which they had themselves selected. Lectures and homilies, sermons and discourses, extempore prayer, broken only by grim psalm singing, went near to eclipse the delicate fabric of Church worship." Religion was made grim and inhuman and worse still it was made ridiculous. That was the Puritans' historic achievement. Religion had been made repellent and cruel before. It had never before been made ridiculous.

Men who cannot laugh are laughable ; men who can never see the joke are themselves a joke. And it was because the English people can always see the joke that, after a bitter struggle, England and the English Church were saved from the Puritans. The men, who were heroes to Carlyle had their virtues, like other men. They had stern courage. They were consistent. Even in their grotesque solemnity they were sincere. But their grim creed compelled them to the rejection of the religion of love. If they had any right to be regarded as Christians (and this I doubt) they were Old Testament Christians. They were untouched by the beauty of the Holy Virgin suckling her divine Babe in the stable at Bethlehem. Their heroine was Jael driving a nail into the head of Sisera. They were great in battle and intolerable in peace. They bullied like Knox ; they slandered like Prynne ; they massacred like Cromwell, and all in the name of the Lord. At their best they were inhuman at their worst they were ridiculous. They trusted in themselves that they were righteous and they despised others And they were utterly indifferent to the sorrows of the poor and the dispossessed.

William Laud, by whom, in his life and through his martyrdom, more than to any other man, the English Church owes its rescue from the Puritans and the retention of its place in Catholic Christendom, went to Oxford on October 17, 1589, as a Commoner of St. John's College. In this same year, Lancelot Andrewes was elected Master of Pembroke College, Cambridge, and three years later Richard Hooker published his *Ecclesiastical Polity*. Andrews was the spiritual child of Colet and Gardiner. In his eloquent sermons he preached traditional Catholic doctrine and he proclaimed the Catholic character of the English Church against the Romanists, while, with scholarship, discretion and charity he attacked the Roman claims and the Tridentine doctrine

as they were proclaimed by Bellarmine, the most distinguished of the counter-Reformation theologians. Andrewes
may properly be regarded as the earliest of the post-Reformation Anglo-Catholics. He held the doctrine of the Real
Presence and all that it implies, but he repudiated the rigid
materialism of transubstantiation, declaring in the true
Anglican manner, " as to the mode we define nothing rashly
nor anxiously investigate."

Andrewes was concerned to save England from the Papists.
Hooker was concerned with the Puritans. His book, " the
first independent work in English prose of notable power
and genius," is a defence of the episcopal system, and the
primitive idea of the Church. It is remarkable that, while
the men who believed that the Christian faith was born in a
conventicle in Geneva, were fanatical, intolerant, and often
coarse and repellent, these two men who held the faith once
delivered to the saints in Jerusalem were human and lovable.
In his youth, the friend of Raleigh and Sidney, Andrewes
was both a scholar and a saint. " No words can express
what true piety, what uprightness of judgment I find in
him," wrote' the French Liberal Catholic, Isaac Casaubon.
" I am attracted to the man by his profound learning, and
am charmed by a graciousness of manner not common in one
so highly placed." Andrewes, believing the doctrine of the
Real Presence always, celebrated the Holy Eucharist wearing
the mass vestments and using lights and incense, the mixed
chalice and wafer bread. He observed the appointed fasts
and days of abstinence, and urged the importance of the
Sacrament of Penance, he, himself, particularly regarding his
duties as a confessor. Despite the growing influence of
intolerant Puritanism, Andrewes was subject neither to persecution nor to denunciation for the doctrines that he taught
and the ceremonial that he practised. That was perhaps
due to the attractive serenity of his character. He was
allowed to live his life of gracious usefulness in peace and
quiet.

Hooker was equally attractive—impracticable, unworldly,
the good country priest who loved " to see God's blessing
spring out of his mother earth " and who ministered to his
people with simple friendliness. The " judicious Hooker "

was an original thinker, an outstanding philosopher and a most felicitous writer. What could be more charming and suggestive than his description of law " whose seat is the bosom of God, whose voice the harmony of the world " ? It was lucky for Laud that when he went to Oxford the influence of Andrewes and Hooker was already affecting the Puritan domination there.

William Laud was born in Reading on October 7th, 1573, the son of a moderately well-to-do clothier. In his later years, the Puritans, most of whom were rich and " well born " and many of whom were pernicious snobs, taunted him with having " poor and obscure parents," and though, as a matter of fact, he was brought up in comfortable circumstances, it is true that his boyhood in a small provincial town, with its contacts with all sorts of men and women, gave Laud as the Dean of Chichester has said, " a sympathy with humble folk that he never lost, and made him their champion against the purse-proud *nouveaux riches* who were his most bitter enemies."

He went first to Reading Grammar School, to which he was afterwards a generous benefactor, where he was given plain Prayer Book teaching ; he was a sickly boy and he was never a strong man. When he went to Oxford at the age of sixteen, he was, we are told, " esteemed by all who knew him (being little in stature), a very forward, confident and zealous person." His school reputation is shown by the fact that he was nominated to a scholar's place at St. John's by the Mayor and Corporation of Reading and that his family was not wealthy is suggested by the other fact that in his early days at Oxford he was supported by a kinswoman.

St. John's, then a new foundation, was one of the few colleges that had escaped from the Puritan influence, and it is, perhaps, suggestive that Edward Campion, the Jesuit, had been educated there and that Laud's most intimate undergraduate friend became a Benedictine monk.

Laud matriculated a receptive boy, eager, intelligent, ready to be moulded, and the moulding came from his tutor, John Buckeridge, a vehement opponent of both Papists and Puritans, who taught his pupils " upon the noble foundation of the fathers, councils and the ecclesiastical historians."

Laud was ordained deacon in 1600 and priest on Palm Sunday 1601. In the next year he held a divinity lecture-ship ; in 1602 he took the degree of Bachelor of Divinity and was appointed Proctor, the mildness of his rule being shown by there being no record of any punishment during his tenure of office. Laud was no recluse ; he took a full part in the life of the college and was particularly interested in the Christmas plays. Years later, in reply to the fanatical Prynne, who regarded the theatre as the gate of hell, Laud said :

" I was never play-hunter, but I have observed at Court some Puritans to be at play because they would not be thought Puritans ; and for better testimony that they have been there have stood under the candlestick and been dropped on by the candles, and so have carried away a re-embrance of the place. If your lordships, after pains taken in the managing of State affairs, grow weary, what is fitter than to take your recreations ? But Mr. Prynne will not allow you to see a play—they are, in his opinion, *mala per se*. But I say, take away the scurf and rubbish which they are incident unto, they are things indifferent."

Laud soon came to be recognised as the leader of the anti-Calvinist party in the University. In everything that he taught and in everything that he did, he had been anticipated by Andrewes, but the full wrath of the Calvinists fell on the head of the Don of St. John's, still in his early thirties. He was assailed for teaching baptismal regeneration. He was actually tried in the Vice-Chancellor's court for super-stitiously urging the duty of bowing at the name of Jesus. ' It was a heresy to speak to me," wrote Laud, " and a suspicion of heresy to salute me as I was walking the street."

Abbot, the Vice-Chancellor and brother of the Archbishop denounced him from the pulpit of St. Mary's.

" Might not Christ say what art thou ? Romish or English, Papist or Protestant ? Or what art thou, a mongrel composed of both ? A Protestant by ordination, a Papist in point of free-will, inherent righteousness and the like. A Protestant in receiving the Sacrament ; a Papist in the doctrine of the Sacrament. What ! do you think there are two heavens ?

If there be, get you to the other, and place yourself there, for unto this where I am ye shall not come."

It can hardly be supposed that Laud had any desire for Abbot's heaven, but he was hurt by the abuse and the misrepresentation. He behaved, however, with Christian dignity and restraint, going about his business and enraging his enemies by ignoring their attacks. In 1611 he was rewarded by election to the Presidency of his college, which he administered with business ability and with a justice that gained the friendship of the Fellows who had opposed his election. In 1615 he became Archdeacon of Huntingdon, in 1616 Dean of Gloucester, and in 1621 Bishop of St. David's.

A. C. Benson says that Laud was a cold man. "The sentiments, the close relations of human life, were wonderfully aloof from him." This may be true, but it was friendship that led him to make the great mistake of his life, a mistake which he bitterly repented. His friend and patron, the Earl of Devonshire, had, when a younger son without prospects, fallen in love with Penelope, daughter of the Earl of Essex, " a most sweet and attractive maiden." Her family would not hear of their marriage and the girl was married against her will to Lord Rich, a harsh creature who treated her cruelly. After the marriage she became Devonshire's mistress and was eventually divorced. Devonshire was naturally anxious to make what reparation was possible, and Laud was persuaded to celebrate what was, according to his own sacramental teaching, a mock marriage. Laud bitterly regretted his mistake, and until he died he kept the anniversary of the unhallowed wedding as a strict fast. If it was ambition that caused Laud to be false to his principles, it was singularly unsuccessful, since it cost him the favour of King James, who held strong views concerning divorce It was more probably pity that led him into error.

Laud found Gloucester as Calvinist as he had found Oxford. Hooper had once been its bishop and his influence remained. The Cathedral was woefully neglected. The services were casual and slipshod. The altar had been removed from its traditional position and a communion table had been set up in the midst of the Choir. Laud promptly

restored the altar, " as was done in His Majesty's Chapels
and in all well-ordered Cathedral Churches," and ordered
the prebendaries to make a humble obeisance " not only
in their first entrance into the Quire but at their approaches
towards the Holy Table." Laud admitted that the Roman
reverence to images was exaggerated, and he wrote :

> " These and their like have given so great a scandal among us, to some
> ignorant, though, I presume, well-meaning men, that they are afraid
> to testify their duty to God, even in His own house, by any outward
> gesture at all ; insomuch that these very ceremonies which by the judg-
> ment of godly and learned men, have now long continued in the practice
> of this Church, suffer hard measure for the Romish superstition's sake.
> But I will conclude this point with the saying of B. Rhenanus : ' Who
> could endure the people,' says he, ' rushing into the church like swine
> into a stye ? Doubtless, ceremonies do not hurt the people, but profit
> them, so there be a mean kept, and the bye be not put for the main ; that
> is, so we place not the principal part of our piety in them.' "

Laud owed his early preferments to the friendship of
Bishop Neile of Durham, the first man with any influence
to appreciate his quality. At Neile's suggestion, James I
appointed him a royal chaplain, but the King was vastly
offended by the Devonshire marriage and had no liking for
the bustling little divine. " The plain truth is," he said,
" I keep Laud back from all place of rule and authority
because I find he hath a restless spirit and cannot see when
matters are well but loves to toss and change and to bring
things to a pitch of reformation floating in his own brain."
This was shrewd judgment. " The wisest fool in Christendom " did not lack shrewdness.

The first Stuart King of Great Britain was an odd, unpleasant person. He was physically repellent. He was a
pedant, who loved to show off his considerable and for the
most part, useless knowledge. He had a crude, boyish
humour, he was a drunkard and a sex pervert, but he was
certainly not the coward that he has been described and he
had the Stuart faculty for gaining the genuine affection of
far better men.

His accession was welcomed by the Puritans, who supposed that his Scottish upbringing would prejudice him in
their favour. During his journey to London he received a
petition signed by 800 of the Puritan clergy asking for the

abolition of confirmation, the disuse of the sign of the cross in baptism, and the ring in marriage, and of the terms " priest " and " absolution " in the Prayer Book. In consequence, James called a conference of the clergy at Hampton Court in 1604, but it was brought to an abrupt end when the King discovered that the real intention of the Puritans was to replace episcopacy by Scottish presbyterianism in the Church of England. James had not forgotten what he and his mother had suffered at the hands of the Presbyterians. He had determined to preserve the church order that Elizabeth had established and he bluntly declared : "A Scottish presbytery agreeth as well with monarchy as God and the devil ; then Jack and Tom and Will and Dick will meet and censure me and my council ; until you find that I grow lazy, let that alone." Wakeman says that the Hampton Conference marks the end of the first great effort of Puritanism to obtain ascendency over England.

In 1616, James went to Scotland. The journey was the beginning of the attempt to establish uniformity in the Churches of England and Scotland that was to prove fatal for his son. Laud was in the royal suite but only in a minor capacity—he was not yet even Dean of Gloucester—and the King's ecclesiastical advisers were Bishop Neile and Bishop Andrewes. Indeed, Laud had to wait for another six years, until he was a man of forty-nine, before he had any great influence either in the Church or in the State.

By 1618, George Villiers, Duke of Buckingham, had become the most powerful man in the kingdom. Buckingham was flamboyant, witty, generous and utterly incompetent as both politician and soldier. James slobbered over his " Steenie," the young Prince Charles had the deepest affection for him, and the Duke, immortalised by Dumas in the *Three Musketeers*, dictated the royal policy for a dozen years.

About 1620, his position and, in consequence, the position of the King were threatened by the rumour that the favourite's mother was contemplating conversion to Rome. James's religion was as flexible as that of Elizabeth's had been. In one of his pamphlets he had denounced the Pope as Anti-Christ, but, as a matter of political policy, he had relaxed the Elizabethan laws against the Roman Catholics and Gondomar, the able Spanish ambassador, was allowed to represent the Pope as well as the Spanish king. James seems to have had dreams of a united Europe with London as its capital and, as steps to this end, he married his daughter to the most influential of the German Protestant princes and planned to marry his son to a Spanish princess. But anti-Romanism was as strong as ever in England, and it was clear that if Buckingham's mother went to Rome there would be an outburst of popular indignation and apprehension that would make the King's plans impossible and might endanger his throne, and it was decided that every effort must be made to keep the lady, who has been described as " a scheming, worldly, pleasure-loving woman," within the bosom of the English Church.

James dearly loved argument and debate and he ordered the lady to attend a meeting at which representatives of Rome and Canterbury should explain the Papal and Anglican claims. The chosen spokesmen were the Jesuit Fisher and Laud, who was then Bishop of St. David's.

Whether or not the lady was edified by the arguments to which she was compelled to listen for many hours, is a matter of no importance. In the end she went to Rome. But in the course of the wrangle, Laud very clearly stated the Anglican attitude to Holy Scripture, which has remained the attitude of the English Church. The Roman contention is that the accuracy of Scripture depends on the authority of the Church. The Anglican contention is that the Church is founded on the Faith, not the Faith on the Church. The Dean of Chichester has summarised Laud's contentions. They suggest that he was familiar with the teaching of his predecessor, St. Anselm :

" There are four grounds on which we say the Scripture is divine. The first is the testimony and witness of the Church and her tradition ; secondly, ' the Scripture may be known to be the word of God by the light and lustre which it hath in itself ' ; the grace of the Holy Spirit, which seals this faith in the souls of men forms a third ground. And last comes the use of reason, since grace is never placed but in a reasonable creature. ' Reason can give no supernatural ground into which a man may resolve his faith, that Scripture is the word of God infallibly : yet reason can go so high as to prove that Christian religion, which rests upon the authority of this book, stands upon surer ground of nature, reason, common equity and justice, than anything in the world which any infidel or mere naturalist hath done, doth or can adhere unto, against it.' Wherever Scripture has been received, it has approved itself as a good thing. The admirable faculty of reasoning has shown men that this was the way to truth. As the various sciences suppose some principles without proving them, we may conclude that Theology is reasonable in giving the like authority to Scripture."

Tradition is not to be disregarded. It is, as Hooker taught, the key that lets a man into the house. But the key is not the house. " Scripture doth infallibly confirm the authority of Church traditions, truly so called," Laud declared, " but tradition doth but morally and probably confirm the authority of the Scriptures."

In the seventeenth century, as now, men were hungry for an infallible authority. The Romans say that the Church, by which they mean the Roman Church, is infallible. The Protestants used to maintain that the literally inspired Scriptures are infallible. But that doctrine has been made untenable by the Higher Criticism, and the Dean of Chichester has rightly pointed out that the real claim was always that the private interpretation of Scripture, or may be the teaching of Calvin, was infallible. Here, as in other things, there is a striking resemblance between Rome and Geneva. The Laudian position is : " Scripture must not be tested by any man's opinions, neither those of the Pope nor those of Calvin. It is itself the test, and the true interpretation is that placed on it from the earliest times. Its main points are determined in the Apostles' Creed."

Laud agreed that the Roman Church was a true Church ; he denied that it was the only Church. The whole Church means a General Council. The Council of Trent was not a General Council, because the Eastern Church, the validity of whose orders Rome admits, was not represented.

Anglicans had broken with Rome because of its errors, and Laud included among the errors transubstantiation, communion in one kind and the invocation of saints, the last of which is, by the way, regularly practised by modern Anglo-Catholics. Rome is intolerant. There is no salvation outside its jurisdiction. Laud, the true Anglican, was tolerant, though his toleration was decidedly patronising. He would not deny salvation to any " ignorant, silly souls whose peaceable obedience makes them safe among any part of men that profess the foundation." Finally, Laud affirmed the belief in the Real Presence that he shared with Andrewes :

> " I quarrel not the words of Thy Son my Saviour's blessed Institution. I know His words are no gross unnatural conceit, but they are spirit and life, and supernatural. While the world disputes, I believe." " Lord, make me worthy of that for which I come—Christ, and remission of sin in Christ." " O Lord God, how I receive the Body and Blood of my most blessed Saviour Jesus Christ, the price of my redemption, is the very wonder of my soul, yet my most firm and constant belief upon the words of my Saviour."

The result of Laud's endeavour to influence his mother was a close association with Buckingham, which resulted in his rise to power in the six years before Buckingham's assassination in 1628. It is difficult to believe that there could have been any genuine sympathy between the reckless aristocratic adventurer and the ascetic divine. But Buckingham realised Laud's outstanding ability and, so far as he was concerned, their association ripened into deep personal regard. On his side, Laud badly needed a powerful supporter. He had many influential enemies. He was convinced that there was work of paramount importance to do and that he alone could effectively do it. He had waited for years for his opportunity. Buckingham provided the opportunity and Laud was properly grateful. In common with many worldlings, Buckingham had his moments of religion. He was a staunch High Churchman, at least occasionally remindful of his duties and one of the relations with Laud was that of penitent and director. In Laud's *Book of Private Prayers* there was a prayer for Buckingham. It ran :

> " Gracious Father, I humbly beseech Thee, bless the Duke of Buckingham with all spiritual and temporal blessings, but especially spiritual. Make and continue him faithful to his prince, serviceable to his country, devout in Thy truth and Church ; a most happy husband, and a blessed father ; filled with the constant love and honour of his prince, that all Thy blessings may flow upon himself, and his posterity after him. Con-

tinue him a true-hearted friend to me, Thy poor servant whom Thou hast honoured in his eyes. Make my heart religious and dutiful to Thee, and in and under Thee true, and secret, and stout, and provident in all things which he shall be pleased to commit unto me. Even so, Lord, and make him continually to serve Thee, that Thou mayest bless him, through Christ, our only Lord and Saviour. Amen."

Dr. Hutton says that Laud's episcopate of St. David's " cannot be said to have left much mark on the Welsh Church." That is not surprising. He was only in St. David's for a few weeks in 1622 and for an even shorter time in 1625. It may be true that during his absence he " kept as close a watch on his see as was possible for a non-resident bishop," but that could not have been of much account in a remote diocese in the seventeenth century.

Laud was very busy in London. With Buckingham behind him, he was able successfully to oppose Archbishop Abbot, who hated him, and he began his intimate association with Prince Charles. James died on March 27th, 1625, and in the following November, Laud was translated to the see of Bath and Wells. He was chosen by the new King to preach the sermon at the opening of his first Parliament, and in the course of it he said : " It is not possible in any Christian commonwealth that the Church should melt and the State stand firm. For there can be no firmness without law, and no laws can be binding if there be no conscience to obey them ; penalty alone could never, or can never, do it. And no school can teach conscience but the Church of Christ." That was to be the motto of the new reign.

King Charles I was a martyr of the English Church. Had he been of the Roman obedience, he would assuredly have been canonised with St. Louis of France. It may be that he was too good a man to be a happy or successful monarch. Even his enemies paid tribute to the sweetness of his personal character. He was, admitted the Puritan Mrs. Hutchinson, " temperate, chaste and serious." Charles indeed took himself, or rather his office, too seriously for his safety. He was, he believed, the Lord's anointed, and, consequently, those who opposed him were the opponents of the Lord. Sometimes he tried to compromise, but he always failed. He was weak and sometimes cowardly. He was cruelly maligned and misunderstood, but he was no fool and he clearly understood the powers arraigned against him. The Dean of Chichester showed a full understanding of the seventeenth century contest and of the character of the King when he wrote that Charles regarded himself as " the last bulwark against the vulgarisation of the national life." He was opposed by men determined to destroy all that made life gracious. Their " opposition to his absolutionism was inspired by a desire to put in its place one much more savage and tyrannical." The fight was between Monarchy and Mammon, and Monarchy, mystically allied with the Church, was the champion of the poor. The Puritan revolution was the bourgeois revolution ; the mass of the people were for the King. It was reported in Bristol that the King's cause was supported by " the basest and lowest sort." " Most of the poorest of the people, whom the other called the Rabble, were for the King," wrote Baxter.

Professor Tawney considers that the assertion that Calvinism in its English version was the parent of capitalism needs considerable modification. I differ with diffidence from so great an authority, but surely the assertion is demonstrably true. Professor Tawney himself agrees that " the triumph of Puritanism swept away all traces of any restriction or guidance in the employment of money." In its hatred of the Catholic religion it derided the Catholic denunciation of the usurer and of him who grinds the faces of the poor. But it did much more than this. The Puritan, being persuaded that fun and laughter and play are contraptions of the devil, had nothing to do but to pray and to work and to him work was as godly an exercise as prayer and the monetary rewards of work were to be regarded as evidence of the divine approval. Professor Tawney quotes from the Puritan Tyndale's translation of the Bible : "And the Lorde was with Joseph and he was a luckie felowe," and he goes on practically to admit my assertion that with Puritanism comes the deification of money. Professor Tawney says :

" For, since conduct and action, though availing nothing to attain the free gift of salvation, are a proof that the gift has been accorded, what is rejected as a means is resumed as a consequence, and the Puritan flings himself into practical activities with the dæmonic energy of one who, all doubts allayed, is conscious that he is a sealed and chosen vessel. Once engaged in affairs, he brings to them both the qualities and limitations of his creed, in all their remorseless logic. Called by God to labour in his vineyard, he has within himself a principle at once of energy and of order, which makes him irresistible both in war and in the struggles of commerce. Convinced that character is all and circumstances nothing, he sees in the poverty of those who fall by the way, not a misfortune to be pitied and relieved, but a moral failing to be condemned, and in riches, not an object of suspicion—though like other gifts they may be abused—but the blessing which rewards the triumph of energy and will. Tempered by self-examination, self-discipline, self-control, he is the practical ascetic, whose victories are won not in the cloister, but on the battlefield, in the counting-house, and in the market."

Piety and ten per cent. was the Puritan's ideal. One of his objections to Catholic practice was that the many saints' days, which were holidays, hampered industry and affected profits. "There is a kind of natural unaptness," wrote a pamphleteer, "in the Popish religion to business, whereas, on the contrary, among the Reformed the greater their zeal the greater their inclination to trade and industry."

"Fervent in business, serving the Lord."

The party that Laud sought to destroy and which sent him to the scaffold was recruited from the men who had benefited from the spoiling of the monasteries and the enclosures, and from the development of manufacture and international trade that began in the sixteenth century. There were country gentlemen among them, like Hampden and Pym. There were propertyless men in the Roundhead ranks—sometimes there against their will—who became the semi-Socialist Levellers, who troubled Cromwell. But the Puritan majority was *bourgeois* and nearly all the considerable Puritans were the *nouveaux riches*. The Puritans' ideal state was plutocratic and individualist. They wanted to establish exactly the order for which the British Federation of Industry and the Carlton Club are planning and plotting to-day to preserve.

Laud's social-political philosophy was totalitarian—one nation, one religion, one party. But as Professor Tawney, a hard critic of Laud, points out, Laud insisted that the sanction of unity is religion, the foundation of unity is justice. "God will not bless the State if kings and magistrates do not execute judgment, if the widows and fatherless have cause to cry out against the thrones of justice." As a member of the Council, he was particularly concerned to redress the wrongs of the peasantry, and to put a stop to the land enclosures, to secure adequate food supplies at reasonable prices, fair wages and generous poor relief. Because of his love of God he never forgot God's poor.

Laud was not a conciliatory man. He was impatient, abrupt, sharp tongued, always positive. He lived a lonely life, happiest when he was left quietly with his books. He shared Charles's love for art and beauty. He knew and admired Orlando Gibbons, Inigo Jones and Vandyck. To the end he retained his love for Oxford and for learning. None of the honours that fell to him pleased him so much as his election to the Chancellorship. Though overburdened with public affairs, he found time to act as the faithful guardian of the university, and the Canterbury quadrangle that he added to St. John's is a beautiful monument of his devotion. The men who served Laud served him with affection. Heylyn, his chaplain and biographer, pays constant tribute to his kindly consideration, and, in his own diary, there are many grateful references to the care of his servants. And the poor of Lambeth loved Laud as the poor of Canterbury had loved St. Thomas.

Few men have been so overburdened by a wilderness of responsibilities. A. C. Benson has suggested that Laud must have often have longed to run away from it all to a life of contemplative peace, knowing all the while that he would not have escaped even if he could. His " call " was to fight. for the Church in the world. He had few intimate friends, but the men whom he sought in his scanty leisure were the men whose lives he envied, devotional men like Cosin and Jeremy Taylor, the gentle poet, George Herbert.

It was Laud who was responsible for Herbert's decision to take holy orders. He was a member of a noble family, well off, a fastidious scholar, something of a dandy, but restless and dissatisfied until, in his early thirties, he met Laud. The Archbishop gave him a new view of the Church, of its character, of its divine mission, of the beauty of its teaching and its ceremonial, of the great part that it might play in the world.

In nothing did Laud serve the Church and the nation better than in turning the steps of " the graceful young courtier " to the divine ministry. As a simple country priest, as the most inspired of England's religious poets, Herbert became the hero of good simple Englishmen, like his biographer, Izaak Walton, that most Christian fisherman. Once a week, Herbert, so Walton related, walked from his rectory at Bemberton to " a private music-meeting at Salisbury." On one occasion he was late and he explained that he had met a poor man with an overloaded horse, and that he had helped the man to unload and reload and sent him on his way with money to refresh himself and his horse. He said that the thought of what he had done would prove music to him at midnight and that the omission of it would have made discord in his conscience. "And now let us tune our instruments ! "

George Sampson says that Herbert's poems " testify to a general intensity of personal religious emotion not confined in that age, as some suppose, to the Puritans." I cannot conceive that anyone should suppose any such thing. Puritan religion was coarse and truculent in its intensity. George Herbert's religion was restful and beautiful, finding its expression in such poetry as :

> These are Thy wonders, Lord of love,
> To make us see we are but flowers that glide ;
> Which when we once can find and prove,
> Thou hast a garden for us, where to bide.
> Who would be more,
> Swelling through store,
> Forfeit their Paradise by their pride.

Sir Henry Wotton, poet and Provost of Eton, was another of Laud's friends, and he demonstrated his affection by leaving him in his will " my picture of Divine Love, beseeching him to receive it as a pledge of my humble reverence to his great wisdom," no mean tribute from the man who wrote the graceful :

> How happy is he born and taught
> That serveth not another's will ;
> Whose armour is his honest thought,
> And simple truth his utmost skill.

It may have been through Herbert that Laud came to know Nicholas Ferrar, and " the domestic monastery at Little Gidding of the strictest rule where the whole Psalter was recited every twenty-four hours and prayer never stopped night or day " and where beautiful books were printed and bound. Laud took the King to Little Gidding, and when he left " those of the family, men and women, all kneeled down and heartily prayed to God to bless him and defend him from his enemies." And Charles, taking off his hat replied with fine and pious courtesy, " Pray, pray for my speedy return ! " Little Gidding was shut up by the Puritans in the days of their domination. To them it was an "Arminian nunnery." Its graciousness was its condemnation.

Laud's intolerance has been grossly exaggerated. Indeed, compared to such men as Prynne he was a monument of toleration. John Cosin, who at the King's request wrote the *Collection of Private Devotions* for the use of the Queen's Protestant ladies, was a Sabbatarian and was by no means sound on episcopacy, but Laud recognised his qualities and secured him preferment which he lost during the Commonwealth. Another priest, John Hales, who " loved Canarie, but moderately to refresh his spirits," had declared that he would leave the Church of England if it required him to believe that any Christians would be damned, and was accused of more damning heresy. Laud was loath to accuse any man of heresy " since it is so easy for us all to err." He sent for Hales and had a long talk with him in the garden at Lambeth, with the result that Hales was appointed one of his chaplains and was afterwards given a prebendaryship of Windsor.

Jeremey Taylor, whose learning was amazing even in his youth, first attracted Laud's notice by a sermon that he preached at St. Paul's when he was twenty-two. Though Taylor was a Cambridge man, Laud secured for him a fellowship at All Souls, and gave him generous help and encouragement. Laud was, indeed, in complete agreement with the man who is accepted as one of the greatest of English casuists. They both insisted on the acceptance of the basic assertions of the faith set out in the creeds, and they agreed that this is consistent with subsequent freedom of opinion. They shared the same attitude to Rome. They denied the power of the Church to determine any new article of faith. Laud said of the post-reformation Roman doctrines : " If we consider the doctrines themselves, we shall find them to be superstructures ill built and worse managed, but yet they keep the foundations." Both Laud and Taylor insisted that religion must be justified by reason. Laud was a St. Anselm rationalist, and one of the causes of his opposition to Puritanism was that it was irrational. As the Dean of Chichester has said : " The Puritans were the enemies of reason. They clamped men's minds down to school points."

Close and sympathetic friendship bound together Laud and Strafford, Charles's two ministers who both paid for their loyal service with their heads. They had a common purpose and they agreed in their estimates of both persons and events. " I have wondered many times," Strafford wrote to Laud, " to observe how universally you and I agree in our judgment of persons, as most commonly we have done since I had the honour to be known to you." There is in existence a number of letters exchanged by the two ministers, most of them written while Strafford was in Ireland, many of them in cipher. All of them suggest mutual affection and understanding.

To return to the incidents of Laud's career. In 1626, on the death of Lancelot Andrewes, Laud became Dean of the Chapels Royal. Soon afterwards, Abbot incurred the royal displeasure and was sequestered from the Archbishopric, which was put into commission in the hands of five bishops, of whom Laud was one, and Buckeridge, his tutor at Oxford, and Neile, his first patron, were two others. In 1627 Laud became Bishop of London. In 1628 Buckingham was assassinated and Laud succeeded to his secular office. His first and very considerable achievement was securing the adherence to the royal cause of Strafford, who, as Thomas Wentworth, had been one of the more moderate of the King's critics in the Commons. When Buckingham was killed, the quarrel of the King with Parliament had grown intense. Twice in three years, Charles had dissolved Parliament and the third was dissolved a few months after Buckingham's death ; but, before the dissolution, it had compelled the King to receive the Petition of Right, in which it was declared that there could be no taxation without the consent of the Commons. This was the beginning of the eleven years of personal rule.

The quarrel was fundamentally religious. The majority in both Houses was fanatically Calvinist. Charles was suspected because of his Roman Catholic French wife and detested because of his determination not to surrender the English Church to the sectaries. It is doubtful whether there could have been anything like harmonious relations whatever political policy the King had followed, but he played into his enemies' hands by sanctioning Buckingham's insensate foreign adventures, with their heavy drain on the royal resources and the consequent necessity for constant appeals to the hostile Parliament for money.

Whether or not Laud approved of the wars with Spain and France, his views of the monarchy made him emphatic in resistance to the attempt of Parliament to limit what to him were divinely instituted royal prerogatives. But it is the sheerest nonsense to suggest that the struggle was between autocracy and democracy. The Puritan Parliaments were not in the remotest degree representative of the English people. They did not pretend to be. They were the spokesmen of a small minority, the champions of money. The Puritans had no thought of securing freedom of any kind for anyone but themselves. They were indeed far more thorough in their hostility to religious freedom than Laud. They were determined to dragoon a laughter-loving nation into a hard, mirthless mode of life which it was believed would make them efficient slaves of the money-making machine.

The days of rule by hereditary monarchs have passed. Most of the kings have departed though the tyrants remain. But in seventeenth-century England, the cause of the King was the cause of the people, and the enemies of the King were the enemies of the people. This is made abundantly clear by two incidents that occurred soon after Laud had become Archbishop of Canterbury in 1633. He was then sixty ; he had had five strenuous years as the King's adviser and confidant ; he was tired of daily attacks and misrepresentations ; he can have had little desire for further preferment and more responsibility. He wrote to Strafford:

> " I thank you heartily for your kind wishes to me that God would send me many and happy days where I am now to be. Amen. I can do little for myself if I cannot say so, but truly, my lord, I look for neither ; not for many, for I am in years, and I have had a troublesome life ; not for happy, for I have no hope to do the good I desire ; and besides I doubt I shall never be able to hold my health there (Lambeth) one year ; for instead of all the jolting which I have had over the stones between London House and Whitehall, which was almost daily, I shall now have no exercise, but slide over in a barge to the Court and Star Chamber. And in truth, my lord, speaking seriously, I have had a heaviness hanging over me ever since I was nominated to the place, and I can give myself no account of it, unless it proceed from an apprehension that there is more expected from me than the craziness of these times will give me leave to do."

The first of the incidents to which I have referred was the trial for high treason before the Star Chamber, of which Laud was a member, of the Lincoln's Inn barrister, Prynne. As A. C. Benson has said, he was a man of almost incredible malevolence and, as he was to show at Laud's trial, utterly unscrupulous, suppressing evidence and lying like a trooper to attain his ends. With the majority of his subjects, Charles was fond of stage plays and his Queen sometimes acted in private productions in the palace. Prynne was a crazy Puritan fanatic, once more to quote the admirable Dean of Chichester, a " representative of a large section of his party in being dominated by a sex-complex." In 1632, he published his notorious *Histriomastix*, the denunciation of all plays as " sinful, heathenish, lewd, ungodly spectacles and most pernicious corruptions." Plays are, Prynne lamented, " accompanied by lust-provoking music and profuse exorbitant laughter," and, like a good Puritan, Prynne hated to hear men laugh. Dancers, too, are generally adulterers and " if our theatres are not bawdy houses, they are at least wise neighbours to them." And the conclusion is : " Carnal, worldly pleasures are no part, no particle of a Christian's comfort ; he can live a most happy, joyful life without them ; yea, he can hardly live happily or safely with them."

A. C. Benson suggests that the book is so " incredibly ludicrous and disproportionate " that it should not have been taken seriously, but the obvious intention was to discredit the Queen, and the Star Chamber fined Prynne £5,000, ordered him to be imprisoned during the King's pleasure, to be degraded from his membership of Lincoln's Inn and to be set in the pillory and to lose both his ears. The sentence was never carried out. Prynne's ears were clipped but not shorn and his imprisonment was short.

Soon after the Prynne trial, Laud successfully prevented the Puritan squires from interfering with the pleasures of the people. At their instigation two judges on the western circuit found that " revels, church-ales, clerk-ales and other public ales " were illegal. The decision caused a righteous outburst of indignation. The people protested that " it was very hard if they could not entertain their kindred and friends once a year to praise God for his blessings and to pray for the King's Majesty," and they added that " they would endure the judge's penalties rather than they would break off their feast-days." The protest brought a summons to the judges to attend a meeting of the Council, at which they were so roughly used by Laud that they tearfully complained that they had been " choked by a pair of lawn sleeves."

To secure his people's rights, Charles published the " Declaration concerning Lawful Sports," still further enraging the Puritans from the fact that these sports were declared lawful on Sundays, after Evening Prayer. Charles and Laud, with all reasonable men, regarded Sabbatarianism as an ugly excrescence on Christian practice.

It is said that, following his enthronement at Canterbury, Laud was assured by a Roman representative that he would be made a cardinal if he would bring England back to the Roman obedience. Rome never has understood English churchmen, and it must have been difficult three hundred years ago to realise that there was an alternative to both Rome and Geneva. Laud recorded that his answer was that " somewhat dwelt within me which would not suffer that until Rome were other than it is."

Laud was now Archbishop of Canterbury, President of the Court of High Commission, First Minister of the Crown, a member of the Treasury Commission and the Foreign Council and Chancellor of Oxford and Dublin Universities. In all these capacities, A. C. Benson says that " he devised, organised, and executed single-handed and indomitable." He was grotesquely overworked and he inevitably made blunders. He approached every problem of administration as a churchman. He resisted the Erastian demand for the subjection of the Church to the State. He never contended for the subjection of the State to the Church. To him the Church and the Crown were together responsible for the well-being of the people.

Laud's personal religion was deep and sincere, and it was because of its intensity that he was determined that the services of the Church, of which he was the chief minister, should be dignified and beautiful. Dean Hutton has said that " praying ever with the tears of a penitent, he still delighted to think of the glory of God and to adore Him in all the dignity and devotion of public worship." There were notorious instances of scandalous irreverence and neglect in many parish churches, and, in the first year of his primacy, Laud ordered a visitation of all the dioceses of his province, among his instructions to his vicar-general being to see to it that the altars should be replaced at the east end of the churches.

To the Puritan the altar has no significance, to him the pulpit (as is evident still in some of the Swiss cathedrals) is the centre of worship. But Laud declared : " The altar is the greatest place of God's residence upon earth, greater than the pulpit, for there it is *Hoc est Corpus Meum*, this is My Body ; but in the other it is at most but *Hoc est Verbum Meum*, this is My Word ; and a greater reverence is due to the Body than to the Word of the Lord."

The Court of High Commission has been accused of intolerably harsh decisions. Its records prove that they were nothing of the sort and its offence was that it punished wrongdoers in high places. Writing of Laud's conduct as one of the Commission, Clarendon says :

" He intended the discipline of the Church should be felt, as well as spoken of, and that it should be applied to the greatest and most splendid transgressors as well as to the punishment of the smaller offences and meaner offenders ; and thereupon called for or cherished the discovery of those who were not careful to cover their own iniquities, thinking they were above the reach of other men, or their power or will to chastise. Persons of honour and great quality, of the Court and of the country, were every day cited into the High Commission Court, upon the fame of their incontinence, or other scandal in their lives, and were there prosecuted to their shame and punishment : and as the shame (which they called an insolent triumph upon their degree and quality, and levelling them with the common people) was never forgotten, but watched for revenge, so the fines were imposed, they were the more questioned and repined against, because they were assigned to the rebuilding and repairing of St. Paul's church, and thought therefore to be the more severely imposed, and the less compassionately reduced and excused."

Laud was always making enemies of the rich, and of the would-be rich. Financial administration was hopelessly corrupt, and despairing of finding an honest layman, Laud caused Juxon, Bishop of London, to be appointed Lord High Treasurer of England. Juxon was scrupulous and capable, but the greedy defeated candidates for the office and their friends and relations were furious. Clarendon comments :

" The Treasurer is the greatest office of benefit in the kingdom, and the chief in precedence next to Archbishop, and the Great Seal ; so that the eyes of all men were at gaze who shall have the great office, and the greatest of the nobility, who were in the chiefest employment, looked upon it as the prize of one of them ; such offices commonly making way for more removes and preferments."

In 1633, Laud went to Edinburgh with the King for his belated Scottish coronation, which took place at Holyrood with full Anglican ceremonial. The result of this visit was the fatal resolve to compel uniformity in the English and Scottish churches. James had desired this uniformity, but, from personal experience, he had learned to understand the Scottish character and he had realised that it would be far too dangerous to endeavour to force the Calvinist ministers, who had become the popular leaders, to accept an ecclesiastical order that they hated. Indeed, hatred was the characteristic of Scottish Reformation religion. Clarendon wrote that " a great part of their religion consisted in an entire detestation of popery, in believing the Pope to be Anti-Christ, and hating perfectly the persons of all papists." That was the heritage of John Knox. The altar, the bishops, the stately traditional ceremonies, even the clerical surplice were the appurtenances of Anti-Christ.

Neither Charles nor Laud understood the strength of the prejudice that they were challenging and they made defeat the more certain by the demand that the nobles should disgorge the lands filched from the Church, though they had been warned by the Marquis of Hamilton that " this could not but touch many of the nobility to the quick, who were too large sharers in the patrimony of the Church not to be very sensible of it." Piety and money were once more allied against the King and the Archbishop.

Under the direction of Laud, a Scottish Prayer Book, a very noble liturgy founded on the Edwardian book with some important emendations, was published, and its use at St. Giles's, Edinburgh, in July, 1627, led to a riot, during which Jenny Geddes became a national heroine by throwing a stool at the head of the Dean. The result was a rising, led by the nobles, to destroy episcopacy in Scotland and the signing of the Solemn League and Covenant.

Charles sent an army across the border, led by a hopelessly incompetent general ; but he was, as usual, badly in need of money. The Scots had many influential supporters in England, and in 1639 he had to sign the Pacification of Berwick, in which he consented to the abolition of the Scottish episcopate. That was for him and for Laud the beginning of the end.

Laud's Prayer Book has remained the official liturgy of the Scottish Episcopal Church, and the liturgies of the American Episcopal Church and the Church of South Africa are based on it ; as was, to a considerable extent, the Revised Prayer Book of 1927, which the House of Commons, by the votes of Calvinists, Presbyterians and unbelievers, refused to sanction.

The complementary attempt of Strafford, the Lord Deputy, to bring the Church of Ireland into uniformity with England was more successful. The conditions were different. In England, the Reformation had left the bulk of the people, delighted with the break with Rome, tepidly attached to the national Church, humorously resentful of the excesses of the Calvinists. In Scotland the Reformation was a genuinely popular movement, which it never was in England. In Ireland the majority of the people were half-starved peasants, ruthlessly exploited by the English landlords settled in the country under the Elizabethan plantation system. The people hated their exploiters and they hated their religion and they remained, as they still remain, faithful to the Roman Church.

The miscalled Church of Ireland was the Church of a foreign minority. Strafford found its clergy miserably poor and ignorant, its services " run over without all Decency, of Habit, Ordre or Gravity," its property appropriated by the laity, its university, Trinity College, Dublin, scholastically dead.

Strafford's administration was notably bold and humane. Always in close touch with Laud, he adopted a policy of gentleness to the Romanists. New and devoted bishops were appointed to the dioceses, church property was recovered and Strafford left the Church £30,000 a year richer than he found it. Laud became the Chancellor of Trinity and his reforms were the beginning of its long and honourable history.

It is a curious fact that, while the Laudian influence has remained strong in the Episcopal Church of Scotland, it was soon lost in the Church of Ireland, to-day the most Protestant of the Anglican communions, almost untouched by the Tractarian movement.

Strafford had raised some money for the King in Ireland, but, early in 1640, the royal treasury was again empty. The levy of ship money with which, as Hilaire Belloc has claimed, Charles laid the foundations of the British navy, was resisted by the rich Puritans, and though the King won his case against the wealthy Hampden, he actually received little from the Puritan money bags and he was advised by Strafford, who had returned home, again to call a Parliament.

The Short Parliament met in April, 1640, refused to vote supplies and was dissolved after three weeks. In August a Scottish army marched into England, was bought off in October, and the Long Parliament assembled in November, the majority being led by men who had been imprisoned during the years of personal rule. In 1641, Parliament passed a bill of attainder against Strafford, his alleged offence being that he had proposed to bring an army from Ireland to subdue the English opposition to the King. Charles, vowing that he'd ne'er consent, consented and signed the bill and his great servant, a man of high character and many parts, was beheaded on May 12th. This was first blood for the Puritans.

Strafford declared that " he died a true son of the Church of England in which he had been born and bred ; for the peace and prosperity whereof he most heartily prayed." He was refused permission to see Laud before his execution, but the Archbishop, by this time himself in the Tower, came to the window of his cell as Strafford was conducted to the scaffold. " My Lord, I crave your prayers and your blessing," said the Earl. Laud, trembling, lifted up his hand and, with a second bow, Strafford bade his friend farewell. Then, with head erect and steady step, he went to his death, an English Christian gentleman.

Laud was far too shrewd a man not to have foreseen what would follow the recalling of Parliament, though he agreed that it was inevitable. He spent the last months of his active life in forwarding the church reforms that were always his principal preoccupation.

The sittings of Convocation, called with the meeting of the Short Parliament, went on, illegally, after that Parliament had been dissolved, and the summer months of 1640 were spent in drawing up a series of canons which were confirmed after the Restoration. During these months, the Puritan leaders busily excited and subsidised popular feeling against both Strafford and Laud, who was assailed in scurrilous pamphlets in which he was described, among other things, as " pander to the whore of Babylon." Convocation had to be guarded by soldiers, and a mob attacked Lambeth

Richard Baxter, a decent Puritan, has candidly exposed the agitation :

"The Londoners petitioned for Justice : And too great numbers of Apprentices and others (being emboldened by the Proceedings of the Parliament, and not fore-knowing what a fire the Sparks of their temerity would kindle) did too triumphingly and disorderly urge the Parliament, crying Justice, Justice. And it is not unlikely that some of the Parliament men did encourage them to this, as thinking that some backward Members would be quickened by Popular Applause."

On December 18th, Laud was accused in the House of Commons of high treason and was committed to the custody of Black Rod, being first allowed to go to Lambeth to collect his papers and " for a book or two to read in." He wrote in his diary :

"I stayed at Lambeth till the evening, to avoid the gazing of the people. I went to evening prayer in my chapel. The Psalms of the day, xciii and xciv, and chap. i of Isaiah, gave me great comfort. God make me worthy of it and fit to receive it ! As I went to my barge hundreds of my poor neighbours stood there and prayed for my safety and return to my house. For which I bless God and them."

Then " the little active figure, the centre of so much life," moved to his waiting barge and to his death.

For ten weeks Laud was in the kindly custody of Black Rod. Then he was summoned to the House of Lords to hear the charges made against him by the Commons. On March 1st, he was committed to the Tower, the usual venal mob following him " with clamour and revilings even beyond barbarity itself." For months the venomous Prynne was busy faking evidence to justify charges, most of them obvious lies, and he was allowed to enter Laud's cell, while he was in bed, to rifle his pockets and to steal his private papers. A. C. Benson, in many respects an understanding critic of the Archbishop, has described Prynne's proceedings :

"He sorted the letters, burning those that might be supposed to tell in Laud's favour. He cut with a knife and blotted out many entries of the same character in the Diary. In one place five pages are removed ; in another there is a great crescent-shaped burn, that extends over many pages, that looks as if it has been inflicted with a red-hot iron. This he called preparing the evidence. Finally, he published a selection, with notes, explaining, according to his own taste, the secret initials and ciphers in the book. It is needless to say that he understood these to mean gross immoralities in nearly every case."

Laud's trial did not begin in the House of Lords until March 12th, 1644, and, in the long months of waiting, he was subjected to every kind of mean indignity. He was ill, he was cold, his stock of wood and coal at Lambeth having been seized with his library, and he was forced to listen to disgustingly abusive sermons by Puritan preachers, one of whom took as his text " Curse ye Meroz." " His abuse," wrote Laud in his diary, " was foul and palpable, but I humbly thank God for it. I bore his virulence patiently and so it vanished."

At his trial he was charged with " having wickedly and traitorously advised His Majesty that he might of his own will and pleasure levy and take money of his subjects without their consent in Parliament," with Popery, superstition, and profanation of the Sabbath. The trial lasted for twenty days ; there were never more than twelve peers present at any sitting and few of them remained until the adjournments. The " evidence " was nearly all ridiculous, and the coarse venom of Prynne, the real prosecutor, may be gathered from his description of Laud's consecration of the City church of St. Katherine Cree in 1630 :

"After the Sermon, which was short, the Bishop and two fat Doctors consecrated and administered the Sacrament, with a number of bowings, duckings and cringeings in manner following :

"At first, when the Bishop approached neare the Communion Table he bowed with his nose very neare the ground some six or seven times ; then he came to one of the corners of the table, and there bowed himself three times ; then to the second, third and fourth corners, bowing at each corner three times (which shows incidentally that the table must have been set out from the wall as he evidently passed round, and so behind it). But when he came to the side of the table where the bread and wine was, he bowed himself seven times, and then, after the reading of many prayers by himself and his two fat chaplains (which were with him, and all this while by him on their knees in surplices, hoods and tippets), he himself came near the bread which was cut and laid in a fine napkin, and peeped into it till he saw the bread (like a boy that peeped after a bird's nest in a bush) and presently clapped it down again and flew back a step or two, and then bowed very low three times to it and the table ; then he came near and opened the napkin again, and behaved as before ; then he laid his hand upon the gilt cup which was full of wine with a cover upon it. So soon as he had pulled the cup a little nearer to him, he let the cup go, flew back, and bowed again, and, lifting up the cover of the cup, peeped into it, and seeing the wine, he let fall the cover on it again and flew nimbly back and bowed as before. After these and many other apish antic gestures, he himself received, and then gave the Sacrament to some principal men only, they kneeling devoutly near the table, after which, more prayers being said, this scene and interlude ended."

Laud defended himself with skill, courage, generally with patience, but sometimes with righteous scorn. Prynne admitted :

" To give him his due," he says, " he made as full, as gallant, and as pithy defence of so bad a cause as it was possible for the wit of man to invent, and that with so much art, sophistry, vivacity, oratory, audacity, and confidence, without the least blush or acknowledgement of guilt in anything, as argued him rather obstinate than innocent."

But the trial was a farce. The Puritans were clamouring for the Archbishop's blood, and on January 4th, 1645, the Lords, six peers only being present, voted that he should suffer as a traitor, the Commons being with difficulty persuaded to allow the sentence of hanging to be commuted into beheading. Laud was beheaded on Tower Hill on January 10th, when he was seventy-one years, thirteen weeks and four days old. His chaplain, Heylyn, has left what A. C. Benson has well described as " a record in grave, grand English of the words and deeds of the last great scene " :

" In the morning he was early at his prayers ; at which he continued till Pennington, Lieutenant of the Tower, and other public officers, came to conduct him to the scaffold ; which he ascended with so brave a courage, such a cheerful countenance, as if he had mounted rather to behold a triumph, than be made a sacrifice ; and came not there to die, but to be translated. And though some rude and uncivil people reviled him, as he passed along, with approbrious language, as loth to let him go to the grave in peace, yet it never discomposed his thoughts, nor disturbed his patience. For he had profited so well in the school of Christ, that ' when he was reviled, he reviled not again, when he suffered, he threatened not, but committed his cause to Him that judgeth righteously.'
"And, as he did not fear the frowns, so neither did he covet the applause of the people, and therefore rather chose to read what he had to speak, than to affect the ostentation either of memory or wit in that dreadful agony, whether with greater magnanimity than prudence can hardly be said."

" Good people," he began, " this is an uncomfortable

time to preach, yet I shall begin with a text of Scripture
'Let us run with patience the race which it set before us,
looking unto Jesus, the Author and Finisher of our faith.' ''
He knew that the God Whom he served was as able to deliver
him " from this sea of blood as He was to deliver the three
children from the furnace," and his resolution was as theirs
was. " They would not worship the image the king had
set up, nor will I the imaginations that the people are
setting up." And he added, adopting the phraseology of
his persecutors, " nor will I forsake the temple and the truth
of God to follow the bleating of Jeroboam's calves in Dan
and in Bethel." He went on to protest his innocence of
the charges made against him and he concluded with moving
dignity :

> " I was born and baptised in the bosom of the Church of England,
> established by law ; in that profession I have ever since lived, and in that
> I come now to die.
> " What clamours and slanders I have endured for labouring to keep
> an uniformity in the external service of God, according to the doctrine
> and discipline of this Church, all men know, and I have abundantly felt.
> Now, at last, I am accused of high treason in Parliament, a crime which
> my soul ever abhorred. This treason was charged to consist of two parts
> —an endeavour to subvert the laws of the land ; and a like endeavour to
> overthrow the true Protestant religion, established by law.
> " Besides my answers to the several charges, I protested mine inno-
> cency in both Houses. It was said, ' Prisoners ' protestations at the bar
> must not be taken !, I must, therefore, come now to it upon my death,
> being instantly to give God an account for the truth of it.
> " I do therefore here, in the presence of God and His holy angels, take
> it upon my death, that I never endeavoured the subversion either of law
> or religion. And I desire you all to remember this protest of mine for
> my innocency in this, and from all treasons whatsoever.
> " I have been accused likewise as an enemy of Parliaments. No ; I
> understand them, and the benefit that comes by them, too well to be so.
> But I did dislike the misgovernments of some parliaments many ways,
> and I had good reason for it ; for *corruptio optimi est pessima*. And that
> being the highest court, over which no other hath jurisdiction, when it is
> misinformed or misgoverned, the subject is left without all remedy.
> " But I have done. I forgive all the world, all and every of those bitter
> enemies which have persecuted me ; and humbly desire to be forgiven
> of God first and then of every man. And so I heartily desire you to join
> in prayer with me.
> " O eternal God and merciful Father, look down upon me in mercy,
> in the riches and fulness of all Thy mercies. Look upon me, but not till

Thou hast nailed my sins to the Cross of Christ, not till Thou hast bathed me in the blood of Christ, not till I have hid myself in the wounds of Christ ; that so the punishment due unto my sins may pass over me. And since Thou art pleased to try me to the uttermost, I most humbly beseech Thee, give me now, in this great instant, full patience, proportionable comfort, and a heart ready to die for Thine honour, the King's happiness, and this Church's preservation. And my zeal to these (far from arrogancy be it spoken) is all the sin (human frailty excepted, and all incidents thereto) which is not known to me in this particular, for which I come now to suffer ; I say, in this particular of treason. But otherwise, my sins are many and great. Lord, pardon them all, and those especially (whatever they are) which have drawn down this present judgment upon me. And when Thou hast given me strength to bear it, do with me as seems best in Thine own eyes. Amen."

I go again to Heylyn for the concluding scene :

" This said, he next applied himself to the fatal block, as to the haven of his rest. But finding the way full of people, who had placed themselves upon the theatre to behold the tragedy, he said, ' I thought there would have been an empty scaffold, that I might have had room to die. I beesech you, let me have an end of this misery, for I have endured it long.' Hereupon room was made for him to die. While he was preparing himself for the axe, he said ' I will put off my doublets, and God's will be done. I am willing to go out of the world ; no man can be more willing to send me out, than I am willing to be gone.'

" But there were broad chinks between the boards of the scaffold ; and he saw that some people were got under the very place where the block was seated. So he desired either that the people might be removed, or dust brought to fill up the crevices, ' lest,' said he, ' my innocent blood should fall upon the heads of the people.'

" The holy martyr was now ready for death, and very calmly waiting for his crown. It was like a scene out of primitive times. His face was fresh and ruddy, and of a cheerful countenance. But there stood, to look on and rail, one Sir John Clotworthy, an Irishman, and follower of the Earl of Warwick. He was a violent and wrong-headed man, an enthusiast, and very furious as a demagogue. Being irritated that the revilings of the people moved not the strong quiet of the holy martyr, or sharpened him into any show of passion, he would needs put in and try what he could do with his sponge and vinegar. So be propounded a question to him, not as if to learn, but rudely and out of ill nature, and to expose him to his associates. ' What,' asked he, ' is the comfortablest saying which a dying man would have in his mouth ? ' To which the holy martyr with very much meekness answered, ' *Dupio dissolvi et esse cum Christo.*' ' That is a good desire,' said the other ; ' but there must be a foundation for that divine assurance.' ' No man can express it,' replied the martyr ; ' it is to be found within.' The busy man still pursued him, and said, ' It is founded upon a word, nevertheless, and that word should be known.'

' That word,' said the martyr, ' is the knowledge of Jesus Christ, and that alone.' But he saw that this was but an indecent interruption, and that there would be no end to the trouble and so he turned away from him to the executioner as the gentler and discreeter person ; and putting some money into his hand, without the least distemper or change of countenance, he said, ' Here honest friend, God forgive thee, and do thine office upon me in mercy.' Then did he go upon his knees, and the executioner said that he should give a sign for the blow to come ; to which he answered, ' I will, but first let me fit myself.' After that he prayed :

" ' Lord, I am coming as fast as I can. I know I must pass through the shadow of death, before I can come to see Thee. But it is but *umbra mortis*, a mere shadow of death, a little darkness upon nature : but Thou by Thy merits and passions hast broke through the jaws of death. So, Lord, receive my soul, and have mercy upon me ; and bless this kingdom with peace and plenty, and with brotherly love and charity, that there may not be this effusion of Christian blood amongst them, for Jesus Christ His sake, if it be Thy will.'

" Then he bowed his head upon the block, and prayed silently awhile. No man heard what it was he prayed in that last prayer. After that he said out loud, ' Lord, receive my soul,' which was the sign to the executioner, and at one blow he was beheaded.

" There was no malice which was too great for his miserable enemies. They said he had purposely painted his face, to fortify his cheeks against discovery of fear in the paleness of his complexion. But, as if for the confutation of this poor malice, his face, ruddy in the last moment, instantly after the blow turned white as ashes.

" Multitudes of people went with his body to the grave, which was borne in a leaden coffin to the church of All Hallows, Barking, a church of his own patronage and jurisdiction. It was noted of many as extraordinary that, although the Liturgy had been by human law abolished, he, the great champion of the church and her ceremonies, was buried by his brave friends according to the old ritual, which it was high treason to use. So that it went to its grave with him. Both only for a while.

" ' For my faith,' saith the holy martyr, in his last will and testament, ' I die as I have lived, in the true orthodox profession of the Catholic Faith of Christ, foreshewed by the Prophets, and preached to the world by Christ Himself, His blessed Apostles, and their successors ; and a true member of His Catholic Church, within the communion of a living part thereof, the present Church of England, as it stands established by law.

" ' I leave my body to the earth, whence it was taken, in full assurance of the resurrection of it from the grave at the last day. This resurrection I constantly believe my dear Saviour Jesus Christ will make happy unto me, His poor and weary servant. And for my burial, though I stand not much upon the place, yet if it conveniently may be, I desire to be buried in the Chapel of St. John Baptist's College in Oxford, underneath the Altar or Communion Table there. And I should be so unhappy as to die a prisoner, yet my earnest desire is, I may not be buried in the Tower.

But wheresoever my burial shall be, I will have it private, that it may not waste any of the poor means which I leave behind me to better uses.'

" So, on the 24th July, being St. James's Eve, 1663, the remains of the holy martyr were translated to Oxford, and laid in one of the four brick vaults beneath the Alter of St. John's. And he has no monument, except his own city of Oxford, and the present English Church.

" ' So the dead which he slew at his death were more than they which he slew in his life.' "

Laud has been grossly maligned by the Whig historians. Carlyle, the eulogist of the unspeakable pervert, Frederick of Prussia, and the worst judge of men among writers of genius, dismissed him as " an ill-starred pedant." On the other hand, Dean Hutton declares that he was " the man who preserved for the Church of England both her Catholicity and her freedom." Laud completed what Elizabeth had begun, and he did much more. He not only saved the English Church from the Puritans ; he established her right to regard herself, not as the creation of either Parliament or King, but as part of the One Holy Catholic and Apostolic Church, national in her liturgy, but faithful to primitive doctrine.

That Laud saved England from Rome as well as from the Calvinists is indicated by the following extract from Evelyn's Diary :

" I was at Rome in company of divers of the English fathers, when the news came of the Archbishop's sufferings, and a copy of his sermon upon the scaffold come thither. They read the sermon and commented upon it, with no small satisfaction and contempt : and looked upon him as one that was a great enemy to them, and stood in their way ; whilst one of the blackest crimes imputed to him was his being popishly inclined."

CHAPTER V

THE CIPHER

IN England, the eleventh century was the century of Lanfranc and St. Anselm, as much as it was the century of the Conqueror ; the twelfth century was the century of St. Thomas, and the thirteenth century of Stephen Langton the 16th of Warham, the champion of the new learning, of Cranmer, of Pole and of Parker ; the seventeenth of Laud and Sancroft. These Archbishops played great parts in the history of the country, and their influence was due not only to their characters and capacities, but to the popular recognition of the authority of the Church. In the eighteenth century the Church had lost both the affection and the respect of the people. During the reigns of the first two Georges it had practically no influence. The names of its leaders find no place in secular history, and the most industrious ecclesiastical historian can find little to say of them.

In choosing John Potter as the typical eighteenth century Primate I have been influenced by the fact that not only does his mediocrity illustrate the general decadence of the Church, but also by the second fact that his Primacy saw the beginning of a great religious movement which might have brought back spiritual vitality to the Church, but which, owing to the blunders of the hierarchy, was unguided, often extravagant and finally schismatic.

First, it is necessary to consider the events that followed Laud's martyrdom.

While Laud was still a prisoner in the Tower, the bishops were excluded by statute from the House of Lords, a commission was appointed to destroy, as superstitious, the painted glass, left in the London churches, the Scottish Solemn League and Covenant was accepted by the Commons and episcopacy was abolished in the Church of England. In 1643, the Westminster Assembly, consisting of English Puritans and Scottish Presbyterians, met to establish a Calvinist uniformity in the two kingdoms. In obedience to the Assembly's decisions, Parliament banned the Book of Common Prayer in the year of Laud's martyrdom, and, in 1646, it ordered the establishment of presbyteries all over England. For some mysterious reason, the tercentary of the meeting of this futile Assembly was celebrated by the BBC, though, thanks to the providence of God, the religious tyranny that it established was destined to last for only fifteen years.

Even before the King's execution in 1649, the Presbyterians in the Long Parliament and the Independents, who were dominant in the Cromwellian Army, were bitterly quarrelling. With the establishment of Cromwell's personal power as Lord Protector Independency became the official religion of England, though it was never more than the religion of a small minority of the English people. Much has been written by his eulogists of Cromwell's toleration. It extended to Jews and Quakers and Brownists and Anabaptists, but it did not extend to Roman Catholics or to members of the Church of England, who, during the Commonwealth, were penalised and persecuted. Cromwell was a great general, a statesman who made his country feared and respected, and an able administrator. But his religion which Landor found mere hypocrisy, is, to the normal judgment, sometimes nauseating and sometimes terrifying. His New Model Army of fanatical fighting men was an admirable military machine which, as J. K. Mozley has said, " rode roughshod over the country, pushing it by main force and simple steel into extremities from which it shrunk." The Roundheads were Cromwell's S.S. men. Indeed, they may have been taken by Hitler as a model, but Hitler has never described his ruthless followers as Cromwell described his as " the poor, weak, despised, jeered saints, poor weak saints, yet saints."

The Puritan religion, with its self-sufficient assurance, had a terrifying expression on Cromwell's deathbed. He asked the attendant minister if it were possible to fall from grace, and when he was told that this was impossible, he said : " Then I am sure of salvation, for I know that I was once in grace."

Cromwell was a true Puritan, too, in his concern for property and his contempt for the propertyless. He dismissed the claims of the Levellers with the remark, " Did not the Levellers' principle tend to the reducing of all to an equality ; what was the purport of it but to make the tenant as liberal as the landlord ? " His wholesale butcheries in Ireland justified by his hatred of the Catholic religion, left a legacy of repulsion that has affected the relations of the two countries to this day, and his selling of British subjects into slavery in the Barbadoes was another anticipation of the methods of Hitler.

Every schoolboy has heard of Pride's purge of the House of Commons. A much more cruel proceeding was Cromeell's purge of the parishes in 1654, hundreds of incumbents being driven from their livings for encouraging dancing and play-acting, for speaking evil of the Puritans, or for using the Prayer Book. The unfortunate men were forbidden to keep a school or to act as private tutors.

None of his admirers, not even Carlyle, has denied that England rejoiced when Cromwell died in 1658 ; never has laughter-loving England more heartily rejoiced than when two years later Charles II was restored to his father's throne. The Church was restored with the King. Juxon, Laud's follower, became Archbishop, the exiled bishops returned to their sees, and learned and pious men were appointed to the vacant dioceses. " Seldom," says Wakeman, " have so many men of mark been found together in one company as was gathered on the episcopal bench of England in 1661." Parliament restored to the Church the property that had been hers at the outbreak of the Civil War, and, by the summer of 1661, " the Church had not only resumed the discharge of her spiritual duties, but had been reinstated in possession of her temporalities and her constitutional heritage." The era of Puritan tyranny had come to an end, vastly to the joy of the mass of the people and even to the relief of the Presbyterians, who disliked Independent Congregationalism only a little less than they disliked episcopal rule.

Still clinging to the old hope for " one nation, one faith," Charles believed that the unanimity, with which he had been welcomed, might make possible the creation of a comprehensive national Church, and twelve of the bishops met twelve Puritan ministers at a Conference at the Savoy. But the old essential differences continued. Baxter produced a Prayer Book, which the bishops found hopelessly inadequate, and it was decided, though with little of the old rancour, that there could be no communion between Churchmen on the one side and Baptists, Quakers, and the adherents of the other sects on the other.

The Church, therefore, set itself to the revision of its own liturgy and the Prayer Book of 1662, still in use in the Provinces of Canterbury and York, was the result. The Book, denounced, rightly from their point of view, for its Papistry by nineteenth century Nonconformists, embodies the faith and requires the practice of Andrewes and Laud, of George Herbert and Nicholas Ferrar. With its publication the Reformation era came to an end in England. Wakeman says :

> " The Church of England reformed on Catholic lines and freed from Puritanism was able to discharge her own duties to her own people in her own way. Puritanism, relieved from its struggle for ascendancy over the Church, was able to develop its principles in the freedom of voluntary societies. For a time, it is true, the toleration which this altered state of affairs demanded was refused by politicians ; but in the purely religious sphere the problems of the Reformation were solved at the Restoration."

This statement needs qualification. There is considerable justification for Bishop Creighton's assertion that religious persecution has been more often an affair of State policy than of religious intolerance, a policy dictated by the belief that national stability demanded uniformity of religious faith and practice. It was for this reason that Elizabeth persecuted the Romanists and, much more mildly, the Puritans. It was for this reason that Cromwell persecuted Romanists and Anglicans and would have persecuted Presbyterians if he had dared. On the other hand, it has to be recognised that the Roman persecutions of heretics had, if not a nobler, a less circumscribed motive. It had indeed a double motive. Men's bodies were burned that their souls might be saved. It was a horrible belief but it was held by honourable and often humane men. It was further held, certainly by an enlightened man like Reginald Pole and, in a muddled sort of way, by Mary that the continuation of one Catholic Church of unchallenged authority was vital for world well-being.

Bernard Shaw has put into the mouth of the Bishop of Beauvais what was a reasonable view, not only in the fifteenth century, but even more emphatically after the Counter-reformation. "What will the world be like," asks Mr. Shaw's bishop, "when the Church's wisdom and knowledge and experience, its councils of learned, venerable and pious men, are thrust into the kennel by every ignorant labourer or dairymaid whom the devil can puff up with the monstrous self-conceit of being directly inspired from heaven ? It will be a world of blood, of fury, of devastation, of each man striving for his own hand : in the end of a world wrecked back to barbarism." This was what was honestly and, as events have proved, most intelligently feared.

The persecution that followed the Restoration had no such excuse. Parliament met, with the nation resentful of the Puritan tyranny from which it had just escaped. There was a national demand that the persecutors should be persecuted. Revenge is always silly. It perpetuates evil. Forgiveness is dictated by common sense, a fact which will probably be forgotten in the coming years with the inevitable fatal consequences. By the Corporation Act, the Act of Uniformity, the Conventicle Act, the Five Mile Act, and the Test Act, Roman Catholics and Puritans were forbidden to practice their religion and were debarred from holding any public office.

The politicians justified these measures by the continued possibility of foreign interference, through the Pope, in English domestic affairs and by the acknowledged fact that Puritanism was anti-monarchic. The Puritan was persecuted not for his religious faith, but for his political opinions. While this is true, it is also true that the Church welcomed, if it did not inspire, the repressive laws with deplorable results to its spiritual life and influence. Wakeman says :

"The history of the Sacramental Test in England is one of the saddest chapters in the whole of Church history. It kept out only the honest and high-minded. It dulled the religious instinct, and lowered irretrievably for generations the whole conception of the Sacraments. It admitted without question—nay, welcomed—the hypocrite, the blasphemer and the libertine, and made the moral discipline of the Church a very by-word of shame. Yet for one hundred and fifty years leading churchmen, clerical and lay, fought for it as the most precious of their safeguards and the palladium of their faith. No wonder if so mistaken a policy brought its own retribution in the deadening of spiritual life, and contributed to the loss of half the English-speaking races to the allegiance of the Church."

This is another over-statement, but it is true that the Church was in sounder spiritual health when Laud went to the block than when a few years after Juxon was installed at Canterbury. The Church persecuted has always been the Church triumphant. The Church dominant has often been the Church impotent.

Charles was both shrewd and good-natured and his qualities made him adverse to religious persecution. Long before his deathbed reconciliation with the Roman Church, he was at heart a Romanist and he was concerned not only to make life easier for men, with whose faith he sympathised, but to secure the succession for his Roman and woefully stupid brother. But the King's efforts for toleration made both his Parliament and his people the more intolerant, and secured influential support for the almost incredible Titus Oates and other similar scoundrels.

James rushed in where his wiser brother had feared to tread, and, unmindful of the fate of his father, he attempted to over-ride Parliament and by a royal edict to suspend the laws against Romanists and Puritans. The Puritans were not beguiled to the King's support. They remained fiercely anti-Catholic. And the Church was compelled, for the first time, into hostility to a Stuart King. The Seven Bishops, headed by Archbishop Sancroft, a Prelate devoted to the Laudian tradition, and Ken, the saintly High Church Bishop of Winchester, presented to the King the famous petition against the Declaration of Indulgence. This was followed by the arrest of the Bishops, their triumphal procession to the Tower and their acquittal by a London jury amid popular rejoicing.

The trial of the Seven Bishops was the King's undoing. The Church, that had fought and suffered for the Stuarts, was finally responsible for the end of the Stuart dynasty.

In the years between the accession of Charles II and the death of Queen Anne, the Church retained much of its noble heritage from Laud. Ken was its most precious ornament, "the good little man," to whom Charles, who never failed to appreciate high character, gave preferment even though he had refused to play the host to Nell Gwynn at Winchester. Jeremy Taylor lived until 1667, in his later years to number John Evelyn among his penitents, and Evelyn himself is evidence of the continuance of Catholic piety in what has been regarded as a Godless age. Throughout England, churches were restored, daily services were again the rule, and the Holy Mysteries were celebrated with due reverence and ceremonial, at Ely Cathedral and elsewhere with the use of incense. Confession was taught and observed, and the traditional restrained veneration for the Blessed Virgin Mary was expressed in Ken's hymn :

> Heaven with transcendent joy Her entrance graced,
> Next to His throne Her Son His Mother placed ;
> And here below, now She's of heaven possest,
> All generations are to call Her blest.

The recovery was by no means complete. The results of Puritan neglect and destruction continued. In some dioceses it was reported that " most of the Houses of God resemble rather stables and thatched cottages than temples in which to serve the Most High," that " some chancels lie wholly disused in more nasty manner than any cottager would keep his house," and that there were churches where there were no surplice, no chalice, no Prayer Book and even no copy of the Scriptures. In some few churches there was a daily celebration, St. Giles's Cripplegate was one of them ; in a few more there was a weekly celebration ; but the usual rule was a monthly celebration.

The quickening of the Church's spiritual life, partial as it was, led to concern for the poor and distressed and the establishment of schools. In the closing months of the century the Society for the Promotion of Christian Knowledge was founded with the objects of supporting religious teaching in schools, assisting the Church in the colonies and circulating good literature at cheap prices. In 1701, the daughter Society for the Propagation of the Gospel in Foreign Parts was founded. It was and it has remained the definitely High Church Missionary body.

It was the tragedy of the English Church that the political events of the year 1688 forced its alliance with the Tory Party which was to continue more or less closely for two centuries. It is impossible to keep politics out of religion. Immense evil has resulted from the success with which religion has been kept out of politics. As I have suggested, the Puritan's faith made him anti-monarchic and the champion of money against the well-being of the people. The Laudian belief that the monarch was the Lord's annointed divinely chosen to guide and serve the nation, did not prevent the Seven Bishops from protesting against the misuse of the royal power, but it did compel these same men, who had sworn fealty to James, from transferring their allegiance to Dutch William, when James absconded. That very wise Pope, Innocent XI, had warned James to be cautious and moderate. In 1688, if there could have been a plebiscite in England, not one Englishman in a thousand would have preferred William to James. If James had not destroyed the popular attachment to the Stuarts, the Dutch Army would never have been permitted to land in England. James committed political suicide.

The Revolution established a Parliamentary monarchy, something fundamentally different to the Catholic conception of monarchy with a spiritual significance. It certainly did not establish popular monarchy or a government in the smallest degree democratic. England hated the rule of a Dutch king as much as it had hated the interference in their affairs of an Italian prelate. They hated William when he arrived at Torbay. They hated him during the fifteen years of his reign. He was indeed a man whom all decent men and women should have hated. But it was not his personal character, of which the common people probably knew very little, that caused him to be detested. It was the fact that the nation, that was every year becoming poorer and more miserable, was being used by a foreign sovereign for the attainment of a continental policy from which it could obtain no advantage and was involved in a war in which it had no interest.

The national spirit had been numbed by James. William was received by a Parliament of intriguers, but the Church would not bow its head. Archbishop Sancroft and five other bishops, among them the lovable Ken, who had had dealings with William at The Hague and knew him for the man he was, and four hundred of the clergy refused the oath and were expelled from their sees and their livings.

The loss to the Church of the Non-Jurors, men of piety and learning, cannot be exaggerated. Sancroft and Ken spent the rest of their lives in retirement. Some of the other Non-Juror bishops, claiming to be the only properly accredited leaders of the English Catholic Church. consecrated others to carry on the succession and what was, at no time, more than an inconsiderable sect, lasted until the beginning of the nineteenth century.

William was a nominal Calvinist and he filled the vacant dioceses with men who rejected the Laudian conception of the Church, and who opposed the measures against the Dissenters which the Church had supported with misguided zeal. The most prominent of these men was Gilbert Burnett, who was promoted to the bishopric of Salisbury. Lecky, despite his dislike of High Church claims, has this candid description of Burnet :

" Scarcely any other figure in English ecclesiastical history has been so fully portrayed, and the lines of his character are indeed too broad and clear to be overlooked. No one can question that he was vain, pushing, boisterous, indiscreet, and inquisitive, overflowing with animal spirits and superabundant energy, singularly deficient in the tact, delicacy, reticence and decorum that are needed in a great ecclesiastical position. Having thrown himself, with all the enthusiasm of his nature, into the cause of the Revolution from the very beginning of the design, he became one of the most active politicians of his time. He was a constant pamphleteer and debater. On at least one occasion, when he advocated the Act of Attainder that brought Sir John Fenwick to the scaffold, he stooped to services that were very little in harmony with his profession. He was one of the last writers of authority who countenanced the fable of the suppositious birth of the Pretender, and in many other points he allowed the passions of a violent partisan to discolour that brilliant history which is one of the most authentic records of the times of the Revolution."

The majority of the clergy, though they did not share the sacrifice made by the Non-Jurors, remained faithful to the Laudian tradition, and, in the reign of William, while the Bishops were nearly all Whigs, the Church as a whole was with the Tories, who for generations were known as the Church party. Lecky says that the Tories had " the sympathy of the country clergy, the country gentry and of the poor."

The Dissenters were the most important section of the party that supported the Dutch King and they were, for the most part, rich traders. In the reign of William, one Lord Mayor of London after another was a wealthy Dissenter. Money, which had begun to talk loudly during the Commonwealth, shouted when William of Orange was King of England. It was William who, needing money for his continental wars, established the Bank of England ; from the point of view of the commonwealth, the most portentous event in modern history, the beginning of the system of paper credit, with all its fearsome consequences.

Fear of the clergy caused the King to refuse for eleven years to allow a meeting of Convocation, but the increasing influence of the Tories forced him to give way and the Canterbury Convocation met, its proceedings being marked by bitter disputes between the two houses. The York Convocation did not meet from 1698 to 1861.

The accession of Queen Anne was an important event in Church history. In matters of faith she was the spiritual heir of her grandfather ; a devoted daughter of the English Church, of whose Catholic claims she had no doubt. She was unaffected by her father's Papist allegiance ; she detested the immoral latitudinarianism of her Dutch brother-in-law ; she could never forget that her grandfather had been murdered by Presbyterians and Independents. Her piety was simple and sincere. She was very obstinate, very generous, very affectionate and often very silly. Her devotion to the Church was proved by her surrender of the first fruits and the tenths originally given to the Pope and afterwards appropriated by the crown, and the continued existence of Queen Anne's Bounty is the evidence of her care for the badly paid clergy. She probably held, though she never asserted, the doctrine of Divine Right. She reigned as the last of the Stuarts, the last legitimate English monarch. And few English sovereigns have been regarded with greater popular affection.

Convocation had lost its power alone to impose taxation on the clergy, but its influence with the Queen and the Tory majority in the House of Commons, backed as it was by the sympathy of the people, was sufficient to secure new and entirely indefensible legislation against Dissenters.

The Test Act made the reception of the Holy Sacrament from an ordained priest of the Church a necessary qualification for public office and many Dissenters, while ordinarily attending their own places of worship, did not hesitate once or twice a year to go to church and to receive Holy Communion, though the practice was condemned by Defoe and regarded as offensive by the Independents and the Baptists. This practice was naturally resented by the clergy and the Occasional Conformity Act was passed with the provision that attendance at a Nonconformist chapel should of itself debar from public employment. The Schism Act imposed the penalty of imprisonment on any man who opened any sort of school without a licence from a bishop, and was not a regular communicant at an Anglican church. Tyrannical as these laws were, they were unquestionably approved by the people, popular sentiment being vehemently expressed after the abortive prosecution of the absurd High Church enthusiast Sacheverell, accused of sedition for preaching the doctrine of non-resistance.

The Queen's death was deeply mourned. The nation had not forgotten the King imported from Holland and it had no desire for another king to be imported from Germany. England owes the Hanoverian dynasty to accident and the Pretender's unshakable loyalty to Rome. If Queen Anne's son had survived, he would have succeeded with the unanimous approval of the nation. If the Queen had lived for another year, she might have secured the abrogation of the Act of Settlement, and, as she certainly wished, the succession would have passed to her Papist step-brother. If the Pretender had been willing to have reverted from Rome to Canterbury, there is little doubt that the crown would have been his. But he was not willing to buy a throne with apostasy, and when the Queen died, the Elector of Hanover succeeded without any effective opposition. He was the King *faute de mieux*. The Pretender would not abandon his loyalty to Rome and would make no promises inconsistent with that loyalty. And the people of England would not have a Popish monarch.

The Whigs had become the dominant party largely because the Tories, and with them the Church, were half and half Jacobites, hating the Hanoverian succession but unable to support the Roman Catholic Stuart. And the Whigs had money on their side. Lecky admits that they could count on " the warm support of the moneyed classes and of the Dissenters, who in this, as in most other periods, were closely united."

Money was now firmly in the saddle and money still feared the Church. Convocation was suspended in 1717 and was not summoned again until 1850. After the suppression, the Church had to go hat in hand to Parliament for all that it needed, with the bishops in the Lords chosen by the Whigs from men whose beliefs were contrary to the Church's accepted formulas. From the Restoration to the death of Queen Anne, it was the Laudian High Churchmen who had been responsible for the spiritual energy of the Church. To the Whigs, High Churchmen were dangerous Jacobites, the enemies of the new dynasty and the potential supporters of rebellion. All religious zeal was accordingly discouraged and none but safe men appointed to positions of authority. Many bishops never went near their dioceses. One Welsh bishop farmed successfully in Westmorland for thirty-four years.

The best of the Whig divines were Latitudinarians. In an age of reason they were concerned to prove that religion was reasonable and they made religion dull and lifeless.

The privileged minority in England prospered amazingly after the arrival of George I and his mistresses, whose exceeding ugliness vastly amused the London mob. Money was added to money. Luxury increased. Fine houses, mostly in execrable taste, were built in town and country. Wages rose and, while the enclosures woefully affected the life of the villages, there was an increased demand for labour in the towns. But in the prevailing materialism and with the Church " extremely phlegmatic and sedate " as it is described by Swift in *The Tale of a Tub*, the general condition of the majority was of neglect, apathy and brutality. Defoe says :

> " There is nothing more frequent than for an Englishman to work till he has got his pockets full of money, and then go and be idle and perhaps drunk, till it is all gone, and perhaps himself in debt ; and ask him, in his cups what he intends, he'll tell you, honestly, he will drink as long as it lasts and then go to work for more."

Remembering Defoe's sympathy with prosperous Dissent and remembering, too, that similar things have always been said by the well-to-do of the poor, it would not be wise to accept this as an entirely accurate description of the mass of the people. It is true, however, that at this time gin drinking increased in the reeking back-streets of London, with the degradation pictured by Hogarth. In 1738, there was a heavy decrease in births and an equally heavy increase in deaths in London, both said to be " the shocking effects of the bewitching liquor," excessive indulgence being obviously due to the dull misery to which the majority were condemned.

The penal laws were brutal and the prisons were infamous. At the end of the Stuart era there were some fifty capital offences. A hundred years later, there were one hundred and sixty. Yet crime steadily increased, owing to the refusal of decent juries to send men, guilty of trivial offences, to the gallows, and to the lack of any efficient police force. When John Howard began his investigation of English prisons he found them pestilential centres of physical and moral corruption. The prisoners were half starved and pitifully cold. They were robbed and tortured by irresponsible gaolers, and Howard found them infinitely more inhuman than the average gaols on the continent, while the number of executions was much higher. In one year ninety-six persons were hanged at the Old Bailey. At the same time, in eight years only five persons were executed in Amsterdam, a city then a third of the size of London. The stinking gaols were crowded with unfortunate debtors —over six thousand were arrested every year in Middlesex alone, one half for debts of less than twenty pounds. Scores of countrymen were arrested for offences against the Game

Laws and many of these were sold to the planters in Maryland and in the last years of the century transported to Australia. The Poor Laws were administered with inhuman harshness, the workhouses were as brutalising as the prisons.

If the Church was impotent, except for a few lucky and indifferent pluralists, its ministers were miserably poor. Swift wrote of the average country priest :

> "He liveth like an honest, plain farmer, as his wife is dressed but little better than Goody. He is sometimes graciously invited by the squire, where he sitteth at humble distance. If he gets the love of his people they often make him little useful presents. He is happy by being born to no higher expectation, for he is usually the son of some ordinary tradesman or middling farmer. His learning is much of a size with his birth and education, no more of either than what a poor hungry servitor can be expected to bring with him from his college."

Such an incumbent was better off than many of his brethren, who were hired as chaplains by the wealthy and treated as servants, often marrying the cook or the housemaid or obliging their patron by marrying his cast-off mistress. They were, complained one of the Non-Jurors, " left to everyone's fancy (and some very unable to judge) to take in and turn out at their pleasure, as they do to their footmen, that they may be wholly subservient to their humour and their frolics, sometimes to their vices ; and to play upon the chaplain is often the best part of the entertainment, and religion suffers with it."

The institution of Queen Anne's Bounty did something to mitigate clerical poverty, and the private chaplain, who was also the family fool, disappeared before the middle of the century, but many years were to pass before the Church and its ministers recovered the respect and authority to exert the spiritual influence that was never needed more. The Church of Andrewes and Laud had become the Church of placemen, half believers and despised dependants on the rich.

Few of the clergy had the smallest interest in the souls or the bodies of the miserable, gin-sodden and oppressed majority. Of one priest, William Romaine, who cared for the people who were always the peculiar concern of our

Lord, it is recorded : " He drew the poor to Church and mainly for this grave offence he suffered annoyance, which amounted to persecution." At St. Dunstan's in the West in Fleet Street, the comfortable parishioners had to push their way to their pews through " a ragged unsavoury multitude," and Romaine was deprived of his lectureship.

It is not wonderful that the deadness of the English Church led to a considerable number of conversions to Rome. It was stated in 1735 that there was " scarcely a petty coffee house in London where there was not a Popish lecture read on Sunday evenings." Doddridge, the hymn writer, was alarmed by the growth of Popery. The Bishop of London seems to have regarded the increase of Popery as a far greater evil than the increase of gin drinking. It was reported that " there is at present a gentleman in the West of England who openly gives five pounds to every person who becomes a proselyte to the chosen Church, and the additional bribe of a Sunday dinner to every such person that attends Mass," a rumour that in view of the fact that " to be reconciled to the see of Rome " was a penal offence is probably quite untrue.

Whether or no, the Roman Church benefited, " a religious languor " had fallen over England when John Potter was enthroned in Canterbury in 1737. He was the son of a Yorkshire linen draper, went to Oxford as a servitor at University College and was elected to a fellowship at Lincoln when he was twenty. When at Oxford, he was responsible for an edition of the works of Clement of Alexandria, which showed an interest in patristics rare in England at this time. He was given various livings, which he held as an absentee pluralist. He served three years as chaplain to Archbishop Tenison, and in 1707 he became Regius Professor of Divinity at Oxford and a Canon of Christ Church. In 1715 he was consecrated Bishop of Oxford and his occupancy of the see is remembered, because in April, 1725, he ordained a handsome young man, John Wesley, as the Bishop himself had been, a Fellow of Lincoln College.

Wesley was one of the nineteen children of a poor Lincoln shire clergyman, most of whom, perhaps fortunately for themselves, died in their babyhood. His father was

feckless and conceited incompetent and a rigid High Churchman ; his mother was an intelligent soured pietist, persuaded
that only by a miracle could any of the children, whom she
had brought into the world, escape an eternity in hell.
The Epworth Rectory must have been an even more miserable home than the Bronte vicarage at Haworth.

Susanne Wesley, who lived to a great age, dominated her
famous son until her death. She was a masterful woman,
who despised her husband and broke the spirit of her
daughters, and whose one human characteristic—it was
carefully repressed—was that she liked " small beer." When
she died, tribute was paid to her in what Miss Bowen has
properly described as " revolting doggerel," which her son
John thoroughly approved.

One verse was :

> The daughter of affliction, she
> Inured to pain and misery,
> Mourn'd a long life of grief and tears
> A legal night of seventy years.

John Wesley was educated at Charterhouse, before going
up to Oxford. There he was the leader of a small band of
serious-minded young men, of whom his brother Charles
was another, who, influenced by Jeremy Taylor and William
Law, lived according to a rigid rule, avoiding all worldly
pleasures, making frequent communions, often fasting and
spending hours a day in prayer. Oxford in the reigns of
the first two Georges had all the characteristics of the coarse
Hanoverian immorality and the lives of these young men—
they were nicknamed Methodists by their fellows—was a
worthy protest against the atmosphere in which they were
forced to live.

After the Wesleys, the most outstanding of the Oxford
Methodists was George Whitfield, who, starting life as a
pot boy in an inn, contrived to get to Oxford, and in his
youth wanting to be an actor, lived to be the most eloquent
preacher of his age, proving by the quality of his converts
that, though it may be difficult, it is not impossible for rich
ladies to enter the kingdom of heaven.

Sir Leslie Stephens has described the Methodist movement as a religious reaction. It was, in fact, a revival and a recovery. The seventeenth century was the age of fervent and pugnacious faith. Romanists, Anglicans and Puritans were all inspired by mystical beliefs for which they were ready to die, and the fervour of their faith gave their lives a dignity and a nobility, apparent in men as different as Laud and Ken and Baxter and Bunyan. The eighteenth century, claimed as the age of reason, was no more than the age of doubt and doubt is the mother of disaster. An ounce of honest conviction is worth a ton of honest doubt.

The genius of the eighteenth century Doubting Castle was David Hume, whom Dr. Johnson scornfully and incorrectly dismissed as " an echo of Voltaire." There had been sceptics, of whom Hobbes was the most considerable, in the preceding century and Hume, as a philosopher, derives from Locke, who was a sincere if unorthodox Protestant. But Hume had the courage to carry Locke's premises to their logical conclusion.

Leslie Stephen has pointed out that the Protestant opponents of Catholicism forged the weapons that Hume and his followers used against themselves. The familiar argument against the doctrine of the Real Presence applies with equal force against belief in the historicity of Our Lord's miracles and indeed against belief in the existence of God.

In the later years of the century scepticism had its crude and vulgar exponents who had their successors a hundred years after in the columns of the *Freethinker* and the speeches in the Hall of Science. But a far more insidious influence was exercised by the men who, differing hardly at all from the Voltairean deists, contrived to remain and to secure preferment in the Church. Typical of these men was Benjamin Hoadly, for twenty-five years Bishop of Winchester, a prolific and portentously dull writer, who denied that the Church and its ministers have any supernatural authority, who agreed with Bolingbroke that a bishop is " a mere layman with a crook," and who taught that the Holy Eucharist is no more than a commemorative rite.

The religious writers of the century, distinguished as thinkers which men like Hoadly were certainly not, were

half-hearted and apologetic. Butler's position was similar
to that of St. Anselm, though he apparently did not accept
St. Anselm's conviction that without faith there can be no
understanding. Butler's God was the human conscience
deified, and Leslie Stephen has said that " he staggers out
of Doubting Castle with trembling knees and wearied
knees." Berkeley's theory of the non-existence of matter
was ridiculed by Johnson with a common-sense example.
Paley's theology has been described as frozen. In his writing
there is no suggestion of the quickening imaginative Christian spirit.

Without a trace of combative faith, the Church was
regarded with contemptuous tolerance by sceptics like
Gibbon, who were concerned with the preservation of the
social and political order. The Church was a useful bulwark
against revolutionary changes and the difference between
unbelieving philosophers and latitudinarian divines was of no
great consequence. Whether the Church's loss of a living
faith was the cause of national degradation or whether it was
one of the aspects of that degradation, of its reality there is
no question. Wesley was more than justified in his condemnation of the corruption of politics, the venality of the
law courts, the drunkenness of the slums, the profligacy of
the rich, the carelessness of the clergy, the worldliness of
the dissenters. Eighteenth-century England was anything
but a merry England. It was a sordid, coarse and cruel
England. The romance of the sixteenth century and the
moral earnestness of the seventeenth had both been lost.

But there are always some good men in every Sodom. In
these years of atheism and deism, of sceptical philosophers
and indifferent churchmen, William Law, ascetic, mystic,
acute thinker, and expert controversialist, kept the lamp of
eternal truth burning in the England of Fielding and
Hogarth. Law was described by Gibbon, in whose family
he lived for some time, as " a worthy and pious man who
believed all he professed and practised all that he enjoined."
He was a Catholic Anglican, with Laud's conception of the
nature of the Church. He was one of the Non-jurors whose
consciences forbade them to take the oath of allegiance to the
Hanoverians, and this refusal deprived him of any chance of

clerical preferment.

The latitudinarians insisted that Christ must not be taken too literally and that much of His teaching was exclusively for the people of His own earthly time. Law believed that Christ meant what He said and that His was the one way of salvation for all men in all times. Law's life was spent in prayer and contemplation and in the writing of an immense number of books, the first of which was published in 1717 and the last in 1761. His biographer says that he devoted " his purified will and intellect to the free, gladsome, active, supercogitative researches of the Spirit of Wisdom and openings of the Divine life."

This simple recluse had a vast influence. His most famous book, *The Serious Call to a Devout and Holy Life*, was a guide and comfort to Samuel Johnson and with Thomas à Kempis and Jeremy Taylor, he was responsible, for the conversion of John Wesley and was thus one of the inspirers of the one vivid religious movement of his century. Law retired from the world. Wesley went out into the world to fight the devil and all his works. Both men believed, I quote Sir Leslie Stephen, that " the ultimate and incontrovertible evidence of Christianity is the evidence of the believer's heart."

When he was thirty-two, Wesley went to Georgia as a missionary to the American Indians, but, when he arrived in the colony, he determined to devote himself to ministering to the colonists and his mission was a distinct failure. In matters of doctrine he was a Catholic ; in morals he was a rigid and intolerant Puritan, and in both capacities he was cordially disliked and entirely disregarded. After two years he returned home, sorrowful, disappointed and doubtful of his vocation.

On the voyage to England, he had long conversations with a leader of the German sect, the Moravian Brethren, and this man became the second great influence in determining the character of the gospel that Wesley was to preach.

In many respects Wesleyanism was a novelty in English religion, differing fundamentally from Puritanism. It rejected the Calvinist doctrine of predestination. It taught that all men may be saved, but that all men, however moral they may be, will be damned unless they are first convinced that they thoroughly deserve to be damned and are then moved by supernatural grace, never denied to the truly penitent, to realise that the death of Christ was the expiation for their individual sins. This double conviction has nothing to do with reason. It is as instantaneous and as mystical as St. Paul's conversion on the road to Damascus.

The fundamental difference between this doctrine and the tenets of the Calvinists need not be stressed. The Calvinists taught that some men are born to be saved, whether they will or not, and that other men, apparently the great majority, are born to be eternally damned. It is impossible to understand how this belief can be reconciled with the existence of the All-loving God, revealed in the New Testament, but it was the fundamental creed of the sixteenth and seventeenth centuries Puritans. Wesley taught that no man need spend an eternity in hell fire, though all men are in danger of that awful fate !

It was admitted that the result of " conversion " might not be lasting. The converted might fall from grace. On the other hand, by persistence, he might arrive at the happy condition of being incapable of sin. This is the doctrine of perfectibility repudiated by both the Roman Church and the Church of England.

Calvinism is as ridiculous as it is repulsive. Wesleyanism is at least more reasonable. Though the belief in eternal punishment has now been abandoned by most Protestants and Anglicans, Wesley taught what is still regarded as the Evangelical faith. In this country Calvinism ceased to exist generations ago—I am told that to-day even the so-called Welsh Calvinist Methodists are not genuine disciples of Geneva—and since this is largely due to Wesley he may be properly regarded as the father of modern English Protestantism. The great achievement of his life was that he saved the nation from the horrors of Calvin and John Knox.

It was the burning conviction that all men may be damned and that all men may be saved that compelled Wesley to use his almost super-human energy in the effort to " rescue the perishing." In fifty-two years he travelled 225,000 miles and delivered 40,000 sermons, at the age of eighty-six preaching to a congregation of 25,000.

The Calvinist could have no real incentive to preach the Gospel in all the world. To him this must have been a waste of energy, since it had already been decided who should inherit eternal life. The Calvinist, too, could not logically accept St. James's estimate of the super-importance of good works, since the elect cannot fall from grace. But Wesley insisted that repentance must be followed by the fruits meet for repentance. Every convert must be a St. Andrew. Having himself answered the call, he must pass the call on to others.

The Methodist banning of all earthly pleasure is entirely logical. Since the Calvinist regards most of his fellows as destined for hell, it might be supposed that, in common decency, he would help them to a good time in this world, in the spirit of the gaoler who provides a substantial breakfast for the man about to be hanged. But to the Methodist the risk of earthly living was so great that there must be complete absorption in the effort to escape damnation.

After his return from America, Wesley was persuaded that, despite his devotion and his faith, he, too, was among the damned, and he believed this until his own " conversion " at a Moravian meeting in London in 1738. The preacher was reading Luther's preface to the Epistle to the Romans, when, Wesley related, " My heart strangely warmed, I felt I did trust in Christ, Christ alone, for salvation and that an assurance was given to me that He had taken away my sins, even mine, and saved me from the law of sin and death."

That was the beginning of his life's work. " He felt," says Wakeman, " that he had a special message to deliver, for which the limitation of the parochial system were too narrow. He took the whole of England for his parish, and set out on preaching tours from place to place in order to announce to a world, still in bondage to sin, the good tidings of the new birth." Wesley remained a priest of the English Church. He never intended to found a new sect. Actually, he was too much an individualist ever willingly to have submitted to Catholic discipline and order, but the direction that he should have had from episcopal authority was never offered to him. He never abandoned the belief in the

Catholic doctr ne of the Sacraments that he had learned from his Laudian teachers, Jeremy Taylor and William Law.

The gentle Charles Wesley, a far more lovable man than his brother, left the English Church some of the most beautiful of her Eucharistic hymns, in which, as in the following verse, the Real Presence is definitely implied.

> We need not now go up to heaven
> To bring the long-sought Saviour down ;
> Thou art to all already given,
> Thou dost e'en now Thy Banquet crown ;
>   To every faithful soul appear,
>   And show Thy Real Presence here.

In enlisting his band of itinerant unordained preachers, like Wycliffe four hundred years before, Wesley's intention was to establish in the English Church a new Franciscan order of friars minor, and this might have happened if there had been the same vision and understanding at Canterbury as there had been in Rome when Innocent III had his historic interview with St. Francis. But John Potter, mild Latitudinarian scholar, had no vision, nor had any of his brethren on the bishops' benches, when John Wesley started out.

The pulpits of the parish churches were soon forbidden to the Wesleys, to Whitefield and the other Methodists, and they preached in the open air to congregations of tens of thousands ; they preached in prisons, they appealed to the most miserable and the most degraded, they were often insulted, often assaulted. Wesley himself was once nearly killed. But they went on.

There was one immense difference between Wesley and St. Francis. The saint of Assisi went out into the highways and the by-ways and made simple men laugh. He was the apostle of gay happiness. Wesley made men howl. The Methodists moved their hearers to repentance by the fear of hell. The conviction of sin that preceded " conversion " was in fact the terror of endless torture which the preachers in burning words warned sinners would be their lot.

Wesley was repeating sound doctrine when he taught that all men may be saved. His insistence that the way of salvation was through hysterical public confession and instantaneous " new birth " was a novelty in England and it could only have had its great popular appeal at a time of social degradation, with the Church forgetful of its traditions and indifferent to its mission. Being " saved " with the accompanying spiritual exhibitionism was a thrilling experience in dull, sordid and unimaginative lives. That was true when Wesley preached in the eighteenth century. It was true when Booth preached in the nineteenth century slums.

It is difficult to determine how far the Wesleys influenced the Church from which they never seceded. It is often said that Wesley was the precursor of the Evangelical revival in the Church at the end of the eighteenth century and the beginning of the nineteenth. In fact, the Evangelicals were " modified Calvinists." They did not insist on the " new birth." They had no sympathy with the extravagances of Methodist conversions. And they had little of Wesley's concern for the poor at their own doorsteps.

To the Latitudinarians who prevailed in the Church during his lifetime, Wesley was an unpleasant eccentric. Bishop Butler, the greatest of them, found any sort of religious enthusiasm revolting and in an interview with Wesley he described the claim to the extraordinary gifts of the Holy Spirit as " a horrid thing, sir, a very horrid thing." And Johnson, the God-fearing High Churchman, was of the same opinion. Boswell records :

> " Speaking of the inward light to which some Methodists pretended, he said, it was a principle utterly incompatible with social or civil security. ' If a man,' said he, ' pretends to a principle of action of which I can know nothing, nay, not so much as that he has it, but only that he pretends to it ; how can I tell what that person may be prompted to do ? When a person professes to be governed by a written ascertained law, I can then know where to find it.' "

This is the characteristic Johnsonian common sense criticism of all " fancy religions."

In the reign of George II, church patronage was to a considerable extent controlled by Queen Caroline, a lady of genuine culture at a time when culture was, as Chesterfield has recorded, generally despised. She corresponded with Liebnitz ; she was the patron of Handel ; she saved Richard

Savage, the poet, from the gallows. In religion she was a Liberal Protestant and she had refused to marry the Emperor Charles because he was a Catholic. Gay wrote of her :

" The pomp of titles easy faith might shake ;
    She scorned an empire for religion's sake."

Butler and Berkeley both owed preferment to the Queen, and she secured the appointment of men of learning and character to more than one bishopric. But after her death, Church patronage was blatantly used to reward political service or was reserved for men with a family pull, who were innocent of any vestige of the religious enthusiasm that the secular rulers found offensive.

As a matter of fact, even while the Queen lived, Walpole had the last word in important ecclesiastical preferments, and he was one of the queerest men ever to have been a bishop maker. He lived in open adultery. " The gross sensuality of his conversation was conspicuous in one of the coarsest periods of English history ; politics and obscenity were his tastes." He governed by corruption. He bribed the King, the Queen, and the Dissenters, and he bought Parliament. He, himself, explained his method of selecting bishops :

> " I would no more employ a man to govern and influence the clergy who did not flatter the parsons, or who either talked, wrote or acted against their authority, their profits or their privileges, than I would try to govern the soldiery by setting a general over them who was always haranguing against the inconveniences of a standing army, or make a man Chancellor who was constantly complaining or threatening to rectify the abuses of Westminster Hall."

It was Walpole who translated Potter from Oxford to Canterbury, though his claims to the Primacy had been urged by the Queen. When Archbishop Wake died, in 1737, it was generally supposed that he would be succeeded by Gibson, the Bishop of London, a man of courage and character of whom even Walpole stood in some awe. But Potter was successfully recommended to Walpole by Lord Hervey. " Sure, sir," he said, " you have had enough of great genuises ; why can you not take some Greek and

Hebrew blockhead that has learning enough to justify the preferment and not sense enough to make you repent it ? " There is no reason to suppose that Walpole ever had any cause to repent his choice.

Potter vastly enjoyed his new position. " When he became Archbishop, not only did he assume a high and pontifical state—having, for instance, half-a-dozen bareheaded footmen by the side of his coach—but also became a courtier in his own ways, and fond of gross flattery in others." Following the habit of his patron, he looked after the interests of his friends and relations. His son-in-law was particularly lucky.

" His Grace obtained for him from the Crown the united rectories of St. Edmund the King and St. Nicholas Axon in Lombard Street, with that of Merstham, Surrey, and the sinecure of West Tarring in Sussex. From the chantorship of Exeter he was promoted to the deanery of that Cathedral. All these preferments he held till his death except that of West Tarring, which he resigned, a few years before, to his son."

Potter was a good, easy man. He was all for a quiet life. He was a good Whig. Otherwise he would never have been allowed by Walpole to go to Canterbury. And he was a mild High Churchman. " He was a good specimen of the prelates of his day " say the ecclesiastical historians of the century, " learned, scholarly, and eminently respectable, but rather slow and not inspiring." If it happened that in 1739 the Archbishop had a gossip with him, while he was journeying in his coach with its escort of running footmen, and he was told of the scene that had taken place at a " love feast " in the Methodist hall in Fetter Lane, at which Whitfield and the two Wesleys were present, His Grace, with his devotion to propriety and decorum, must assuredly have been extremely shocked. Miss Bowen has described what happened :

"After hours of prayer, groans, cries and sobs, in the stale air of the gloomy meeting room—there were sixty brethren besides the leaders present—a wave of hysteria swept over the gathering ; the half crazed men turned to one another with shouts and cries, many fell in convulsions on the dusty floor ; the coarse, yellow lamplight shone on contorted faces and foaming lips. John, unaffected himself, stared in awe and amazement, then exclaimed in words that all repeated : ' We praise Thee, O God ; we acknowledge Thee to be the Lord.' "

But while the Archbishop must have shuddered at Wesley, he never condemned him. He does not seem ever to have condemned anyone. He wanted to be at peace with all the world. Moreover, he never forgot that he had ordained Wesley ; he was always very friendly to him, and he once, so Wesley related, gave him good advice. " If you desire to be extensively useful, do not spend your time and strength in contending for or against such things as are of a disputable nature, but in testifying against open vice, and in promoting holiness." It was the advice that came naturally from a man who hated trouble, though the Archbishop, himself, carefully avoided testifying against open vice in high places. Wesley was of a different mettle. He contended, notably with Whitfield, in matters of a disputable nature; he denounced vice and in his own way he endeavoured to promote holiness, counting himself holy.

Potter died in 1747. Wesley died in 1791 at the age of eighty-nine. But thirty years before, the Methodists had definitely broken with the Church, the lay preachers taking it upon themselves to administer the Sacraments. In the same year, 1761, the highly respectable George III became King. The era of coarse Teutonic vice came to an end, and the evangelical movement, encouraged by the novelty of a moral if exceedingly dull court, began to affect the life of the Church. Clerical abuses continued for a time. The first Archbishop appointed in the new reign, Frederick Cornwallis, was as tolerant as Potter and much more self-indulgent. His wife was a leader of fashion, " who eclipsed everybody by the splendour and magnificence of her equipages and her entertainments," and the balls given by the lady at Lambeth Palace brought a severe reprimand from the King. He wrote to the Archbishop :

" I hold these levities and vain dissipations as utterly inexpedient, if not unlawful, to pass in a residence for many centuries devoted to divine studies, religious retirement, and the extensive exercise of charity and benevolence—a place where so many of your predecessors have led their lives in such sanctity as has thrown lustre on the pure religion they professed and adorned. I trust you will suppress them immediately, so that I may not have occasion to show any further marks of my displeasure or to interpose in a different manner."

Cornwallis was succeeded by John Moore, the son of a grazier, a simple cautious man, much more to the heart of King George, and another chapter in the history of the Church may be regarded as having begun.

CHAPTER VI

THE HIGH CHURCHMAN

JOHN WESLEY was a man of great and varied ability. He was a born leader and a first-rate organiser. He had, indeed, the qualities that, if he could have curbed his histrionic extravagances, might have made him the distinguished head of the Church, which he never left, at a time when its leaders were tepid half-believers. As it was, he was the creator of what has become the most powerful of the English-speaking Protestant sects. With all the other Protestant bodies, Methodism has become mainly a middle class society, but, at the beginning, it was the religion of the poor and it is not to be forgotten that the most effective leaders of the Labour Party at the beginning of this century were recruited from Methodist local preachers.

Unlike the Wesleys, George Whitefield had his following from what he himself called (he was a shocking snob) " tip-top gentility." He was financed by the Countess of Huntingdon, and listening to his sermons was a fashionable diversion. Whitefield, far more than Wesley, was the father of the evangelical movement that flourished in the Church of England (so far as anything flourished in it) from the accession of George III. Its theology was Whitefield's modified Calvinism, not Wesley's humane Arminianism.

The revival was confined to the well-to-do. It never touched the imagination of the poor, though it endeavoured to dragoon them into unnatural Puritanism. It encouraged a narrow self-satisfied individualistic piety well illustrated by an incident in the life of Toplady, remembered as the author of the hymn, " Rock of Ages cleft for me." Toplady exchanged a living with a friend and soon afterwards the vicarage was burned down and all his friend's goods were destroyed. And Toplady gratefully recorded in his diary : " What a providential mercy was it that I resigned the living before this misfortune happened. O God, how wise and how gracious art Thou in all Thy ways ! "

The most conspicuous of the evangelical clergy was Charles Simeon, who lived almost the whole of a long and ascetic life in King's College, Cambridge, preaching to undergraduates with occasional visits to adjacent villages with the object of " humbling the sinner, exalting the Saviour, promoting holiness." The " classism " of Simeon's gospel is indicated by the grace that he habitually said before breakfast : " We pray not ourselves alone but also for the poor ignorant creatures who wait behind our chairs." Macaulay says of Simeon : " If you knew what his authority was, and how it extended from Cambridge to the most remote corners of England, you would allow that his real sway over the Church was far greater than that of any primate." But there was no preferment for Simeon. Indeed, his devotion was resented by authority.

Almost the only bishop who was sympathetic with the Evangelical revival was Beilby Porteus, Bishop of London, who vastly annoyed George III by objecting to the band playing on the terrace at Windsor Castle on Sunday afternoons.

The Evangelical laity were more distinguished than the clergy—Hannah More, Cowper and the Unwins at Olney, Wilberforce and the Clapham sect—and there is, therefore, considerable interest in the clergyman who had most influence with them. He was a strange person, John Newton, who was responsible for Wilberforce's " conversion " and for the beginning of Cowper's long residence at Olney, and who was Hannah More's spiritual adviser. Newton was the son of a master mariner. He went to sea when he was a boy of twelve, and was the captain of a slave ship when he was suddenly converted. Mr. R. Coupland, the biographer of Wilberforce, naively says :

" Oddly enough the transformation of his beliefs and his morals brought with them no sense of repugnance to his occupation. On one side of a partition in his ship the slaves lay packed in chains, many of them dying, all of them in appalling filth and discomfort, while on the other side, from time to time, the lord and master of the infernal vessel conducted the prayers of his European crew."

Subsequently, with some difficulty, Newton obtained Holy

Orders and was for sixteen years the curate of Olney, where he was cordially disliked by the majority of his parishioners. Among his other proceedings was the habit of regularly preaching at the village fair. " Sometimes," he wrote, " I depreciate the wares and objects of the fair, and endeavour to convince them that all is vanity and vexation of spirit, in comparison to what is set forth to view and to sale, without money or price, in the ordinances of the Gospel ; but alas I have the fewest spectators and the fewest buyers."

Hannah More was more susceptible to the ex-slaver than the Olney villagers. She was converted by him when she was a woman of thirty-six, after having been a close friend of David Garrick, for whom she wrote a play that was produced at Covent Garden. Johnson grossly over-praised Hannah More's verse, but he found the lady's habit of fulsome flattery distinctly irritating. " She is in the right to flatter Garrick," he said to Boswell, " first because she has the world with her and secondly because she is rewarded for it by Garrick. Why should she flatter me ? I can do nothing for her. Let her carry her praise to a better market."

To Newton she was a brand plucked from the burning. Under his influence she devoted herself to practical and exceedingly arrogant philanthropy and to the writing of religious tracts—one had a circulation of two millions—in which she taught the poor " in most ingenious rhetoric to rely on the virtues of content, sobriety, humility, industry, reverence for the British constitution, hatred of the French, trust in God and in the kindness of the gentry." This was the religion of Wilberforce and the Clapham sect.

Wilberforce was able, sincere and rich. He has his honourable place in English history for the part he played in the anti-slavery agitation. He was the intimate friend of Pitt and might have held the highest offices in the State if he had not largely abandoned politics for philanthropy. But he was hated by Cobbett, denounced by Hazlitt and jeered at by Sydney Smith and not without reason.

The English comfortable classes were terrorised by the French Revolution, which they supposed was a proletarian and not, as it was, a *bourgeois* rising. They knew, though they tried to forget, that the English people were suffering grievously from the Corn Laws, from the Enclosures Acts, from low wages and increasing unemployment. They were fearful of Jacobin outrages and the destruction of property. Jacobinism was a nightmare in St. James's in the seventeen nineties as Bolshevism was in Mayfair and the City after 1917.

The war against the Bourbons was, so they believed, a war against the Church. There were scores of emigrant French priests in England to justify the belief, and, again as in Russia one hundred and twenty-eight years later, religion seemed to be threatened with property and Wilberforce and his pious Clapham friends were convinced that the rich Englishman's neglect of personal religion was bringing on him the divine wrath and that, if he did not repent, the rich Englishman would lose his property if he did not also lose his head. Wilberforce wrote in 1792 :

> " I will frankly own that I entertain rather gloomy apprehensions con-cerning the state of the country. Not that I fear any speedy commotion —of this I own I see no danger. Almost every man of property in the kingdom is, of course, the friend of civil order, and if a few mad-headed professors of liberty and equality were to attempt to bring their theories into practice, they would be crushed in an instant. But yet I foresee a gathering storm, and I cannot help fearing that a country which, like this, has so long been blessed beyond all example with every spiritual and temporal good, will incur those judgments of an incensed God which in the prophets are often denounced against those who forget the Author of their mercies."

The dwellers in the London stews and the village hovels had few temporal mercies for which to be thankful and, therefore, little to lose from the wrath of God. But in the commodious mansions on Clapham Common there was an ample excuse for believing that England had been " blessed beyond all example," and it was to the rich that the call to repentance was properly made. Since the poor had nothing to lose why should they bother to repent ?

Wilberforce accordingly wrote a tract with the formidable title, " A Practical View of the Prevailing Religious System of Professed Christians in the Higher and Middle Classes contrasted with Real Christianity." Society, wrote Wilber-force, is condemned for its " utter forgetfulness of its being the great business of life to secure our admission into heaven and to prepare our hearts for its service and enjoyments." England, that is Clapham Common, was " much indebted " to the commercial spirit, and they who benefitted from commercial success should be liberal and beneficent. At the same time, true religion, he declared,

> " . . . renders the inequalities of the social state less galling to the lower orders whom she also instructs in their turn, to be diligent, humble and patient : reminding them that their lowly path has been allotted to them by the hand of God ; that it is their part faithfully to discharge its duties contentedly to bear its inconveniences ; that the present state of things is very short ; that the peace of mind which religion offers indiscriminately to all ranks affords a more true satisfaction than all the expensive pleasures which are beyond the poor man's reach."

This nauseous smugness would have been less offensive if it had been mere hypocrisy. The very devil of it was that it was the sincere belief of a good and kindly man. He recognised that hunger, ignorance, filth and insecurity were mightily " inconvenient," but the inconvenience will soon be over.

> A few more toils, a few more tears,
> And we shall weep no more.

Wilberforce urged that everything should be done to insure the poor felicity in the world to come in the hope that the assurance would prevent them from being a nuisance in this world. He supported the demand for the building of more churches after the French Revolution, where Arthur Young pointed out the poor may " learn the doctrines of that truly excellent religion which exhorts to content and to submission to the higher powers."

Wilberforce urged his comfortable friends to mend their ways and fervently prayed for their conversion. But he tried to compel the poor to abandon their naughtiness. To this end he started the Society for the Suppression of Vice, which excited Syndey Smith's righteous scorn. Smith described the Society as " a corporation of informers, supported by large contributions," intent on suppressing not the vices of the rich, but the pleasures of the poor, on reducing their life " to its regular standard of decorum," while " the gambling houses of St. James's remain untouched."

Wilberforce spent his life in fighting for liberty for heathen blacks. He cared nothing for the liberty or the earthly content of Christian whites. He bitterly opposed the first Trade Unions, " as tending," his biographer says, " to force up wages to the detriment of trade." Trade unions would have been politically dangerous. They might cause the workers to forget the lowly estate ordained for them by Almighty God and the Paris Terror might be repeated in London. If, too, it were once admitted that " the inequality of property " is wrong, the next step would be the attack on Christianity ! The English poor must not be allowed to suppose that their earthly lots could be materially improved. He wrote :

> " I declare my greatest cause of difference with the democrats is their laying and causing the people to lay so great a stress on the concerns of this world as to occupy their whole minds and hearts and to leave a few scanty and lukewarm thoughts for the heavenly treasure."

Lazarus must endure his hunger and his sores or he will never have his place in Abraham's bosom. No wonder that Cobbett, who hated humbug with all his rugged English soul, regarded Wilberforce as a mere hypocrite, and there was ample excuse for Hazlitt's assertion that Mr. Wilberforce " would willingly serve two masters, God and Mammon."

Wilberforce was in the fullest sense the heir of the Puritanism that has alienated the mass of the English people from the Church. He denied himself the cakes and ale. He avoided all " earthly amusements." And he endeavoured to rob the poor of their few miserable opportunities for laughter and amusement while urging them to degrading content. The evangelical revival made the Church of England at the end of the eighteenth century the Church of the classes more definitely than it had ever been before. For all his good intention, Wilberforce represents the complete surrender of the instrument of God into the hands of Mammon. Wilberforce and his fellows stood for property and piety as Prynne and Pym and Hampden had stood for them.

It would be an exaggeration to say that the life of William Cowper, " the saddest and sweetest life in English literature," was primarily saddened by the dour teaching of the Evangelicals, for he had had his first attack of madness before he met the dreadful Mr. Newton, but George Sampson is justified when he writes : " Newton's influence upon an ill-balanced mind always inclined towards religion and suicidal mania was thoroughly evil : Cowper became assured of his eternal perdition." Other men and women less gifted than Cowper, but of the same sensitive character, have had their lives warped and made miserable by hell fire Christianity. Love is the note of Cowper's poetry. He had both exquisite tenderness of feeling and a great sense of fun, but his religion encouraged his morbidity. He was persuaded that hearts are made only to be broken.

> O make this heart rejoice or ache,
>   Decide this doubt for me ;
> And if it be not broken, break,
>   And heal it, if it be.

George Crabbe, the parson-poet, was outside the inner Evangelical circle, but he, too, was impressed by the theory that a man's life on earth can be nothing but a wearing pilgrimage. But Crabbe is remembered by his realistic description of rural life in " The Village," of which Johnson warmly approved. " Its sentiments as to the false notions of rustic happiness and virtue were quite congenial with his own."

Though the Evangelical movement, with its crudities and exaggerations, was the only spiritually alive influence in the Church until Keble preached the famous Assize sermon in 1833, it never represented more than a small minority of the clergy and the well-to-do laity. The prevailing churchman-ship was represented by Burke and it only became more than formal subscription when it was believed that the Church was a bulwark against revolution, and the nation was summoned to rally round " the altar and the throne." Burke is said to have been greatly edified by Wilberforce's " Practical View," but he had none of Wilberforce's religious enthusiasm.

Burke was a pure Erastian. Religion was necessary for political stability. The Church existed for the preservation of the State. He wrote in his *Reflections on the Revolution in France :*

" They (the people of England) do not consider their Church Establishment as convenient, but as essential to their State ; not as a thing heterogeneous and separable—something added for accommodation—what they either keep or lay aside, according to their temporary ideas of convenience. They consider it as the foundation of their whole constitution, with which and with every part of which, it holds an indissoluble union. Church and State are ideas inseparable in their minds, and scarcely is the one mentioned without mentioning the other."

This is the theory, accepted by nineteenth century Erastians, that the function of the Church is to assist the maintenance of law and order. Burke opposed the repeal of the Test and Corporation Acts because "it was not the time to weaken the safeguards of the Established Church," not because the Church's spiritual activities might be hindered but because she might be a less effective ally of the established political order.

But while the Laudian tradition had been almost lost in a welter of Latitudinarianism, Erastianism and individualistic piety, it was cherished by a minority of whom Johnson was the most famous example. To Johnson the Church of England was the Church Catholic. He resented the State domination. He warmly advocated the recalling of Convocation. He insisted on regard for the creeds. He held the offices of bishop and priest in high regard. " I do not envy a clergyman's life as an easy life, nor do I envy the clergyman who makes it an easy one." He ridiculed the common Protestant claim that every individual, even the least instructed, has the right to interpret Holy Scripture for himself. He described the New Testament as " the most difficult book in the world for which the study of a life is required." He defended the expulsion of six Methodist undergraduates from Oxford for persisting in "publicly praying and exhorting." They were at the university to be taught, not to presume to teach, and when Boswell suggested that they were very good young men, Johnson snorted, " a cow is a very good animal in the field, but we turn her out of a garden."

He refused to go into a Protestant chapel even in Scotland, where he was invited to listen to a sermon by Principal Robertson. " I will hear him," he said, " if he will get up into a tree and preach ; but I will not give a sanction, by my presence, to a Presbyterian assembly." Johnson's own prayers were humble, fervent and often beautifully phrased, but he himself declared that he knew of no good prayers but those in the Book of Common Prayer.

He was a moderate Sabbatarian. " Sunday should be different to another day. People may walk but not throw stones at birds. There may be relaxation, but there should be no levity." Believing in religious authority and guidance in training in the faith, he was sceptical as to the value of of death-bed religion. " A man who has never had religion before no more grows religious when he is sick than a man who has never learned figures can count when he has need of calculation."

Johnson had no sympathy with the prevailing anti-Romanism, which Wesley condoned if he did not encourage, and which led to the Gordon riots in 1780. He said that he preferred the Popish to the Presbyterian religion since the Presbyterians had no " apostolical ordination." His attitude to Catholic doctrine and practice is indicated by the following quotation from Boswell :

" I proceeded : ' What do you think, Sir, of purgatory as believed by Roman Catholics ? ' Johnson : ' Why, Sir, it is a very harmless doctrine They are of opinion that the generality of mankind are neither so obstinately wicked as to deserve everlasting punishment, or so good as to merit being admitted into the society of blessed spirits ; and therefore that God is graciously pleased to allow of a middle state, where they may be purified by certain degrees of suffering. You see, Sir, there is nothing unreasonable in this.' Boswell : ' But then, Sir, their masses for the dead ? ' Johnson : ' Why, Sir, if it be once established that there are souls in purgatory, it is as proper to pray for them, as for our brethren who are yet in this life.' Boswell : ' The idolatry of the mass ? ' Johnson : ' Sir, there is no idolatry in the mass. They believe God to be there, and they adore Him.' Boswell : ' The worship of saints ? ' Johnson : ' Sir, they do not worship saints ; they invoke them ; they only ask their prayers. I am talking all this time of the doctrines of the Church of Rome I grant. you that in practice, purgatory is made a lucrative imposition, and that the people do become idolatrous as they recommend themselves to the tutelary protection of particular saints. I think their giving the sacrament only in one kind is criminal, because it is contrary to the express institution of Christ and I wonder how the Council of Trent admitted it.' Boswell : ' Confession ? ' Johnson : ' Why, I don't know but that it a good thing. The Scripture says, Confess your faults one to another, and the priests confess as well as the laity. Then it must be considered that their absolution is only upon repentance and often upon penance also. You think your sins may be forgiven without penance, upon repentance only.' "

Laud and Andrewes, Pusey and Keble would have approved Johnson's assertion, though they would have been more positive. Anglo-Catholics to-day regard Johnson as one of themselves.

On hearing that an English clergyman had 'verted to Rome, Johnson exclaimed, " God bless him," and he went on :

"A good man of a timorous disposition, in great doubt of his acceptance with God, and pretty credulous, may be glad to be of a church where there are so many helps to get to heaven. I would be a papist if I could. I have fear enough ; but an obstinate rationality prevents me. I shall never be a papist, unless on the near approach of death, of which I have a very great terror."

Johnson had a reverent understanding of the religious life. " I never read of a hermit, but in imagination I kiss his feet : never of a monastery, but I could fall on my knees and kiss the pavement." Strong Church of England man as he was, with the belief in the valid Apostolic orders of her priests and the validity of her sacraments, Johnson had a far greater toleration than either the Evangelicals or the Latitudinarians of his time. " For my part, Sir, I think that all Christians, whether Papists or Protestants, agree in the essential articles, and that their differences are trivial and rather political than religious." So far as the Church of England and the Church of Rome are concerned that is truer today even than it was in the eighteenth century.

The foregoing extracts from Boswell show that in the years of religious extravagance on the one side and indifferentism on the other, the Laudian tradition continued. In Johnson's case—and this must be true of many of his contemporaries—religious conviction affected political opinion. Because he regarded bishops as divinely commissioned, he held, too, the Divine appointment of the anointed king, and it was hard to suppose that the Hanoverians had any such approval. Johnson admired George III. He thought him " the finest gentleman I have ever known." He was grateful for the pension that had made his life easy. But he was a Jacobite at heart.

> "A Jacobite, Sir, believes in the divine right of kings. He that believes in the divine right of kings believes in a divinity. A Jacobite believes in the divine right of bishops. He that believes in the divine right of bishops believes in the divine authority of the Christian religion. Therefore, Sir, a Jacobite is neither an atheist nor a diest. That cannot be said of a Whig ; for Whiggism is a negation of all principle."

Jacobitism, as a serious political creed, died before Johnson, but his High Church Toryism remained and was the note of the hierarchy certainly until the accession of Queen Victoria. The High Church divines had nothing of Laud's conviction nor of Ken's saintliness. They were slack in their administration, comfortable and easy-going in their lives, and they cordially disliked the pietistic fervour of the Evangelicals. The Evangelicals cared next to nothing for the bodily well-being of the poor, but they were concerned for their souls' salvation. The High Church folk were uninterested in either the bodies or the souls of the majority. They opposed every sort of change and every kind of reform. They stood for " High Church, high Toryism and old port," and they seem to have valued the old port most of all.

During Johnson's life and for some years after, the see of Canterbury was held by nonentities, but William Howley, who became Bishop of London in 1813, and succeeded to the Primacy in 1828, was a man of some parts. He has been described as " an old-fashioned High Churchman," and Canon Ollard says that he was more old fashioned than High Church. He was, indeed, typical of the men generally chosen at the time for ecclesiastical preferment. But though Archbishop Howley carefully avoided any action that might have annoyed the comfortable and never expressed any convictions that might have disturbed the indifferent, his friendships suggest that he had convictions that he was too timid and too time-serving to advertise.

He was on intimate terms with Joshua Watson, a remarkable layman, who may be described as a Catholic-minded Wilberforce. Watson founded the Clapton sect of High Churchmen in imitation of Wilberforce's Clapham sect of Evangelicals. He was a Laudian in his conception of the nature of the Church. He believed in the Apostolic succession and, before the beginning of the Tractarian movement, he held the traditional Anglican doctrine that, in the words of Dr. Darwell Stone, " the consecrated Sacrament is the Body of Christ and that the Eucharist is the sacrificial pleading of Him, Who for our redemption took human life and died and rose again."

Watson's faith saved him from Wilberforce's other-worldliness. It inspired him, indeed, with a zest for social service and he lives in Church history as the founder of the National Society, the Church's instrument for the education of the poor, which founded schools fifty years before elementary education became the concern of the State.

Watson was a link between the churchmen of the school of Johnson and the Tractarian fathers. Pusey wrote to him : " I cannot say how cheering it was to be recognised by you as carrying on the torch which we had received from you and from those of your generation who had remained faithful to the old teaching."

As I have said, it is indicative of Howley's private sympathies that Watson was his friend. Another indication of these sympathies was the Archbishop's appointment of Hugh James Rose as his chaplain. Rose was a sort of John the Baptist to Hurrell Froude and Newman, the latter of whom dedicated a volume of his sermons to him with the words, " To Hugh James Rose, who, when hearts were failing, bade us stir up the strength that was in us and betake ourselves to our true mother."

Howley was a contemporary at Winchester of Sydney Smith, whom, it is related, he " knocked down with a chess board for cheeking him." This, says George Russell, was the only violent action in a timid and gentle life. The association is interesting, since while the future Archbishop was to be recognised as a consistent if compromising High Churchman, Sydney Smith, with his delightful caustic

humour, was the heir of the eighteenth century Latitudinarian
Erastians. He detested religious enthusiasm, jeered at
Methodists and missionaries, accepted the teaching of
Paley and valued the Established Church as the safeguard
of national stability.

From Winchester, Howley went to New College, Oxford,
and when he was forty-three, he became Regius Professor of
Divinity—" his scholarship is said to have been admirable,
but he never displayed it," says George Russell—with the
comfortable addition of three substantial livings. And so,
in due course, to the bishopric of London. In the House
of Lords Howley demonstrated his High Church Toryism
by vigorously supporting the Bill of Pains and Penalties
against Queen Caroline, the unfortunate wife of George IV,
on the grounds that " the King can do no wrong either
morally or politically." Johnson would probably have
agreed with him, but it must have been a difficult doctrine
for a churchman to defend when the King was a notorious
debauchee and a political blunderer.

George was not ungrateful. He always knew how to
placate the pious, on one occasion earning the warm apprecia-
tion of Wilberforce by denouncing Cobbett's " infidelity,"
and it was the sovereign himself who secured the Primacy
for Howley. It was odd that a man, who held the traditional
regard for high ecclesiastical office, should have been enthroned at Canterbury by proxy for which he was sternly
reproved by Sydney Smith, who may not have forgotten the
incident of the chess board. Smith wrote :

> "A proxy sent down in the Canterbury fly, to take the Creator to witness
> that the Archbishop, detained in town by business or pleasure, will never
> violate that foundation of piety over which he presides—all this seems to
> me an act of the most extraordinary indolence ever recorded in history.

Howley was the last Prince-Archbishop of Canterbury,
with a princely income which on his death was reduced by
the Ecclesiastical Commissioners to £15,000 a year. There
were regular stately banquets at Lambeth to which the
guests invited themselves and " the domestics of the Prelacy
stood, with swords and bag-wigs, round pig and turkey and
venison." The Archbishop always drove out in a coach and

four. No woman was allowed in the official apartments of the Palace, and in the evening, after the chapel service, the Archbishop crossed the courtyard to " Mrs. Howley's lodgings," preceded by footmen carrying flambeaux.

But with all this splendour, Howley retained a simplicity of character. He enjoyed giving private dinner parties at which Southey and other literary men were sometimes his guests, and the author of the *Memoir of Joshua Watson* says that on these occasions, his guests noted " how capable he was of guiding the conversation into a channel which would call forth the literary powers of his guests, how cultivated a taste he had in old English lore and how he designedly avoided topics of public agitation." The famous Dr. Chalmers was taken to one of the stately entertainments and it was feared that his Presbyterian soul would be shocked by the magnificence. But the Scottish divine agreed that the Archbishop, like the three Israelites, was untouched in the midst of fire. " It is," he said, " as if the smell had passed over him."

Howley was indeed naturally modest and good natured. Gladstone described him as " gentle among the gentle and mild among the mild," and even Sydney Smith paid tribute to his " gentleness, kindness and amiable and high-principled courtesy." It was sometimes his fate to be concerned in heated political and ecclesiastical wrangles, but he shrank from controversy, and he once said that he was often impelled to sustain his soul by repeating the text, " Leave off from wrath, and let go displeasure : fret not thyself, else thou shalt be moved to evil." This mixture of sensitivenes and laziness made him disinclined to give public support even to the good causes of which he approved. He was a good, easy man, never out for trouble.

When he died at the age of eighty-two, Watson wrote that he had found less of human infirmity in the Archbishop than in any man without exception he had ever known, and he referred to " the exquisitely beautiful traits which lay so open to those who lived with Him."

The Archbishop took an active part in the proceedings of the House of Lords. Unlike Dr. Johnson, he had no sympathy with religious tolerance. He led the opposition to the Roman Catholic Relief Bill, and he moved the rejection of the Bill for removing Jewish disabilities. He opposed all political and social changes and he was one of the twenty-one bishops who voted in 1831 against the Reform Bill, the bishops having the support of the bulk of the country clergy. The Radicals indeed declared quite justifiably that there was " a black recruiting sergeant in every village." As a result of the popular indignation against the reactionary action of the Church, the mob burned the bishop's palace in Bristol, and Howley was mobbed in the streets of Canterbury, and was hit in the face by a dead cat, the Archbishop meekly remarking that he was glad that it was not a live cat.

Perhaps because of the cat, Howley changed his mind, and next year he voted for the Reform Bill when it was again introduced into the House of Lords.

Keble's sermon was preached five years before Howley's death. The publication of the Tracts for *The Times* began in the same year. It seems certain that Howley must have heard of what was to be the beginning of a new era in the history of the Church from his chaplain, but there is no evidence that the Archbishop appreciated the significance of the new awakening. Just before his death, however, he joined the protest led by the Tractarians, against the nomination of the heretical Hampden to the see of Hereford, and he declared to the Prime Minister that he would sooner go to the Tower than consecrate him. This is the only recorded instance of Howley's opposition to secular authority. He had before protested that he would never consecrate the equally heretical Arnold, but, as a matter of fact, he was never asked to do so.

In 1841, Howley was partly responsible for the institution of the Jerusalem bishopric, which has its historic interest since it was " one of the three blows which broke Newman and finally shattered his faith in the Anglican Church." The King of Prussia had proposed to the English Government that the two nations should establish and endow an Anglican-Lutheran bishopric in the Holy City, the bishops to be nominated in turn by the Crowns of England and Prussia. Howley introduced a Bill creating the bishopric in the House of Lords and it became law, despite vigorous protests that were supported by *The Times*. In his own solemn protest, Newman insisted that Lutheranism and Calvinism were heresies and that the English Church was admitting heretics to communion without the renunciation of their errors. Newman prayed that " the measure may utterly fail and be as though it had never been," and his prayer was answered. Only one Lutheran, and he was an eccentric Swiss, ever held the bishopric, only two Germans were ever ordained under the scheme, and the treaty was dissolved after eighteen years. But it helped to take Newman to Rome.

As Bishop of London, Howley baptised the Princess Victoria. As Archbishop, he went with the Lord Chamberlain in the early morning to Kensington Palace to announce to the Princess that her uncle was dead and that she was Queen. And he crowned the Queen in Westminster Abbey. But, though he lived for another ten years, he was never a Victorian. There is almost as much fundamental difference between Howley and Tait as there is between Howley and Laud.

I have described Howley as a High Churchman. It has been the common habit to divide English churchmen into High, Broad and Low. The Low are inclined to Calvinism, live in dread of the Scarlet Woman, and are in close sympathy with the Nonconformists, with a general inclination to vote Tory at Parliamentary elections. The Broad were in the Victorian age men like Arnold and Stanley and are now men like Dr. Inge and the Modern Church Unionists, who have always ached to " translate the creeds into modern terms " and whose ideal is that contradiction in terms, an undogmatic religion. High Church, as a descriptive term, fell into disrepute after the Tractarian revival. It represented rejection far more than acceptance. The High Churchmen of the Howley school were repelled by the doctrines of the Calvinists and shocked by the enthusiasm of the Methodists. They certainly did not agree that the Church was only one of the many Protestant sects ; they valued their Orders, not because they derived from the Apostles, but because they assured them a privileged position in the State.

The followers of Keble and Pusey claimed to be Catholics and, after a hundred years, they at last succeeded in persuading *The Times* that their brethren of the Roman allegiance are not the only Catholics in this realm.

But the Church of England remains comprehensive. That is at once its strength and its weakness.

CHAPTER VII

THE ERASTIAN

ARCHBISHOP HOWLEY died in 1848. Archbishop Tait succeeded to the Primacy in 1868. To understand his reign in Canterbury it is necessary to go back to the birth of the Oxford Movement in 1833.

When Keble went into the pulpit of the University Church on July 14th of that year, the Church was discredited, popularly detested and weakened by the influence of men like Thomas Arnold, who scoffed at every aspect of sacramentalism. Its services were casual ; its ministers were, for the most part, indifferent. Its spiritual impact on the nation was a thing of the past. The High Churchmen were described as " two bottle orthodox." The Evangelicals still had their wealthy followers, but their religion, Dean Church says, had become "poor and thin and unreal."

The character of the clergy is suggested in the fiction of the period. In his *Short History of the Oxford Movement*, Canon Ollard says that the clergyman at the Dingley Dell party in the *Pickwick Papers* was " part of the Christmas decorations along with the holly and the mistletoe," and that the clergy in the Jane Austen novels are " amiable and respectable gentlemen, who were satisfied to read morning and afternoon service on a Sunday and to dislike Dissenters." Canon Ollard has collected stories of episcopal methods. The chaplain of Dr. Brownlow North, who was bishop from 1771 to 1830, on one occasion examined two candidates for Holy Orders in a tent on a cricket field while he was waiting for his innings. The chaplain of Dr. John Douglas, who was a bishop from 1787 to 1807 examined candidates while he was shaving. In 1822, George Spencer, son of the then Lord Spencer, who sought ordination in order to take up a family living, wrote to the chaplain of the Bishop of Peterborough to ask what books he should read. The chaplain replied : "As far as I am concerned, it is impossible that I could ever entertain any idea of subjecting a gentleman with whose talents and good qualities I am so well acquainted to any examination except one as a matter of form for which a verse in the Greek Testament and an Article of the Church of England returned into Latin will be amply sufficient." And, Canon Ollard says, it was.

The Oxford Movement was founded by four remarkable men, as saintly as they were learned. John Keble, was the Professor of Poetry at Oxford. George Saintsbury, no mean judge, describes him as " a true poet and a critic of very unusual insight and catholicity." Edward Bouverie Pusey, Regius Professor of Hebrew and Canon of Christ Church, was a man of massive learning, an ascetic and a divine of unbounded devotion. " Something in Pusey's voice always reminded me of something in Shelley's poetry —the colour-key of both being found in moonlight," wrote Saintsbury. Newman, that always harassed saint, was among other things one of the great masters of English prose. The fourth leader, Richard Hurrell Froude, the brother of J. A. Froude, who died when he was thirty-two, was an extremely handsome young man, a good sailor, a fine rider, a brilliant conversationalist, a hater of shams and humbug, and a devoted Christian. With all this, Froude was given to humorous indiscretions that were sometimes an embarrassment to his friends, as when he said that there was little good to be recorded of Cranmer except that he burned well. These were the men who nearly set the English Church alight.

The most distinguished lay adherent of the Oxford Movement was W. E. Gladstone, and, as I have suggested that Dr. Johnson represents all the little that was good in the English Church in the eighteenth century, so Gladstone is the finest example of the English Church laity in the nineteenth. It was the moral issues that were his concern as politician and statesman. When he was stirred to righteous wrath by the Balkan atrocities he was regardless of political expediency in his denunciation of the unspeakable Turk. When, as an old man, he was convinced that the British government of Ireland was morally wrong, he spent himself in the struggle to give Ireland self-government. For a generation he brought moral fervour into the world of secular affairs. This gives Gladstone his pre-eminent place in modern English history. When he died, moral leadership died with him. In a very few years men of all political parties were more concerned with what was expedient than with what was right. Opportunism replaced principle. Courage was lost ; compromise prevailed.

To-day we are paying the consequences. If Gladstone had been alive in 1933, when Hitler began his systematic torturing of the Jews, the country would have been stirred, from end to end, to indignation by his burning words. Statesmen would have been compelled to much more than mild and polite protests. Hitler would have been stopped in the first stage of his wickedness and Poland and Czecho-slovakia, Russia and France, Greece and Yugoslavia would not have been drenched in blood and tears. But in 1933, " behold there was no man there, neither voice or man," only Simon and Hoare, Baldwin and Chamberlain.

In all that he did, Gladstone was inspired by his faith. He was the devout son of the English Church. His religion was the religion of Keble and Pusey. And it is of importance to know what were for him the tenents and teaching of his Church. In a valuable essay in the volume *The Household of Faith*, George Russell, who was one of Gladstone's intimates, has summarised some of his confessions of faith :

Here is what this great English churchman believed :

THE INCARNATION
"All I write, and all I think, and all I hope, is based upon the Divinity of Our Lord—the one central hope of our poor, wayward race."

THE NICENE CREED
" The Creed elaborated at Nicea and Constantinople represented, even more than any other document, the prolonged, concentrated, and most severely-tested action of the mind of the Universal Church. In the last of these particulars it stands alone. It was through the agonies of the fourth century—the hardest of all the trials, the noblest of all the victories, of the Church of God—that this Creed made its way to a position unrivalled alike in loftiness and in solidity. In the East it may be said to enjoy an exclusive dominance. In the West, through the Eucharistic Office, it holds the grandest of all position in Christian worship."

THE HOLY CATHOLIC CHURCH
" No doubt (as I for one believe) the Church began with a clergy ; nay, began in a clergy. It had its centre of life and of self-propagating power

in the Apostolic College, which gradually called into being those orders that form the full equipment of the Christian Ministry."

THE APOSTOLIC SUCCESSION

" The Bishop conveys the power of administering Sacraments, whereby the Church is constantly replenished with children ; of ordaining Priests, by whom Sacraments are administered ; and of consecrating Bishops, by whom in turn these powers may be communicated anew to others, who may replace the actual holders, and hand them on from one generation to another. In this line, therefore, alone it is that the effectual principle of continued propagation is carried down from the Apostles of Christ to the latest age."

THE CHURCH OF ENGLAND

" In England . . . the course of events was widely different (from that on the Continent). Her Reformation, through the Providence of God, succeeded in maintaining the Unity and Continuity of the Church in her Apostolical Ministry. We have, therefore, still among us the ordained hereditary witnesses of the truth, conveying it to us through an unbroken series, from our Lord Jesus Christ and His Apostles. This is to us the ordinary voice of Authority ; of authority equally reasonable and equally true, whether we will hear or whether we will forbear ; of authority, which does not supersede either the exercise of private judgment, or the sense of the Church at large, or the supremacy of the Scripture ; but assists the first, locally applies the second, and publicly witnesses to the last.

" She (the Church of England) gives credibility to her doctrines, and clear authority to her ministrations, but the fact that she teaches no articles of faith but such as have been drawn out of Scripture by the universal consent of the Church from the beginning, and that she is to this day historically the same institution through which the Gospel was originally preached to the English nation—preached then, and it is preached now, by the ascertained commission of the Apostles of Christ, and through them by the Will of Christ Himself."

HOLY BAPTISM

"A spiritual power and operation belong to Baptism. The exercise of a spiritual power, whose office it specifically is to impart a principle of spiritual life."

THE HOLY COMMUNION

"As regards the Holy Communion, our Church teaches a similar doctrine. She does not feel that the solemn words of the Institution of the Eucharist are adequately, that is Scripturally, represented by any explanation which resolves them into mere figure. . . . She believes that there is a real, though not carnal, truth in the solemn words, THIS IS MY BODY, and THIS IS MY BLOOD ; in just conformity with the precept in which St. Paul desires us to discern, that is discriminate from common elements, the Body and Blood of the Lord. . . . Here is also comprised the idea of a spiritual power feeding that new life, which we have in the Church or body of Jesus Christ our Redeemer, and which was first given us at our Baptism, when we became by covenant, whether for good or evil, members of that Church or body.

" The word preached is mingled with human imperfection ; whereas That which is received in the Sacrament is wholly Divine."

PURGATORY

" The strong and just reaction from the Purgatorial system prevailing in the Latin Church of the period (the Reformation) went far to account for, and even excuse, that stark and rigid conception of the effect of death on the state of the human being, which led to an abandonment of the uniform practice of the earliest ages of the Church, as testified by the Liturgies, in the commendation of the Faithful Departed to God for an increase of their rest and peace. But what caused—nay, even what might excuse—the violence thus done to Nature as well as to Religion did not frustrate its mischievous effects in narrowing the range of Christian sympathies, and establishing an anomaly in the general doctrine of prayer. With the obscuration of an universal tradition, there came indeed manifold confusion of doctrine ; the Final judgment, with its solemn import, seemed to have no place left for it when the Intermediate State of Souls had been reduced almost to a cypher. Worst of all, the new standard appeared to be in hopeless conflict with the widest experience ; for it implied that the entire work of discipline was in every case fully accomplished on this side of the grave—that every soul passed away into the unseen in a state of ripeness for a final destiny of bliss or woe."

Like Johnson, Gladstone was appreciative of the Roman Church, but he was alive to the many Roman abuses. He was an Anglican Catholic. He believed that the ordained priest has ghostly authority to grant absolution to the penitent, but George Russell says that " nothing is more conspicuous in his writings on the grave subject of repentance than his apprehension lest spiritual laziness should lead people to substitute a merely mechanical process for the saving realities of heart-searching and self-abasement."

With Gore and the present Archbishop of Canterbury, Gladstone rejected the awful doctrine of eternal punishment. He believed in conditional immortality, which he contended does not conflict with the Catholic creeds. He was a reasonable Sabbatarian. " Sunday should be reserved for religious employment." He cared very little for ritual. " No ritual is too much, provided it is subsidiary to the inner work of worship ; all ritual is too much unless it ministers to that purpose." Erastianism was to Gladstone the accursed things he wrote in 1876 :

" If we follow the Erastian idea, it does not matter what God we worship, or how we worship Him, provided we derive both relief and worship from the civil ruler, or hold them subject to his orders. Many most respectable persons have been, or have thought themselves to be, Erastians, but the system, in the developments of which it is capable, is among the most debased ever known to man."

Father Figgis has defined Erastianism :

" Its later developments are due partly to Selden and Hobbes, partly to the growth of toleration. Selden asks : ' Whether is the Church or the Scripture the judge of religion ? ' and replies,' In truth neither, but the State.' This is precisely the view of Hobbes and would make all religious truth the sport of political expediency. . . . With the development of toleration, Parliament has come to consist of men of all religions and of none. Modern Erastianism claims the right of a body so composed to adjudicate on matters of belief either in person or by deputy, and would allow ecclesiastical causes to be decided by civil judges, who might everyone of them be agnostics."

Accepting this definition and all that it implies, it is not unfair to describe Archibald Campbell Tait, Bishop of London in 1856 and Archbishop of Canterbury from 1868 to 1882, as the supreme Erastian. In the years when the English Church, after generations of lifeless apathy, was recovering its birthright and was acquiring vivid spiritual activity, its chief shepherd regarded the Church as a branch of the civil service.

Tait was a capable, stubborn, Scottish Presbyterian, the first Scotsman to be Archbishop of Canterbury. He established a precedent. Two of his five successors were born north of the Tweed. Tait left the church of his Scottish fathers because in his day the Presbyterian Kirk was still nominally Calvinist and he could not accept the doctrines of Reprobation and Assurance. But on questions concerning the Sacraments, the nature of the Church and the authority of the ministry his views remained Presbyterian until his death, and the bareness of Presbyterian worship appealed to him more than the stately traditional Anglican ritual. It is notorious that Queen Victoria was of the same mind and their agreement was one of the reasons why Tait enjoyed so large a measure of the royal favour and confidence. But as I have said, Tait was above all other things an Erastian. He had made his home in England. He had attained high office in the English Church. He regarded the defence of the Establishment as his first duty to his adopted country and his adopted church.

Tait was born in Edinburgh in 1811. In 1830, he went to Oxford with a Snell Exhibition for Balliol. In 1834, he became a Fellow of Balliol, and as such he was bound to take Holy Orders, which seems to be the only reason why he was ordained. In 1842, he followed the great Arnold as Headmaster of Rugby, and in 1849, he was appointed by Lord John Russell as Dean of Carlisle. Lord John Russell was the determined enemy of the Catholic Revival, and Tait doubtless owed his deanery to the fact that he was one of the four Oxford dons who, eight years earlier, had published a protest against Newman's famous Tract No. 90, in which, so they alleged, Newman had contended that the 39 Articles do not condemn the doctrines of purgatory, the invocation of saints and the Mass. This protest was posted in Oxford in the buttery hatches of all the colleges and at the gates of the schools and aroused a fierce campaign of denunciation, one fiery Protestant declaring that he would be sorry to trust Newman with his purse. The abuse nearly broke Newman's gentle heart. He retired to Littlemore and in 1845 he was received into the Roman Church. And the Carlisle deanery was the first small reward that Tait received for the part he had played in driving from the English Church one of the most splendid of her sons. Other and greater rewards were to follow.

The hunt for the Tractarians was now up. In 1843, Pusey was suspended from preaching in the University for two years for a sermon on the Holy Eucharist. Newman's secession naturally led lesser men to take a similar step. The Gorham judgment in which the Judicial Committee decided that the denial of the doctrine of Baptismal Regeneration was " not contrary or repugnant to the doctrine of the Church of England as by law established " took many others to Rome, including Manning and Archdeacon Wilberforce, one of the sons of the famous Evangelical. But the movement inside the Church did not lack leadership. Pusey and Keble remained faithful to their allegiance and there were new men of distinction, among them Church, afterwards Dean of St. Paul's, and King, afterwards Bishop of Lincoln.

The secessions fanned the No Popery scare, encouraged by Lord John Russell, and, with other persecutions, Archdeacon Denison was charged with the " offence " of teaching the Real Presence, the trial being noteworthy from the fact that the court, over which Archbishop Sumner, Howley's immediate and virulently Protestant successor, presided, specifically repudiated the Eucharistic doctrine taught by Andrewes and Laud. In 1851, the Anti-Catholic party, led by the good Lord Shaftesbury, started the Protestant Alliance, the persecuting zeal of which continues to this day. Its objects were :

> " Not only to oppose the recent aggression of the Pope . . . but ' to maintain and defend, against all the encroachments of Popery the Scriptural doctrines of the Reformation.' This was to be effected (1) ' by awakening British Christians of various classes . . . to regard the interests of Protestantism as the paramount object of their concern ; (2) by uniting the Protestants of the Empire in a firm and persevering demand that the national support and encouragement given to Popery of late years shall be discontinued . . . ; and (3) by extending as far as may be practicable the sympathy and support of British Christians to those in foreign countries who may be suffering oppression for the cause of the Gospel.' "

Tait had taken a leading part in the condemnation of Newman. He was recognised as a leading Evangelical and he was invited to join the Alliance. But the canny Scottish Dean of Carlisle was disinclined for any party entanglements that might interfere with further preferment, and he wrote that in his opinion, " Popery in this country is better met by every Protestant clergyman and layman zealously doing his duty in the position God has assigned to him than by the agitation which seems implied in the formation of a society for the defence of Protestantism."

Apart from his duties as Dean, which he performed with business-like thoroughness, while at Carlisle, Tait was mainly concerned with the Royal Commission, of which he was a member, appointed by Lord John Russell to inquire into " the State, Discipline, Studies and Revenues of the University of Oxford." The appointment of the Commission was opposed by Gladstone, then the member for the University and by the Heads of Colleges, who boycotted its proceedings, but was strongly supported by the Prince Consort. No one will now question that Oxford badly needed reform. The recommendations of the Commission, drawn up by Tait, were embodied in an Act of Parliament passed in 1854 after being vehemently opposed in the Commons by Lord Robert Cecil, afterwards the famous Marquis of Salisbury whose hatred of any interference with the vested interests of " ancient seats of learning " is today inherited by his son, Lord Quickswood. The principal objective of the Commission was to open the University " to a much larger and poorer class than that from which the students are at present almost entirely taken."

Membership of this Commission was the beginning of Tait's public life, and the associations that he made greatly affected his future. The Prince Consort and consequently the Queen recognised that he was largely responsible for the reforms that they desired, and his name was added to the Windsor list. In the work of the Commission, he was in close touch, for the first time, with Stanley, who was its secretary, and with Goldwin Smith, the historian, its assistant-secretary. After subscribing to the popular Victorian undenominational religion, Goldwin Smith repudiated Christianity altogether in his old age. Stanley was " the most absolute Erastian in the Church of England." Lord Bryce has said of Stanley, remembered, of course, as a famous Dean of Westminster :

> " He had two leading ideas : one that the Church of England must at all hazards continue to be an Established Church, in alliance with, or subjection to, the State (for his Erastianism was unqualified), and recognising the Crown as her head ; the other, that she must be a comprehensive Church, finding room in her bosom for every sort and description of Christian, however much or little be believed of the dogmas contained in the Thirty-nine Articles and the Prayer Book, to which she is bound by statute."

Stanley and Tait were closely allied for thirty years. They died within a year of each other. They both had the confidence of the Queen. They shared the same Erastian opinions, and, when they disagreed, it was because Stanley was always courageous and outspoken and Tait always played for safety.

Tait was thirty-nine when he went to Carlisle and he was in bad health, with morbid anticipations of an untimely death. He wrote in his diary in 1853, " In the midst of life we are in death. O God make me ready." " I have often thought that I may soon die. My many bodily ailments, though not perhaps serious, seem to show a very weakly constitution, shattered by illness. Whether Thou callest me soon or late, make me ready." And so on.

At Carlisle, too, Tait suffered a grievous bereavement. Five of his six daughters—the eldest was ten—died of scarlet fever within a month. Five months after this tragedy, Tait was nominated to the bishopric of London by Lord Palmerston, with the warm approval of the Queen. George Russell calls this elevation " sudden and surprising." Tait's biographers ascribe the preferment to Lord Shaftesbury, who regarded the Dean as " very much the best " of the Liberal Latitudinarians, for whom the Prince Consort had a great regard, and they add that not the least of the influences that helped Tait was " the widespread sympathy and interest which had been aroused from the throne downwards by the tragic illness in the Carlisle Deanery." It seems odd to have thought of a bishopric as the balm for personal sorrow.

The biographers admit that " it would not, perhaps, be possible to find another instance in the last half century in which a man with so little training of a technical sort has been placed at one step in a position at once so responsible and so independent." Tait had never sat in Convocation. " About strictly Episcopal work he knew nothing." He knew nothing of the great diocese that he was chosen to rule. George Russell asserts, indeed, that he never really knew the England in which he was to become the chief ecclesiastical figure. " He never took root in it—never thoroughly understood the English people in some of their moods and tenses ; never quite comprehended the thought, on some important topics, of those with whom he worked or over whom he bore rule." Scottish Tait was part of the price that the English Church has paid for the State connection.

Bishop Blomfield, whom Tait succeeded, was a vigorous prelate, with, as Sydney Smith said, "an ungovernable passion for business," who, during his episcopate consecrated nearly two hundred new churches, but who, according to Dean Church, was "singularly unsure of his own mind." When he was forced by illness to resign the see, it was generally thought that Samuel Wilberforce, by far the most distinguished of the bishops, would be offered London, but Wilberforce was unpopular at the court, and, thanks to the cynical Palmerston and the masterful sovereign, greatness was thrust upon the Dean. Lord Bryce, himself a Scotsman, who vastly admired Tait, has summarised the qualities of the man to whom fortune was so kind. That I may not be thought partisan in my judgment, I quote this judgment of Tait by an admiring Scottish friend :

> "He had no original power as a thinker. He was not a striking preacher, and the more pains he took with his sermons the less interesting did they become. He was so far from being learned that you could say no more of him than that he was a sound scholar and a well-informed man. He was deeply and earnestly pious, but in a quiet, almost dry way, which lacked what is called unction, though it impressed those who were in close contact with him. He showed slight interest either in the historical or in the speculative side of theology. Though a good headmaster, he was not a stimulating teacher. Had he remained all his life in a subordinate position, as a college tutor at Oxford, or as canon of some cathedral, he would have discharged the duties of the position in a thoroughly satisfactory way, and would have acquired influence among his colleagues, but no one would have felt that Fate had dealt unfairly with him in depriving him of some larger career and loftier post. No one, indeed, who knew him when he was a college tutor seems to have predicted the dignities he was destined to attain, although he had shown in the theological strife that then raged at Oxford the courage and independence of his character."

Tait was consecrated on November 23rd, 1856, and on December 4th he did homage to the Queen. Referring to this incident in his diary, he recalls that, when the Bishop of Ripon did homage to William IV, as soon as he had risen from his knees, the King said to him in a loud voice, "Bishop of Ripon, I charge you, as you shall answer to Almighty God, that you never by word or deed give encouragement to those damned Whigs, who would upset the Church of England."

Tait at once began to take a constant part in the House of Lords debates, warmly supporting the Divorce Act of 1857, which abolished the ecclesiastical jurisdiction over marriage and allowed divorce *a vinculo* for the wife's adultery and for the husband's adultery with aggravating circumstances. No clergyman was legally compelled to re-marry the guilty party, but every incumbent was under obligation to allow the use of his church if another clergyman could be found to perform the ceremony.

The Divorce Act was opposed by Gladstone and Wilberforce and, of course, by the Catholic party. Tait's support is indicative of his indifference to the traditional teaching of the Church.

In 1860, the publication of *Essays and Reviews* caused a storm among the Orthodox, both High and Low. The seven writers included Frederick Temple, then the Headmaster of Rugby, Mark Pattison and Jowett. The volume was the expression of religious liberalism. Most of the essays were innocuous, but together they threw the pious High Churchmen and the pious Low Churchmen into a pother of indignation, the pious of both parties being apparently most upset by the cautious suggestion that " a judgment of eternal misery may not be the purpose of God." Wilberforce violently attacked the essayists, Stanley defended them. The Bishops censured the writers. Convocation condemned the publications. Two of the essayists were prosecuted.

Tait kept his head and for once his Scottish caution was of real value. He wrote : " I deeply deplore and indeed execrate the spirit of much of the *Essays and Reviews*." But he equally deplored the spirit of their critics. He detested all extreme men, and his wise conclusion from the controversy was " what is wanted is a deeply religious liberal party ; the great evil is that the liberals are deficient in religion, and the religious are deficient in liberality." The Church had to wait for Charles Gore to supply the leadership that Tait properly believed was needed.

No sooner were *Essays and Reviews* condemned and forgotten than Bishop Colenso, known to schoolboys of my generation for his book on arithmetic, again upset the

Anglican apple-cart. Colenso was consecrated the first Bishop of Natal in 1853. He set the example that has been faithfully followed by the English Church in South Africa of real care for the social welfare of the Zulus in his diocese, to whom he was known as " Father of the People," but he published books of heretical criticism of the Bible and he protested that he could not use the baptismal service because of its reference to the deluge, which he did not believe ever happened. The heterodox are often as silly as the orthodox.

Tait succeeded in preventing a general condemnation of Colenso, but he drew up a letter signed by all the English diocesans, begging him to resign, which he refused to do. He was subsequently tried and condemned by the Bishop of Cape Town, sitting as the Metropolitan of South Africa with very doubtful jurisdiction.

Colenso sat tight in England and did nothing, and when he returned to South Africa he was formally excommunicated. The English bishops, influenced by Tait, refused to recognise the excommunication, and Colenso retained the endowments of his see until his death in 1883.

The Colenso case raised the whole question of the relations of the colonial churches with the English primacy, and Tait addressed the following *questionnaire* to all the bishops, deans and archdeacons of the overseas churches :

> " I desire very much to know what is your feeling, and what you believe to be the feeling both of the clergy and of the laity in your diocese, on the following points :
>
> " *First :* The desirableness, or otherwise, of all Bishops in British Colonies receiving their mission from the See of Canterbury, and taking the oath of canonical obedience to the Archbishop.
>
> " *Second :* Whether it is desirable that there should be an appeal in graver cases from the judgments of Church Courts, or decisions of Bishops or Synods in the Colonies, to any authority at home ; and if so (1) to what authority, (2) under what restrictions ?
>
> " *Third :* How far the Royal Supremacy, as acknowledged by the United Church of England and Ireland, can be maintained in our Colonial Churches.
>
> " *Fourth :* What seems the best guarantee for maintaining unity of doctrine and discipline between the different scattered branches of our Church in the Colonies."

The upshot of the trouble was the calling of the first
Lambeth Conference in 1867, Tait, with his Presbyterian
prejudice urging at the preliminary meeting that " the
Romeward tendency is more dangerous for our clergy than
the tendency to free thought."

The English bishops had no enthusiasm for the Conference. Six of them refused to attend, four others were
conveniently ill. Despite Tait, the Conference, thanks to
the votes of the colonial and American bishops, approved
Colenso's deposition, and the Bishop of Cape Town consecrated a second Bishop of Natal.

It is clear that Tait was mainly influenced in this controversy by his care for the rights of the crown. It was the
State more than the Church for which he was concerned.
This is made clear by a letter published in *The Times*, which
his biographers suggest had Tait's approval :

> " If the notion is sanctioned that the jurisdiction of the Queen is a
> mere vulgar, secular jurisdiction, which must give way, in all graver
> questions, to the jurisdiction of a Bishop or Metropolitan, I believe the
> minds of the Colonists will be perplexed as to their political allegiance,
> and as to their moral duties, I believe the minds of the natives will be
> still more perplexed ; that there will be no continuance of faith among
> the first, and no spread of faith smong the second. . . . (Bishop Gray)
> seeks to establish in his colony one law for the clergy and one for the
> laity—the first to be administered in the name and by the authority of
> the Metropolitan ; the second to be administered in the name and by the
> officers of the Queen. I do not say that these two laws will be equally
> administered. I believe the Queen's officers will struggle, under great
> obstructions, to follow some standard of justice. They will be said to
> obey a secular instinct. The other tribunal will be what such tribunals
> have been in other countries ; what they have already proved themselves
> to be in South Africa. Those who are zealous for the well-being of their
> countrymen and of the heathen among whom they dwell, should ask
> themselves whether they will be parties to so fatal a contradiction. If
> they are, they may expect to see the example which has been afforded by
> the colonies copied here ; in England, a jurisdiction will be restored
> which neither we nor our fathers have been able to bear."

The argument of this letter seems to be that, unless the
spiritual authority is subordinate to the secular, the heathen
will remain in their blindness and the Christians will lose
their faith. I should think that it is extremely likely that
Queen Victoria held this odd belief ; it is hard to suppose

that it was really accepted by the level-headed ecclesiastic whom she trusted.

Colenso and the essayists and reviewers were of secondary importance in Tait's career. The principal preoccupation of his episcopacy at both London and Canterbury was his attempt " to put down ritualism " in the Church of England, and the chief interest in his life today is that, not only, as he himself obviously realised at the end, was the attempt a complete failure, but that all the details of Catholic teaching and practice, that he condemned, often with comic exaggeration, are now commonly accepted in the Church of England. The point that I wish most to emphasise is that in his prolonged anti-Catholic campaign, Tait was carrying out the wishes if he were not directly obeying the orders of the court, while the statesmen most in sympathy with his efforts were Palmerston and Disraeli, two cynics without any pretence to a personal interest in religion.

Lord John Russell shared Shaftesbury's extreme Protestantism, though with less fervour, and he was sincere when, in a letter to the Queen, he quoted with approval Arnold's " I look upon a Roman Catholic as an enemy in his uniform. I look upon a Tractarian as an enemy in disguise." The Tractarians were to these men the religious fifth column. And the Queen and her Lutheran husband fully agreed. The Queen wrote to her uncle that the Tractarians were doing immense harm, and she told Lord Derby, when he was Prime Minister, that no " ritualists " must be recommended for appointments in the Church as bishops or clergymen. The Prince Consort apparently believed that promulgating " principles likely to disturb the peace of the Church " was due either to foolish eccentricity or to a temporary naughtiness, which would be cured, if it was made clear that the offenders must choose between Andrewes and Laud and the ecclesiastical loaves and fishes. He believed that even the most active, ambitious and talented of the High Church party were not likely long to hold principles which permanently excluded them from preferments. A greater libel has rarely been written.

Following the established rule, the Catholic revival flourished on persecution. It began in the Oxford cloisters.

In the year in which Tait settled in Fulham, Charles Lowder carried Anglo-Catholicism into the East End slums. With inspiration and courage derived from the services of the altar, Lowder went into the highways and byways to minister to the hungry, the miserable and the degraded, and for years he and his associates were abused and assaulted. Sunday after Sunday, there were organised riots in church, which the police did little to stop. The rioters were ruffians, paid by the sweaters, whom Lowder had denounced, and the brothel keepers whom Lowder would have suppressed. This is admitted by Tait's biographers, who write : " The keepers of the dens of drink and infamy who reap their nightly harvest from the sailors and others in the neighbour-hood of the London docks were doubtless ranged to a man under the so-called Protestant banner." Indeed, the Victorian Protestant mobs were much the same as they are described by Dickens in his story of the Gordon riots.

The excuse of the organisers of the riots and the paymasters of the rioters was that Lowder indulged in practices that had been forbidden by ecclesiastical and secular authority. He wore the Eucharistic vestments, which the Bishop of London described as " dresses and ceremonies mimicking of popery." He used altar lights, condemned by the Privy Council. He encouraged the practice of sacramental confession, according to the Anglican tradition, and confession was denounced by the good Lord Shaftesbury in a frenzy of indignation and banned by the Bishop in a letter so characteristic that it is worth quoting at length.

" If any clergyman so preaches to his people as to lead them to suppose that the proper and authorised way of a sinner's reconciliation with God is through confession to a priest, and by receiving priestly absolution ; if he leads them to believe (I use the illustration I have found employed by an advocate of the Confessional) that, as the Greek Church has erred by neglecting preaching, and the Church of Rome by not encouraging the reading of the Scriptures, so our Church has hitherto been much to blame for not leading her people more habitually to private auricular confession ; if he thus stirs up the imagination of ardent and confiding spirits to have recourse to him as a mediator between their souls and God, and when they come to seek his aid receives them with all the elaborate preparation which is so likely unduly to excite their feelings, and for which there is no authority in the Church's rules of worship—taking them into the vestry of his church, securing the door, putting on the sacred vestments, causing them to kneel before the cross, to address him as their ghostly father, asking a string of questions as to sins of deed, word and thought, and imposing penance before he confers absolution ; the man who thus acts, or—even if some of these particular circumstances are wanting—of whose general practice this is no exaggerated picture, is, in my judgment, unfaithful to the whole spirit of the Church of which he is a minister."

Condemned by those who should have understood and encouraged, misunderstood by those whom he was eager to help, Charles Lowder went on, never losing his courage or his humour. In 1866 he became the first Vicar of St. Peter's, London Docks, and there he remained until his death in 1880, still on occasion the victim of Protestant malice, but gaining the love and veneration of his people. The East End streets were lined with weeping men and women when Lowder was buried, as they were when Father Wilson went to his rest and as Holborn was on the day of Father Stanton's funeral. Steadfastness in the faith and holiness of living had won the people's hearts.

Work, similar to that of Lowder in the East End, was begun in 1862 by Alexander Heriot Mackonochie in Baldwin's Gardens off the Gray's Inn Road, in those days a squalid and mainly criminal slum. For some months, Mackonochie held services in a room over a fried fish shop, and in 1863 Tait consecrated the beautiful church of St. Alban's, Holborn, a part of the site of which had been occupied by a notorious thieves' kitchen. From the beginning, the mixed chalice, unleavened bread, lights and vestments were used. Mackonochie, a curious mixture of strength, courage and humility, gathered round him a band of devoted priests and laymen, and St. Alban's, now, alas, largely destroyed by Hitler's bombers, became in a short time the centre of splendid spiritual and social activity.

With the spiritual ministrations—the Holy Eucharist, confessions and hearty Evensong Services—the agencies for good included a Sisterhood ; a Burial Society ; Guilds and Associations for Men, Boys, Women and Girls ; a Workingmen's Club ; an Infant Nursery ; a Choir School, Parochial Schools, Night Schools for Boys and Girls ; a Soup Kitchen ; a Blanket Loan Fund ; Lying-in Charity ; a Clothing Fund ;

a Coal Charity ; a Savings Bank, and Clothing Club, a Shoe Club, provision and food for the destitute and relief for the sick.

The services were crowded and there was a large number of faithful communicants.

After four years, the Church Association, well described by Archbishop Magee as " Persecution Limited," contrived a suit against Father Mackonochie, and Tait exercised his discretion as a bishop and sent the case to the Court of Arches. Fortunately the judge, Sir Robert Phillimore, the father of the future Lord Phillimore, was a lawyer with real knowledge of the Church of England, and, while deciding against Mackonochie on some of the issues, he pronounced that altar lights, kneeling at the Consecration and the elevation of the Blessed Sacrament, all of which had either been deprecated or condemned by Tait, were legal. The persecutors appealed to the Erastian Judicial Committee of the Privy Council, the spiritual jurisdiction of which has never been recognised by Catholics in the Church of England. Russell says that " an enquiry, touching the niceties of Eucharistic ritual, was conducted by a tribunal, including a Presbyterian, an ex-representative of the Orange town of Belfast, a partisan Archbishop, a lay Low Churchman and a theologian who talked about ' the Inferior Persons of the Trinity.' " Mackonochie was condemned by the Committee on all counts and was ordered to pay monstrously high costs. And the work of St. Alban's went on much as before.

Perhaps because they were both Scotsmen, Tait was courteous and kindly to Mackonochie, but it had been in his power to have scotched the proceedings at the beginning by refusing to send the Letters of Request to the Court of Arches.

The judgment of the Judicial Committee was delivered in 1868, and before further developments, Tait had gone up higher and London had another bishop. In 1867 Disraeli, hoping to dish the Whigs, had passed a Reform Bill which considerably enlarged the electorate. In the next year he dissolved Parliament, believing that the gratitude of the newly enfranchised would give the Tories a majority. But

the Liberals were returned and the Queen, much against
her inclination, was obliged to send for Gladstone.

Early in the year, Archbishop Longley had died. It was
known that Gladstone would have nominated Wilberforce
for Canterbury, but Longley lived just long enough to give
Disraeli the nomination. He suggested Tait to the Queen
she gladly agreed, and Tait removed from Fulham to
Lambeth. This was the last and the most important instance
of the good luck that, professionally at least, never deserted
him.

The first business of the Liberal Government was the
disestablishment of the Irish Church, the Church of an
inconsiderable minority of the Irish people. Archbishop
Longley had been foremost in the opposition to the measure
to which, before the election, Gladstone was pledged. When
the Bill passed the Commons, Disraeli tried to persuade Tait
to lead the opposition in the Lords, but he was too wary.
His condescending attitude to Gladstone was amusingly
expressed in his remark, " I wish that he was not so strangely
impetuous, for he is certainly a good Christian man." He
was strongly in favour of established churches whatever their
quality might be. But he was far too shrewd to fight for a
losing cause.

The Queen dreaded a conflict on this issue between the
two houses and she employed Tait as mediator. In his
speech in the Lords debate he said : " I cannot agree either
with those who advise us to accept the measure that is now
before us without alteration or with those who advise us at
once to cast it aside." He did not vote in the second reading
division, but, with his political astuteness, he succeeded in
obtaining valuable financial concessions from the Government before the Bill became law.

In 1870, an attempt which at first Tait warmly approved
was made to excise the Athanasian Creed from the public
services of the Church. Dean Stanley was, of course
vehement in his support of the demand, which was as
vehemently opposed by Pusey and Liddon, who both declared
that they would resign their Orders and go into lay communion if the proposal was carried. I cannot profess to
regard the controversy, which was revived in 1927, as o

supreme importance. As I have written elsewhere, I can repeat the Athanasian Creed because of its traditional authority, enjoying its sonorous sentences without understanding the meaning of them. But there can be no doubt that the attack seventy years ago was inspired by men who rejected what are generally accepted as fundamental Christian doctrine. The result of what has been properly described as a tedious controversy was another of the compromises for which Tait was famous. The Athanasian Creed remained in the Prayer Book with an innocuous explanatory note.

In 1873, the anti-Catholic agitation came to a head again. It was excited by a petition, signed by four hundred and eighty-three priests, to the Upper House of Canterbury Convocation, praying the House " to consider the advisability of providing for the education, selection and licensing of duly qualified confessors in accordance with the provisions of Canon Law." The practice of habitual private confession had been steadily increasing ; it was obviously undesirable that penitents should go to callow and uninstructed curates and the recovery of a laudable practice made it the clear duty of the episcopate to make adequate provision for its proper fulfilment. The need for qualified confessors particularly applied to the religious communities which had come into existence as the result of the Oxford Movement. The Sisterhoods had little encouragement from the Victorian episcopacy, and, on occasion, the holy women were assaulted by paid Protestant mobs, and the bishops, including Tait, deprecated while, in view of awkward passages in the Prayer Book, they could not forbid confession. While he was still Bishop of London, Tait wrote :

> " There is no warrant for supposing that I in any way approve of Sisterhoods in which perpetual vows are administered. I have on more than one occasion stated publicly my belief that all vows or oaths administered under the circumstances you describe, not being sanctioned by the legislature, and being taken by persons not authorised to receive them, are of the nature of illegal oaths. It is a grave question whether a clergyman of the Church of England, administering such an oath, does not make himself amenable to prosecution before the magistrates."

Tait was not concerned as to whether the taking of life vows was right or wrong, but only as to whether the receiving of such vows was legal. Two years later, he consented to the settlement of a community in his diocese on the condition that the vows were not regarded as permanent.

The presentation of the confessions petition to Convocation stirred what Bishop Hensley Henson called years afterwards the Protestant underworld to its depth. The usual meeting was summoned at Exeter Hall and auricular confession was denounced as an unclean and disgusting thing. The outcome was a statement from the bishops in which the clergy were forbidden " to require private confession previous to receiving the Holy Communion or to enjoin or even encourage any practice of habitual confession to a priest, or to teach that such practice of habitual confession, or the being subject to what has been termed the direction of a priest, is a condition of attaining to the highest spiritual life."

The matter flared up again owing to the publication of a silly manual and again Tait and the bishops thundered, but the comfortable practice of the Sacrament of Penance has continued in the English Church. All that happened was that many devout people were made unhappy and that many devoted priests were discouraged, for Tait's biographers are honest enough to admit that among the clergy who were censured were those " whose daily work in overcrowded and poor parishes brought them into contact with the grossest form of vice," though it is certainly not true that the grossest forms of vice flourish in poor parishes and or that the rich have no need for repentance, confession and absolution.

While Gladstone remained in power Tait's " reforming " zeal was checked, but in 1874, the Tories swept the country and the return of Disraeli ensured Tait Parliamentary support. The result was the Public Worship Regulation Act, the supreme achievement of Tait's career well described by an American churchman as " the most unpopular ridiculous and unworkable of modern Acts of Parliament." The provisions of the Act were as follows :

" In every Diocese in England a Council or Board of Assessors was to be formed, under the presidency of the Bishop, consisting of three incumbents and five lay Churchmen, elected respectively by the clergy and the church-wardens of the Diocese, such elected members holding office for five years, in addition to the Chancellor, the Dean, and the Archdeacon, who were to sit *ex officio*. Any complaint made to the Bishop as to ritual irregularity might be referred by him to this Council, which should, if necessary, hear evidence, and advise the Bishop whether, in the light of local circumstances, it seemed desirable that further proceedings should be taken. In the event of the Bishop being advised to proceed, he was to issue such admonition or order, if any, as he deemed necessary, and this order was to have the force of law unless the clergyman affected should himself appeal to the Archbishop against it. The Archbishop was in person to hear the appeal, and to determine, with the aid of his Vicar-General, whether the Bishop's admonition should be confirmed or annuled. From the Archbishop's decision thus given there was under this Bill to be no appeal either to the Privy Council or elsewhere."

After the decision by the Privy Council in 1871, in what is known as the Purchase case—a decision that was ignored and never enforced—the aims of the ceremonial revival consisted of six points, the eastward position of the priest at Holy Communion, the Eucharistic vestments, altar-lights, the mixed chalice, unleavened bread and the use of incense. Tait's purpose was to create an effective machine for finally suppressing these practices, as well as of securing the punishment of priests who encouraged confession and the invocation of the Blessed Virgin Mary and the saints.

The Bill did not go far enough for Shaftesbury. It did not specifically condemn confession, and " unless the Church can cleanse herself of the foul thing she and all her children will sink into the dust," and in committee in the Lords he carried an amendment providing that a lay judge should be appointed by the Archbishops to hear and determine all representations under the Act. Shaftesbury had no confidence in bishops. It is another amusing example of Erastianism in practice that the first lay judge was Lord Penzance, an ex-judge of the Divorce Court !

The Bill was warmly approved by the Queen, and, in his constant desire to secure royal favour, supported by Disraeli, who cared for none of these things, when it reached the Commons. It was vehemently opposed by Gladstone, but William Harcourt made his debut as a Protestant champion, and with Tory and Liberal support the Bill passed into law. It should be added that the Public Worship Regulation Act never had the formal approval of Convocation. After the final division in the Commons, Tait noted in his diary : " I wrote in the House of Lords to the Queen—' Thank God the Bill has passed.' I received congratulations on all sides. So ends a work which has given me no rest for six months. May God grant that the peace and lasting good of His Church may follow from our labours ! " His prayer was not granted.

The first victim of the Act was the vicar of St. Peter's, Folkestone. He was condemned by the ex-divorce judge, condemned by the Privy Council on appeal and condemned by the Archbishop, who was his Diocesan—and submitted. The next victim was the Rev. Arthur Tooth, who lived to a great and venerable age to be universally regarded for his saintliness. Tait noted : " I fear I shall not find him so amenable as Mr. Ridsdale." He was right. Father Tooth was made of sterner stuff. He was persistent and was finally sent to gaol.

Three other clergymen were imprisoned. In one case, religious feelings were outraged by a consecrated wafer, stolen by some wretched creature, being regarded as a legal exhibit and retained with " other materials of evidence." This abominable outrage was described by Tait as " most reprehensible." With many difficulties and after having legal quibbles, the consecrated wafer was, after four months, rescued from the ex-divorce judge and reverently consumed by the Archbishop. Mackonochie was prosecuted under the new Act and deprived of his living. But the work he had begun at St. Alban's still went on. What God had blessed, no ex-divorce judge could destroy. Here is George Russell's description of the ministry which Tait's Act of Parliament was devised to hinder :

" Men of good position, of private fortune, of University education, of abilities certainly not below the average—in some respects, which conduce to professional success, conspicuously above it—they gave up, to the work of the Church and the service of the poor, health, means, ease, comfort, the countenance of their ecclesiastical superiors, and all hope of preferment. They made the surrender, not in a sudden gust of soon-repented enthusiasm, but by a deliberate and sustained act of calculated sacrifice. And the sacrifice was not more deliberate than complete. In youth and middle age and advancing years, at morning, at noon, at night, in summer and winter, in sickness and in health, in workdays and holiday time, in popularity and in persecution, these men gave themselves, body and mind and soul, to the work which they had undertaken. Indefatigable in the duties of their sacred office, they laboured far beyond its limits for all that could serve the material and moral interests of their fellow-men. They worked for public health, for higher and wider education, for all innocent and rational recreation. Not content with teaching, and preaching and visiting the sick, and guiding the perplexed, they instructed the ignorant, and comforted the sorrowful, and fed the hungry, and clothed the naked and helped—without pauperising—the industrious poor."

Other great and good men suffered. John Mason Neale, a gentle scholar and the author of many famous hymns was mobbed, persecuted and insulted, and died, worn out at the age of forty-eight. His hymns, mostly translations from the Greek and Latin—" Jerusalem the Golden," " Art Thou Weary," " O Happy Band of Pilgrims," and a dozen more— are known throughout the world, but because of his Catholic opinions, all the English Church gave Neale was the warden-ship of a small almshouse at East Grinstead with a stipend of twenty-eight pounds a year. John Bacchus Dykes was the author of over fifty hymn tunes made familiar in " Hymns Ancient and Modern." They include " Nearer my God to Thee," "Eternal Father, strong to save," "Holy, Holy, Holy," " Jesu, Lover of my soul," and " the King of Love, my Shepherd is." And the life of Dykes was embittered and his work cut short by a persecuting bishop.

These men are remembered. But it was an obscure parish priest, of whom little is known except that his faith was strong and his courage indomitable, who made the Public Worship Regulation Act ridiculous and compelled the Archbishop on his death bed practically to admit that he had been beaten. Sidney Faithhorn Green was the rector of St. John's, Miles Platting, in the diocese of Man-chester. He was prosecuted by the tireless Church Associa-tion in December, 1878, and after the usual protracted proceedings, he was committed to prison for contempt of court in March, 1881. The Bishop of Manchester had refused to veto the prosecution and was, therefore, at least partly responsible for the imprisonment. It was easy enough to get Mr. Green into gaol. He refused to obey the orders of the ex-divorce judge, and as Tait ruefully wrote, " if a man is determined to go into gaol it is very difficult to keep him out." It proved equally difficult to get him out, and the indefinite imprisonment of a harmless parish priest became a national scandal. The case was discussed in the newspapers and mentioned in Parliament and a Bill was actually introduced into the Lords, with the support of the Archbishop, to secure Mr. Green's release. It was passed in the Lords but killed in the Commons by a count-out.

Then the Archbishop tried to persuade the Bishop of Manchester to take steps to open Mr. Green's prison doors. But the Bishop was quite content that a tiresome priest with strong convictions should stay quietly under lock and key. Then Tait appealed to the Home Secretary, only to be told that the Minister " having consulted the law officers of the Crown is advised by them that the powers of the Crown to discharge persons from custody would not be rightly, or even constitutionally, exercised in the case of a person imprisoned for contempt of court committed by persistent disobedience to the lawful commands of a competent tribunal." Finally Tait tried to influence the fanatic heart of the Church Association and naturally failed. In a speech in Convocation he said :

> " The great objection to the imprisonment of Mr. Green is (besides the natural feeling one has that he really has had more than enough punishment for whatever he had done), that it is an anachronism, and that the thing is out of date. The world has outlived the idea that offences of that kind are to be punished by incarceration, and though it is perfectly true, and has been argued in the most logical manner, that it is not for any opinions that he has been imprisoned, yet, still, you will never get the people to draw an accurate distinction between the two things ; they know that he held certain unusual opinions, and they know that, as a direct or indirect consequence of holding those opinions, he has been put into this unpleasant position. . . . Therefore, even if there were no other reason than that, I should certainly give my vote for releasing him from imprisonment as speedily as possible."

Meanwhile Randall Davidson, Tait's chaplain and son-in-law, and later himself to be Archbishop, was endeavouring to persuade Mr. Green to release himself. The correspondence between the chaplain and the prisoner is instructive and not unamusing. Mr. Green's position was perfectly clear. He wrote :

"As the Archbishop has by you expressed a wish to understand my position, I can state it very simply—

"(1) It is demoralising, degrading, and incompatible, with the very existence of a Church that any three persons who ignore all their own religious responsibilities should dictate to God's faithful people in matters as to which they have no concern whatever.

"(2) That it is absolutely impossible for an assembly like the House of Commons, upon which the supreme power has now devolved, and which is officially ignorant of the very existence of its God and Saviour Jesus Christ, to be in *any sense whatever* a source of ecclesiastical jurisdiction.

"It has been my misfortune to have both these aspects of the Public Worship Act thrust upon me ; they are alike so monstrous that I have never had the least doubt how I ought to act."

Davidson answered that, of course, Mr. Green could not change his conscientious opinions, but that the Archbishop was anxious to know " whether there at present exists any authority, ecclesiastical or civil, to whose commands you would be disposed to conform your actions." To this came the reply :

"Practically your letter resolves itself into this, does it not ? Can I suggest a way of surrendering the Rubrics of the Prayer Book which will not cause me to feel that I have betrayed a trust ? I regret to say that I can offer no suggestion whatever.

"I assure you that if I had known of any way of escape I should not have been in prison for ten months, and that is only the least part of what I have been called upon to undergo.

"You will, I hope, pardon my saying plainly that I fail to see how, if I do an action which I believe to be wrong, I mend matters by *proclaiming* that belief and saying ' I believe so and so to be indefensible, still I do it.' I think people would say, and rightly too, ' The more shame for you.'

"To submit to loss of life, goods, liberty, etc., under protest is plain enough, but to *do wrong one's self,* under protest is another matter altogether.

"How sad to think of the thousands of lives wasted on account of a grain of incense as in the early persecutions, for a mere shibboleth, as in those of a later age, when such a simple means of escape was ready at hand."

Davidson persisted, and Mr. Green replied :

"I can only say in reply that I should deem it sinful to recognise Lord Penzance in any shape or form as having authority in Christ's Church, and that to introduce ' an authority ecclesiastical or civil ' as an *excuse* for doing so, would, from my point of view, make matters ten times worse, for that would be to *compromise* ' the authority ' without in any sense clearing me. I am, dear Sir, faithfully yours."

The correspondence concluded with the prisoner pointing out :

> " It is somewhat unprecedented to require one who believes himself illegally punished by an incompetent tribunal, to point out some other authority whose *condemnation* he would prefer.
>
> " Even Festus did not say ' Wilt thou go up to Jerusalem and there be condemned for these things ? ' In Japan, I believe, there does exist an arrangement by which a person distasteful to the Government is invited to be his own jury, judge and executioner, but I must decline to offer myself as a subject, especially as I know myself ' neither against the law of the Church, neither against the law of the land, to have offended anything at all.' "

There was evidently nothing to be done with " poor Mr. Green," and the Archbishop made a second attempt to move Parliament. He, himself, introduced a Bill this time to give the Archbishop of the Province power to order the release of any one imprisoned for contumacy to the Act for which he was responsible. This Bill was passed in the Lords and killed in the Commons. Then Tait, already a very sick man, threw himself on the mercy of his brother of Manchester, who, after protesting that he would sooner resign his see than be responsible for Mr. Green's freedom, at last consented to approach the ex-divorce judge, and Mr. Green was released after sixteen months in gaol.

I do not suggest that Tait was not sincerely moved by " poor Mr. Green's " suffering, though his letters show that Mr. Green did not fail to find some enjoyment in the hopeless position in which the Public Worship Regulation Act and the ex-divorce judge had brought the bishops. But Tait's principal concern was the fillip that Green's imprisonment had given to the demand for disestablishment. There was a considerable Radical wing in the Liberal majority returned at the 1880 election, and what seemed to Tait an unseemly alliance of Dissenters and atheists was agitating for disestablishment and disendowment. The ritual prosecutions had also convinced many Catholics, including Pusey, that the highest spiritual considerations made it necessary that the Church should be entirely freed from State control. Establishment was evidently in danger.

Lord Bryce says that " Tait's policy and personality

counted for something in prolonging the time-honoured connection of the Anglican Church with the English State." To preserve that connection was Tait's main objective. He endeavoured to destroy the doctrinal and ceremonial developments of the Tractarian Revival for three reasons. The first was that, remaining in all essentials a Presbyterian, he rejected the Laudian conception of the nature of the Church largely recovered through the influence of Keble and Pusey ; that he rejected most of the accepted traditional Catholic doctrines and that he had no conception of the beauty and significance of Catholic ceremonial. The second reason was that, regarding the Church as a branch of the civil service, he was convinced that there must be a limit to the variety of teaching and practice that could be tolerated within the Church.

The third reason was that the Catholic movement and all that it implied was detested by the head of the State. I think that it is quite certain that, with all the Protestant clamour, Parliament would not have passed the Public Worship Act had it not been for Queen Victoria. Had not the royal wishes been very clear Disraeli would not have bothered his head with a matter in which he did not profess to have the smallest personal interest.

The tragedy of Tait's last days was that he was compelled to realise that the Act for which he was responsible had definitely weakened the cause that he had planned to strengthen. The ritual controversy annoyed and bored the Archbishop. It seemed to him much ado about nothing. He declared that to him the Church of England was " the bulwark of the Reformation," but it was not so much the preservation of " Reformation principles " for which he cared, as the preservation of law and order. He was definitely, if politely, anti-Roman, but he had no sympathy with the undisciplined extravagances of popular dissent. He was a Scottish Presbyterian, not an English Methodist. This is shown in an interesting comment on the Moody and Sankey mission that drew great crowds in 1877. He wrote :

" That addresses urging in whatever homely language, the great truths of the Gospel on our people's consciences should be delivered by layman is no innovation amongst us, and I heartily rejoice that the present movement is conducted on so great a scale and with such apparent success. It is chiefly from the ' after meetings for confession of sin and for guidance of the conscience ' as they have been described, that I am apprehensive lest evil may arise. I cannot think that the delicate and difficult duty of thus ministering to anxious souls ought to be entrusted to anyone who has neither been set apart by the Church for this especial office, nor has given proof of such a spiritual insight as may in certain cases be held to take place, in this particular, of the regular call to the cure of souls. I cannot but fear, from what I have heard, that the counsel given at these meetings must often be crude, and founded upon no knowledge of the real circumstances and state of mind of those to whom it is addressed, while there is danger also lest some self-constituted advisers of others may do harm to themselves, seeking to be leaders, when in truth they have much need to be led. I learn, also, that in the organisation for addressing God publicly in prayer, a great deal too much is trusted to the readiness of any one who may be present to accept, without due preparation, the grave responsibility of guiding the devotions of the multitude assembled. These objections are quite independent of others, which I have heard urged upon good authority, against particular statements as to doctrine said to be made without sufficient guard or explanation. I am not alluding so much to any depreciation of the ordinances which Christ has established for the edification of His Church, but rather to the allegation, that in the discourses of the missionaries, there are unwise and untrue representations of the almost universal necessity of instantaneous conversion, and an ignoring of the full Scriptural teaching as to the nature of repentance."

His conception of the responsibilities of his office and of his paramount obligations caused him to be a constant attendant at the debates in the House of Lords, and there can be no doubt that he immensely enjoyed his position in the legislature. Indeed, he constantly regretted that his example was followed so rarely by his suffragans, who preferred to go about their Master's business in their dioceses.

Tait was an astute politician, a good debater, a deft negotiator. But his Parliamentary record does not suggest that any spiritual or moral cause benefitted from the fact that the English Primate was a Peer of Parliament. He never showed the smallest desire to persuade the State that it should be guided by moral and religious considerations in determining national policy. He had none of Gladstone's Christian enthusiasm. In the earlier years of the century the bishops in the House of Lords had been among the steady opponents of political and social reforms. And they were properly and reasonably detested. Tait was as much concerned, as they had been, to keep things as they were and to resist anything and everything that in his judgment was calculated to weaken the Church as the chief buttress of the crown. He was determined to destroy the Catholic revival because it was feared and detested by the Queen, by important politicians of all parties and by the rich dissenters, and, if it were allowed to leaven the whole lump of the Church, disestablishment would, he feared, have been inevitable. So " poor Mr. Green " had to go to gaol.

Reviewing the Archbishop's political activities, George Russell asked, " What is the use of bishops in the House of Lords ? " Since Tait's time they have happily become of great use. To-day the Archbishop of Canterbury, the Archbishop of York and the Bishop of Chichester stress in frequent speeches the claims of national and international righteousness, and the urgency of radical social changes to save the many from the greed of the few.

Tait died before the London dock strike began the history of the modern English Socialist movement and before, with the birth of the Guild of St. Matthew and the Christian Social Union, the crusade for social regeneration was started within the Church. But, while he was still Archbishop, Maurice, for whom in other respects he professed unstinted admiration, had denounced unrestricted competition and had declared that " a true Socialism is the necessary result of a true Christianity " ; and Kingsley, whose name is not mentioned in Tait's voluminous correspondence, had fought for the abolition of sweating, for better schools for the people and for sanitary reform. Apparently Tait cared for none of these things, and the majority of the people did not care a jot for the things for which he fought. It is easy to forget the silly twaddle that the good Lord Shaftesbury talked about confession when his struggle for the Factory Acts is remembered. There is no such care for Christ's poor in the life of the Erastian Tait.

" Poor Mr. Green " was released from gaol on November 4th, 1882. A temporary peace at St. Albans was patched up on December 1st. Tait died the next day. And, for all

practical purposes, the Public Worship Regulation Act died
with him.

CHAPTER VIII

SIXTY YEARS AFTER

TAIT was succeeded at Canterbury by Edward White Benson, who, after being the first headmaster of Wellington College, the school founded by the Prince Consort, had been chosen by Beaconsfield as the first Bishop of Truro. Gladstone was Prime Minister when Benson was elevated to the Primacy, and he was sharply criticised by his party for the choice of a Prelate who was a strong Tory. As a matter of fact, Benson was the selection of the Queen more than of her Minister. The Prince Consort had thought highly of him, and Tait, whom she trusted, sent a message to her from his death-bed, urging that the Bishop of Truro should go to Canterbury.

The message was conveyed by Randall Davidson, the Archbishop's chaplain and son-in-law, and his interview with the royal lady was the beginning of an intimate association that lasted until the Queen's death. Tait was the complete Erastian. Davidson, who was to become Archbishop in 1903, was equally convinced of the super-importance of the establishment.

Benson was much more a churchman. He was, indeed, intent on saving the Church from State domination. Benson has been described by George Russell as " intensely hard-working, copious in great designs, eager to extol the Church as the divine safeguard of our national life, intolerant of contradiction or criticism, and, as far as circumstances permitted, imperious." He was " a man of fervent piety, an æsthete, an artist, an antiquary, and a ritualist, delighting in Christian art and tradition, and loving to use ancient forms of devotion and hymns from Breviary and Missal." Incidentally, he was the father of three gifted sons.

Benson's love of ritual was purely artistic. Like many other Englishmen he loved ritual for ritual's sake, but disliked it when it had deep spiritual significance. He had no sort of sympathy with the Oxford Movement and was intensely anti-Papal.

This was shown in 1894, when, owing to the boldly expressed opinions of the French theologians, Abbé Duchesne and the Abbé Portal, and the enthusiasm of the late Lord Halifax for reunion, Pope Leo XIII appointed a commission to consider the validity of English orders. The commission reported, as Benson had anticipated, that the orders were entirely invalid. Despite this authoritative pronouncement, a number of French and Belgian theologians remained unconvinced, and the question was raised again and considered in Rome in 1924 with the same result. In both years the prevailing hostile influence was the Roman hierarchy in England. If Rome were to recognise Anglican orders, as she recognises the orders of the Eastern Orthodox, the Roman Church in England would evidently be no more than the " Italian mission," as it was described by Canon Liddon.

Benson's anti-Erastianism compelled him to bold action when, in 1888, the venomous Church Association inspired the prosecution of Bishop King of Lincoln for the use at Holy Communion of the eastward position, altar lights, the sign of the cross at the absolution and the blessing, the mixed chalice, the ablutions at the altar of the sacred vessels and the repetition of the *Agnus Dei*. Edward King was the finest flower of Anglicanism in the later Victorian era. He was " a saint, simple, sane, sensible, strong." In his modesty, his kindliness, his charm and his intellect, he has been justly compared to St. Anselm. The persecution of such a man outraged churchpeople throughout the English-speaking world, and to decent men with no Church interest it seemed, as it was, an example of outrageous fanaticism.

Instead of allowing the case to be heard by a secular tribunal, Benson cited the bishop to appear in his archi-piscopal court, which had not sat for two hundred years. Dean Church described the court as " a distinctly spiritual court of the highest dignity."

In the findings, the decisions of the Erastian Privy Council were ignored, and the Archbishop and his assessors were influenced only by the Prayer Book rubrics and traditional practice. The verdict was almost entirely in Bishop King's favour, and Dean Church wrote that it was " the most courageous thing that has come from Lambeth for the last two hundred years." It was indeed a Laudian triumph, the considered assertion by the highest Anglican authority of the continuity of the English Church from St. Anselm and St. Thomas. The persecutors appealed from the Archbishop to the Judicial Committee of the Privy Council, which claiming that it was not bound by its former decisions, dismissed the appeal.

This was by far the most important event of Benson's primacy. Intermittent Protestant persecutions have occurred since. On occasion hired Protestant rowdies have interrupted church services. But Bishop King's practices have become the rule rather than the exception in the Church of England.

Benson served the Church well with the Lincoln judgment. He served it very badly in his vehement opposition to the Welsh Disestablishment Act, which confirmed the popular belief that the Church was the Sunday edition of the Tory party.

Frederick Temple was seventy-five when he followed Benson, and his six years at Canterbury were the least successful period of a long and useful life. In 1898, acting on Benson's precedent, he sat as judge in another ritualistic prosecution and condemned the use of incense and portable lights and of reservation of the Blessed Sacrament for the communion of the sick and dying. Temple had none of Benson's knowledge of traditional practice, and he seems to have doubted his own competence to act as judge by declaring that his decisions were only " opinions," which his suffragans were free to adopt or to reject. The question of reservation was to become the main controversy in the Church, and the refusal of an ever-increasing number of parish priests to obey Temple and abandon a practice, vital for the spiritual health of the people entrusted to their care, was responsible for the abortive efforts in 1927 and 1928 for Prayer Book revision.

Benson was Archbishop and Frederick Temple was Bishop of London in 1886 when the London Dock Strike began a new era in the history of English Trade Unions, and Manning's mediæval faith made him the champion of the poor. The Bishop of London was approached by the strikers, who were making the extravagant demand for " a tanner an hour," but he gave them no efficient support. The imperious Archbishop does not appear to have been interested. The industrial organisation of unskilled labour was a triumph for the men, most of them members of the Social Democratic Federation, who were regarded with suspicion by the leaders of the skilled Trade Unions, who were politically mild Radicals. And from this strike came the spread of Socialism in England, the foundation of the Independent Labour Party and of the birth of the Labour Party.

The real fathers of English Socialism were not Marx and Engels, but Kingsley and Maurice, two clergymen, and in 1887, the Christian Social Union was founded by the great Bishop Westcott, of Durham, who was courageous enough to call himself a Socialist, and to organise opinion within the Church in support of the demand for radical social reform. The Union and the more " advanced " Guild of St. Matthew had considerable clerical support, among their members being Charles Gore, then a canon of Westminster, Canon Scott Holland, of St. Paul's, and Stewart Headlam, a man of great parts and boundless courage, who never became more than a curate. But the agitation for the application of the gospel to the incidents of the common life had no episcopal support from Canterbury in the days of Benson and Frederick Temple.

The end of the century saw the Boer War a blatant Imperialistic adventure, waged with cynical candour for the benefit of shareholders of the African mining companies. But while Kipling was twanging his banjo and spluttering in a frenzy of " patriotism " the worst doggerel that ever came from the pen of a writer of genius, the bishops of the English Church made not even a mild protest against the sacrifice of their fellow countrymen on the altar of Mammon.

The events of the primacies of Randall Davidson and Cosmo Lang are outside the range that I have set for myself in this book. From 1924 until his resignation in 1928, I had frequent interviews with Archbishop Davidson and was vastly impressed by his strength of character, his dignity and his acute judgment. He was one of the few really great men whom I have ever met. I think that the Archbishop will be remembered as the last of the Erastians. I have written, and I think not unfairly, that he believed in the Holy, Catholic and Established Church. His was a dominant personality. He was always strong enough to take his own line however unpopular it might be. During the first world war he denounced the clamour for reprisals after the German air raids. Though he disliked Catholic practice and had little sympathy with Catholic doctrine, he was ready for the peace of the Church to make the concessions to Anglo-Catholics in the revised Prayer Book of 1927. And for this he was assailed as if he had been another Laud. To Archbishop Cosmo Lang I have been indebted for much gracious kindness, and all will agree that he fulfilled his high office with sympathy and dignity.

But it has to be admitted that in the years between Davidson's accession and the second world war, the Church progressively lost its influence in the life of the nation. This is not only true of the Church but of the " churches," if one may use the term. Nonconformity was the soul of Victorian Liberalism. The early leaders of the Labour Party were largely recruited from Methodist chapels. Today the Liberal Party is a museum piece and the Labour Party has lost its spiritual inspiration.

At the beginning of the century, the English Church had already to a considerable extent become a class church. Its bishops sat with the Lords and were the spiritual ornaments of the court. The congregations in its often beautiful churches were mostly prosperous and content. Politically it was the valuable ally of the men with money. When the moneyless man was moved to public worship he went to an ugly Methodist conventicle or to an uglier Salvation Army barracks. It is true that Anglo-Catholic priests, like Lowder and Dolling, carried the saving beauty of the Catholic faith into the dark places, but, as the century went on, the social fervour of these holy men was lost and the appeal that had been gladly heard in the slums was politely repeated only in the squares and the more comfortable suburbs. Much for which Laud died had been recovered, but not for the benefit of the people for whom Laud cared most.

Good men in the Church tried hard to stay the rot. The ecclesiastical machine was overhauled and reformed. But the people remained aloof and indifferent. The eminent Jewish scholar, Dr. Charles Singer, says : " What Christians regard as the moral decay of our time appears to those outside Christianity to have arisen as a disease within the Christian body itself." As Christ Himself declared : " Salt is good, but if the salt has lost its saltness, wherewith will ye season it ? "

Professor John Macmurray says that religion must be either conservative or creative. It must be both. Indeed, unless it is conservative it cannot be creative, and unless it is creative it is dead. Creative religion, Professor Macmurray says, is concerned with the new community and its creation. But it is only by conserving all that is vital in the old that something new and better can be ensured. The Oxford movement was the Church of England's recovery of the understanding of its birthright. It emphasised the supreme value of the sacramental means of grace, and its early adherents understood that the intention of the means of grace was not only to secure eternal felicity for the individual, but also to secure ephemeral joy and satisfaction for the earthly community. The Anglo-Catholic slum priest, therefore, was eager to take his full part, in the name of the Lord, in the crusade against foul housing, half-filled stomachs, constant unemployment and the whole Mammon-ridden economic system that makes these evil things inevitable. The grievous misfortune has been that Anglican Catholicism has become more and more concerned with the means and more and more indifferent to the objective. It has tended to become a selfish æstheticism, a narrow spiritual method of self indulgence, a comfortable religion for comfortable people.

"The task of the Church is to christianise the State and Society," writes T. S. Eliot. This entails destruction as well as construction ; it entails the upsetting of a great many apple-carts, and the apple-carts often belong to people who say their prayers, are regular communicants and generous contributors to the Easter offerings.

Christianity is a revolutionary religion or it is nothing. Because it is creative it is uncomfortable. There are no births without pangs. As Professor Macmurray asserts, Christ insisted on economic democracy. In the *Magnificat* the Almighty is adored because He puts down the mighty from their seats and exalts the humble and the meek. The supreme value of liberty, equality and fraternity is implicitly proclaimed in the Gospels. The Christ ideal is brotherhood on this earth. The Church was divinely created to establish the fraternal human society. It should, therefore, be the relentless enemy of oppression, aggression, and privilege. When it has condoned any of these things, when it has patched up peace with the devil, whom it is its business to destroy, when it has petted and fondled the fat sheep in the sheepfold and forgotten the hungry sheep lost on the mountains, it has become " as sounding brass or a tinkling cymbal." The Church impotent is the Church pathetic. The Church must be either sublime or ridiculous.

The pious are now holding up their hands in holy horror because many of the men, who are spending their strength in the attempt to pull down the mighty from their seats and to exalt the humble, have no faith in God and are untouched by the Christian revelation. They should abase themselves in the dust, since they have left to others the task that would have been theirs had they answered the call of the Master.

There is an individual other-worldliness that is a dedication. But the other-worldliness of the Church has been an abdication. By its indifference to the earthly well-being of the majority, it has rendered unto Caesar the things that are God's. The Church has allowed the sword of the Lord and of Gideon to fall from its nerveless hand. We should be thankful that it has been picked up and sturdily wielded by other hands. The Church has been halting, ineffective, Mammon-tied and unfaithful to its high calling, and the tragedy is—this is admitted by non-Christian writers— that its mission cannot conceivably be fully accomplished by any other institution. The sword of the Lord cannot be used, as it might be used, except by the Church that was created to war against the devil.

We are living in a catastrophic era of history. The old order is dead. Men are fearfully wondering what the new order is to be. Without question its character can be largely determined by the Church if it recovers the courage, the faith and the vision of St. Anselm, St. Thomas and Laud.

For me the wide acceptance of the Malvern Findings is the most comforting and the most heartening of recent happenings. With all the studied moderation of the wording and the sometimes illogical qualification of the condemnations, the Findings are a Christian declaration of war against the inherent evils of monopolist capitalism. This is clearly realised by a prelate like the Bishop of Bradford ; it is equally realised by the Tory members of Parliament, who have been moved to wrath by the Findings and by the present Archbishop's speeches.

We are being constantly told that the objective of the war is the destruction of Fascism. The only practical alternative to some sort of Fascism, which is the latest and perhaps the last form of capitalist monopoly, is some form of Socialism. The Church of England, which used to be the Church of the English people and which still retains, to a surprising extent, the respect of the English people, has to choose whether it is to be a triumphant instrument in the establishment in this country of economic democracy, which its influence can make Christian in the finest sense of the term and not mere Marxism, or whether it is to be, as it has often been, the ally of the power of money. In the circumstances of the world, the choice is between new and abundant life or lingering death.

To St. Anselm and St. Thomas the unity of Christendom, which in their day meant the unity of the European peoples, was the matter of first importance. Rome was valued because Rome stood for unity. The unity was destroyed by the Reformation ; arrogant nationalism came into being and war has followed war, the horror and destruction ever growing greater. Now it is perfectly clear that, with the development of the mechanical means of killing and destroying, future wars must be made impossible or the continent will sink into a general condition of semi-starvation and moral degradation. Unless there is a United States of Europe, European civilisation is doomed. That is commonly recognised and, with the failure of the League of Nations in mind, men are wondering on what basis international unity can be established.

The only unification with any chance of peaceful permanence must be democratic and Professor Macmurray, hard critic as he is of the Christian Church, declares that such a unification must have its roots in Christianity.

" If it fails us," he writes, " then the unification will still take place, but it will be merely political and therefore totalitarian." I believe that this is true. And it makes the responsibility of the Church obvious.

As in the Dark Ages, the individual Christian may well despair of the world. In the welter of brutality and lies, he may feel that the cause of kindness and truth is, at least for the time, quite hopeless and that all that is left for him is, so far as that is possible, to hide from the world, like the hermits in the desert, and to spend his time in fasting and prayer. But if the individual Christian may escape from the world, the Christian Church cannot. It was created to be the light of the world. It may be an effective lighthouse or a monument of failure. But it will remain in the world. It has not only to declare that it has an ethic which must control social action, if the common life is to be decent and dignified, but it has to have a realistic understanding of how that ethic must be applied in contemporary conditions.

Today it must stand unequivocally for democracy, not because of any intrinsic value in democracy as a vague idea, but because it is the only practical political method of creating a society freed from frustration, insecurity and premature death. Democracy is a way to an end, the only way to the Christian end set out at Malvern.

Religion has to be political if it is to be effective. Of the seven Archbishops, of whom I have written in this book, five were politicians as well as ecclesiastics. The two who were not politicians were nothing else of importance. The Church must now pledge itself to a definite political programme for the destruction of the power of money and of the consequent inequality, injustice and suffering and the securing of the chance for the good life for all, the simple as well as the gifted, the humble and not the proud. If the Church finds the courage for this outspoken championship, it will be faced by denunciation, misrepresentation, and the loss of its material possessions. The bishops will have to give up their lawn sleeves and their places on the seats of the mighty if they are to contrive victory for the champions of the poor.

Every reform suggested in the Beveridge Report, every attempt to bring to an end the payment by the many for the privilege of the few, is going to be stubbornly resisted. Mammon is going to fight like the devil that he is, before he is dethroned. While I have been writing this chapter, I have been reading an indignant outburst from the Earl of Selborne, a pious churchman and the lucky possessor of considerable inherited wealth, who denounces the demand for even " the partial confiscation of mining royalties and tithes," the implication being that the Church must selfishly side with Mammon ; and I have seen the following appalling extract from the *Bankers' Magazine :* " Workers of the future will require fears of unemployment and poverty to ensure the necessary drive in this world of internal and international competition."

The end of the war will not necessarily mean a period of peaceful reconstruction. The character of the new society will be determined only after struggle that may be long and bitter, and the Church will have to decide " under which flag, Bezonian ? " In the contests of the sixteenth and seventeenth centuries, men like Laud fought to keep the English Church and the English nation English. Puritanism was a foreign importation, more alien to the English character than Papalism. As I have asserted, Puritanism has been largely responsible for the establishment in England of the supremacy of money. That supremacy has been, I believe, permanently destroyed in the continental economy. It is threatened here, but, in association with American capitalism, the financiers may contrive to retain their stranglehold on the national life. If they fail, as Christopher Dawson has said, the problem will be " to re-interpret the English ideals of freedom and toleration in accordance with the require- ments of a post-individualist and post-capitalist age." There is no reason why the country that escaped from both Rome and Geneva should, in the next chapter of its history, adopt

Marxism which George Orwell has called " a German theory interpreted by Russians." There is a world of difference between the Christian Socialism that derives from Kingsley and Maurice and the Socialism that derives from Marx and Lenin.

I am convinced that it is the mission of the English Church, as it is within its powers, to make it possible for the distinctive English way of life, cleansed, strengthened and ennobled, to continue in a new co-operative industrial order. My faith was expressed by Maurice at a far less momentous time. He wrote : " The Church, I believe, can only profit by this great crisis in the history of mankind if she be ready to acknowledge that, according to the will of her Author and her Lord, she is not meant to be extra-national : that she has no commission nor powers which dispense with the necessity of positive formal law and with outward government : that her highest honour is to be the life-giving energy to everybody in the midst of which she dwells."

INDEX